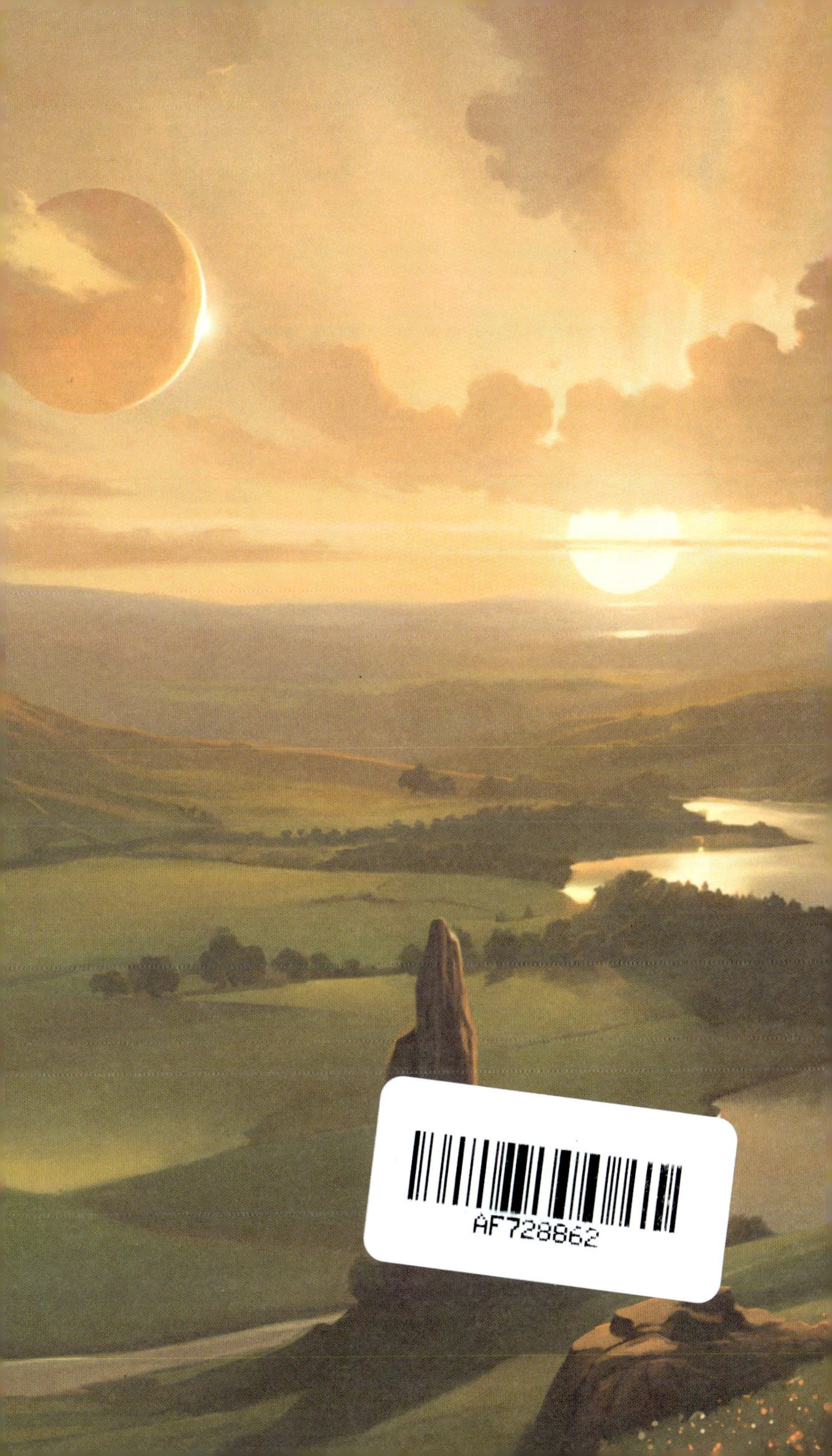

The Mind of the Doctor

across the neurodiverse universe of Doctor Who

lillian crawford

HERNE BOOKS

'If you have ever felt "other", "outside of the norm", confused by social signals, unrepresented, alone ... then Doctor Who is for you. And ... this book is for you. Acknowledging neurodiversity, the pluses and the minuses, the total acceptance (and indeed admiration) of anything that doesn't conform. This is a brave and exceedingly knowledgeable piece of work. Lillian Crawford you have my love and respect.'

Louise Jameson, 'Leela' in Doctor Who, 1977-78

'A brilliant read for the Neurodiverse Doctor Who community.

'A brilliant read for the Neurotypical Doctor Who community.

'This is a beautifully researched, fascinating deep dive into the mind of the Doctor in all their shapes and sizes and forms. It's also a very personal account of one fan's journey with autism which will strike a chord with so many readers. A must read in fact.'

Sophie Aldred, 'Ace' in Doctor Who, 1987-89, 2022

'Part memoir, part study of fan sensibility, part critical study of six decades of television, this is a dazzling work of scholarship. Doctor Who, captured in all its impossible and frustrating and beguiling multiplicity.'

Matthew Sweet, writer, broadcaster and cultural historian

'Intelligent, warm and hugely insightful. It's a joy to travel with the always thoughtful Lillian Crawford through time, space and television.'

Samira Ahmed, journalist and broadcaster

'In this age of blowhards and bullies amplified by algorithms and technologies, it's a relief to hear this gentle, sometimes acerbic, always curious voice grapple with life, emotions and The Doctor. If anyone tells you Doctor Who doesn't matter, this book will make you realise right away, of course it does.

'There is a lot to learn in this book – about typical minds and untypical minds, about Doctor Who, about the consolations and power of art to help overcome the challenges of life, about growing up and, in the end, about getting used to change.

'It's written with a great deal of heart, wit and wisdom. Towards the end, I became worried that the relationship between the author and The Doctor was on the rocks but I think it is still in good health. If there's a message in here, it's that life entails change and many of these changes are uncomfortable and unwelcome but that there's a way of coping if you stay curious and open. It is by no means a fawning portrait of The Doctor. On the contrary it holds a mirror to all their flaws and complications and in doing so, invites us to consider our own selves. I found myself asking a number of times, what is that weird thing in my head doing the reading and thinking anyway, and how does it relate to me.

'It is simultaneously a critical and exhaustive monograph about the ever-evolving nature of The Doctor, the experience of being a fan and, most moving of all, a personal meditation and window into the challenges and superpowers of untypical minds.'

Murray Gold, composer for Doctor Who, 2005-17, 2023-25

'By turns joyous and poignant, impressively researched and personal, Lillian Crawford's highly readable study is a deep-dive celebration of difference and the Doctor.'

Stephen Gallagher, writer of Doctor Who stories 'Warrior's Gate' (1981) and 'Terminus' (1983)

'A fascinating premise to present a neurological diverse analysis of Doctor Who. It's a bold, detailed analysis and one I really enjoyed.'

James Strong, director of several episodes of Doctor Who, 2006-09 (including 'The Impossible Planet', 'Daleks in Manhattan' and 'Voyage of the Damned')

'This is a fascinating read, insightful, expertly written and intertwined with the deeply personal in the best way. Sci-fi is a means of telling a bigger human story and this is exactly what this book does. It opened my eyes yet again to the power of the Whoniverse to accept each other's differences and find a place to belong outside the social norms. Lillian Crawford not only leads us through the history of this phenomenal show but enlightens us as to how it helps the isolated individual form a relationship with fiction that is more real than their reality. A must read for Doctor Who fans.'

Catherine Tregenna, writer of Doctor Who: 'The Woman Who Lived' (2015) and several episodes of Torchwood (2006-2008)

'This book builds a thorough and insightful case for how and why there's a neurodivergence/Doctor Who connection in the show itself and in the fandom. It has just the right amount of poignant personal memoir and authoritative show exposition

- helping it provide a powerful, nuanced and enjoyable take on this long running show and the sometimes complex relationship it has with its audience.'

Kate Fox, stand-up poet, broadcaster and writer (including Bigger on the Inside)

'This book is Cleo Proctor approved!'

Charlie Craggs, 'Cleo Proctor' in Doctor Who: Redacted (2022-23)

First published in 2026 by
Herne Books
Unit 1, The Exchange
6 Scarbrook Road
Croydon CR0 1UH
info@hernebooks.com

This product conforms to the requirements
of the European Union's General Product Safety Regulations (GPSR).
EU Authorised Representative for GPSR:
Easy Access System Europe –
Mustamäe tee 50, 10621 Tallinn, Estonia
gpsr.requests@easproject.com

ISBN: 978-1-917665-10-0

Cover and endpaper artwork by Daryl Joyce.

A catalogue record for this book is available from the British Library.

Printed and bound in Great Britain by Bell & Bain, Glasgow

For six-year-old Lilly,
on 26 March 2005,
across space and time.

Sugar MacAuley: Can't you hear it?

The Tenth Doctor: Like distant voices crying out from a very long way away?

Sugar MacAuley: Yes.

The Tenth Doctor: No I can't. But that doesn't mean you can't. Auditory interstitial echoes could be part of this phenomenon. Whether you can hear them or not could depend on how neurotypical your mind is.

Sugar MacAuley: What are you saying exactly?

The Tenth Doctor: I'm many things, Sugar MacAuley, but neurotypical has never been one of them.

The Last Voyage **by Dan Abnett**

CONTENTS

INTRODUCTION

THE WOMAN WHO FELL TO EARTH

I can see you've been doing the TARDIS up a bit. Hmm. I don't like it.

The Second Doctor in 'The Three Doctors'

On Sunday 3 April 1977 the BBC broadcast a documentary in its *The Lively Arts* series entitled *Whose Doctor Who*. Presented by Melvyn Bragg, the programme chronicled the production of *Doctor Who* from its origins in 1963 to the peak of its popularity during the tenure of the Fourth Doctor, played by Tom Baker. One of the talking heads is introduced as 'educational psychologist John Miller' who visits children at schools in Oxfordshire. He describes a young boy 'who had originally been autistic' but he observed had 'gotten a lot better' by being relocated to a 'special school.' Miller says that the boy described a recurring nightmare in which Daleks gathered in the bushes outside but were unable to attack due to the protection of his teachers. Miller reflects that 'the Daleks are a superb representation of [...] 'autistic behaviour', if you like; of mechanical, mindless, emotionless behaviour.' Miller felt that, despite the boy being 'cured' of autism, there was a constant threat of it returning to invade his mind.

Miller's outdated understanding of autism, as an affliction which might be suppressed or even cured, calls to mind the most explicit representation of mental disability in the classic era of *Doctor Who*. In 'Planet of the Spiders', a young man named Tommy lives at a rural Buddhist meditation centre at which Mike Yates recuperates after being discharged from UNIT. In a narrative similar to *Flowers for Algernon* by Daniel Keyes, Tommy is introduced trying to encourage others to look at a 'pretty flower' he found while weeding the garden, becoming sad when he accidentally crushes it. When he meets Sarah Jane Smith, Tommy admires her 'pretty' silver brooch and she gives it to him, an action which Mike derides as 'a shameless display of feminine wiles'. Tommy steals the blue crystal from Metebelis III to add to his collection of 'pretty' things, which later glows when Tommy is trying to learn to read. The crystal 'cures' him of his disability, and he finds himself capable of more complex speech. He goes to the library and reads 'The Tyger' by William Blake, at first describing it as 'pretty' before correcting himself – 'No, that's beautiful.'

In his 1887 work *Mental Affections of Childhood and Youth*, John Langdon Down described the 'idiot savant', a person in which 'extraordinary memory' is associated with a 'very great defect of reasoning power.' Tommy suddenly has excellent reading ability, but the effects of the crystal do not give him comprehension. In the 1940s, Down's 'savants' were described almost simultaneously by Leo Kanner in Baltimore and Hans Asperger in Vienna as having a condition they both called autism. Both men described aloneness and isolation as the essential factor of autism, and Kanner found 'an obsessive insistence on sameness', such as through repetitive movements which we now identify as self-stimulating behaviour, or stimming, as well as strict routines and hyperfixation on specific details or subjects. While today Tommy appears a clumsy representation of what we would now identify as a neurodivergent man, he was a more sensitively written and empathetic character than Miller's identification of autism with Dalek kind.

In 2014 I came home from school and walked into my bedroom. The walls and ceiling were plastered with posters of the Eleventh Doctor and my first crush, Amy Pond, included as free gifts with my subscriptions to *Doctor Who Adventures* and *Doctor Who Magazine*. Two prints had been purchased from HMV: a mock World War II poster emblazoned '–TO VICTORY!' featuring one of Professor Bracewell's Ironsides on the door to the airing cupboard, and Vincent van Gogh's prophetic painting of an exploding Police Box amidst a starry night framed above my TARDIS-blue chest of drawers. Hundreds of Character Options action figures formed a battalion on the windowsill, standing watch over a painting of K9 my mother created for the family to 'pin-the-tail-on' at one of my childhood birthday parties. There was also the collection of classic-era VHS tapes my uncle gifted to me, and the DVD collection I accumulated over many Christmases and birthdays. These objects and images which brought me such comfort over the years suddenly nauseated me, and I went into meltdown. I tore down the posters, boxed up the figures, and promptly despatched the videos online.

It breaks my hearts to describe this event, given that nine years prior nothing could have come between six-year-old Lilly and the Doctor's adventures through space and time. I knew I would love it even before the broadcast of 'Rose' on Saturday 26 March 2005, having heard my parents describe with fondness the eras of Tom Baker and Peter Davison they watched religiously as children. Immediately I was hooked; but the next week we went on holiday and I missed the transmission of the aptly-titled second episode, 'The End of the World'. Without the godsent gifts of scheduled recording or BBC iPlayer, in those early years I remember furiously fidgeting and whining at my parents to get us home in time for seven o'clock – often hurriedly saying goodbye to Nan, and then running into the house only to moan for hours after I realised I had missed the first three minutes. I was not content merely to watch the show – I filled scrapbooks with clippings from the *Radio Times*, spent all of my pocket money on toys, compendia, and *Battles in Time* cards, and wrote my own stories in my school journal. No one was allowed to know more about *Doctor Who* than I did – undoubtedly one of the reasons why I struggled to make friends.

It will come as no surprise to the reader that it was around this time when my parents first suspected I was autistic. Yet the doctors who examined me used the narrow-minded, male-focused Simon Baron-Cohen diagnostic methods which did not take into account my skilful masking, my sense of humour, and in particular, my love of history and literature rather than science and mathematics. I was diagnosed with dyspraxia, accounting for my lack of coordination. My formal diagnosis of Autism Spectrum Condition did not come until my early twenties after, like Amelia Pond, I had seen countless psychologists and spent years on waiting lists. The process has made me sceptical of the institution of diagnostic practice. Nonetheless, I here present my credentials for writing this book, as both dedicated Whovian and confirmed autist. I recall one doctor telling me that I was too 'normal' to be autistic, and too autistic to be 'normal'. I was 'quirky', 'eccentric', and, always, 'interesting'. He questioned why my parents were pushing for a diagnosis – did they want their daughter to be labelled as abnormal? I have never seen being identified as neurodivergent as limiting. Rather, it gives me the language with which to express myself and make my needs known to others. It is profoundly liberating.

I do not wish to limit the scope of this book, however, to autism. Instead I embrace the neurodiversity model, that there is a constellation of neurodivergent conditions which are naturally occurring cognitive variations. These often have associated strengths rather than being seen as deficits or dysfunctions. I object to the othering of neurodivergent individuals by self-proclaimed 'neurotypicals', many of whom will likely identify with aspects of neurodivergence discussed in this book. There is a common error whereby neurodivergent individuals are referred to as 'neurodiverse' – a singular person cannot in and of themself be 'diverse'. I have subtitled this book *Across the Neurodiverse Universe of Doctor Who* because I am writing not of a singular form of neurodivergence, but acknowledging and celebrating a diversity of experience. That being said, like the Doctor, I have some ground rules, and, like the Doctor, I am bound to break them. I am not diagnosing anyone as neurodivergent, fictional or otherwise; rather, I am offering personal sites of relatability and resonance with *Doctor Who* from my neurodivergent perspective. I am a cultural writer and historian, not a neurologist, and my knowledge of neurodiversity is experiential rather than scholarly. I have interviewed an array of fans and creatives with a relationship to the show to broaden the scope of interpretation, although I must of course acknowledge that these quotations have been curated in line with my own argument. The scope of the book is mostly limited to the main television series from 1963 to 2025, with a smattering of references to spin-offs and other media. The Whoniverse is simply too large to contain in a single volume, although the analytical framework I set out here can certainly be applied beyond the confines of the small screen.

TALKING ABOUT REGENERATION

My meltdown in 2014 and rejection of fandom was the result of too much change. Amy Pond was my favourite companion, and when she suddenly vanished mid-series I was heartbroken.

Just as the Doctor feared at first, Clara Oswald was never going to be good enough because she simply was not Amy. On 23 November 2013, the fiftieth anniversary of *Doctor Who*'s first broadcast, I went to see 'The Day of the Doctor' in 3D at the local Odeon with my mother and brother. Wielding my emerald sonic screwdriver, I watched in awe as my favourite Doctor, the Eleventh, reunited with my favourite Doctor, the Tenth, and even briefly with my favourite Doctor, the Fourth. My favourite Doctor was and is, of course, whichever Doctor I am currently watching. There was something special about the Eleventh, however. I started wearing tweed blazers and my wristwatch upside down, which I claimed made it easier to read when standing on the bus. He blundered through life, not caring that his passionate ramblings made little sense to others, and embraced everything with childlike wonder. Then on Christmas Day he died, and he turned into a scary old man who did not even know how to fly the TARDIS.

This was my third regeneration, but as the Doctor always says, it felt different this time. 'What did you say, my boy? It's all over. It's all over. That's what you said. No, but it isn't all over. It's far from being all over.' The First Doctor stumbles into the TARDIS at the end of 'The Tenth Planet' and his body metamorphoses into the Second. The ability of a Time Lord to regenerate is what has allowed *Doctor Who* to survive, but it has never been an easy concept to accept. In 'The Power of the Daleks', Ben says that it is not only the Doctor's face which has changed, 'He doesn't even act like him.' He forces the Doctor to try on a ring which his previous incarnation had always worn, but it slips off. 'I'd like to see a butterfly fit into a chrysalis case after it's spread its wings', the Doctor explains. 'Life depends on change and renewal.'

Michael Troughton, the son of Patrick Troughton, told me that he was nine when *Doctor Who* began and had instantly become a fan. He loved the First Doctor, as portrayed by

William Hartnell, and he described the bizarre experience of seeing 'my dad trying to emulate the man, a family favourite that had grown and established himself in the hearts of a viewing public.' Few can relate to Michael's exact experience of watching the first regeneration in 1966, but right from the beginning there has been a collective grief when the Doctor alters their appearance. Anneke Wills, who plays Polly, had a different experience, telling me that when she first saw Troughton walk into St Helen's church hall in October 1966 with 'a hopeful grin on his face', everyone cheered. She is quite right when she says that, 'If it hadn't been for Patrick Troughton, we wouldn't be talking about *Doctor Who* today.'

The Doctor often expresses sadness at their change, and has been particular about their new appearance. At the end of 'The War Games', when the Second Doctor is sentenced to exile on Earth for meddling in the affairs of other planets, he is forced to regenerate and is shown several options for his new self. He dismisses them all as too old or young, too fat or too thin. When the Third Doctor eventually sees his face in the sick bay at UNIT in 'Spearhead from Space', he says that it is 'not me at all' before quickly deciding it is 'rather distinctive', even thinking it would be useful on Delphon where they communicate with their eyebrows. The Fourth Doctor explains the process as being like moving into a new house in 'Robot' – 'It takes a little bit of time to settle in.' When he regenerates in 'Logopolis', he comforts himself by saying, 'It's the end. But the moment has been prepared for.' By now audiences were familiar with the Doctor's transformative power.

The Fifth Doctor struggles with his new self in 'Castrovalva', imitating the behaviours of his previous selves before finding a look of his own in cricket whites and a Panama hat – 'Well, I suppose I'll get used to it in time.' His regeneration bucks the trend, however, with the Sixth Doctor bearing a radically different personality at the end of 'The Caves of Androzani'. Peri appears terrified, and says, 'Doctor?' 'You're expecting someone else?' he rebuts. She stammers in response, and he cuts her off. 'That's three 'I's in one breath. Makes you sound a rather egotistical young lady.' 'What's happened?' she manages. 'Change, my dear. And it seems not a moment too soon.' For once, change seems easy for the Doctor to accept. Peri dislikes the Sixth Doctor's appearance in 'The Twin Dilemma', while he calls it 'a positive triumph' and says that his 'outward appearance is of no importance whatsoever.' Peri says that she has to live with it, and when he eventually takes her compact mirror to admire himself he is thrilled, describing it as 'the most extraordinary improvement.' He suddenly becomes overwhelmed and curls into a ball on the floor before dressing in his ghastly coat of many colours. His behaviour is erratic and violent, even strangling poor Peri in a display entirely uncharacteristic of the Doctor. While in 'Time and the Rani' the Seventh Doctor similarly shows confusion, firing off an absurd chain of malapropisms including 'fit as a trombone' and 'absence makes the nose grow longer', his predecessor's vanity is gone, demanding all mirrors to be removed from the TARDIS. The Seventh Doctor is more endearingly feckless than the Sixth, a deliberate retread which makes change palatable.

The first regeneration I watched occurred sooner than anyone anticipated, at the end of the Ninth Doctor's first and only series in 'The Parting of the Ways'. He distracts himself with humour, telling Rose he was going to take her to the planet Barcelona. Bella Madge, an autistic fan who like myself started watching *Doctor Who* from the 2005 series, expressed the difficulty of witnessing the transformation:

> *You get so attached to that character and get a lot of comfort from them. So much of the show doesn't change: there's the*

> *Doctor and his companion, there is a problem and it gets resolved. But with regeneration the change is so abrupt. You're just launched into a brand new personality which can be jarring.*

That new personality, with his bright toothy smile, seeks to find out who he is in 'The Christmas Invasion'. When the Tenth Doctor asks Rose how he looks, she says, 'different.' Not good different or bad different, 'just different.' He is disappointed that he's not ginger, and tells Rose off for giving up on him – 'Oh, that's rude. That's the sort of man I am now, am I? Rude. Rude and not ginger.' When the Doctor puts on his suit and long brown coat, 'Song for Ten' plays over the scene: 'I wish today was just like every other day / 'Cause today has been the best day / Everything I ever dreamed.' Change is something to be feared, and to be embraced. 'Time Travel Coach' and neurodivergent Whovian Carolyn Arnold says that regeneration has always hit home – 'Growing up feeling like an alien child trying to survive in a neurotypical world, the idea that you could completely reinvent yourself without losing who you were was deeply comforting. Still is.' Regeneration is change, but it is also continuation, a paradox peculiar to *Doctor Who*.

By the time the Tenth Doctor regenerated, it was clear that his incarnation needed to change – the Time Lord Victorious had gone too far. With his tearful expression of 'I don't want to go' in 'The End of Time Part Two', I remember my mother emotionally responding, 'Then don't!' The Eleventh Doctor's humour quickly won me over, making the change an easy one to accept. In 'The Eleventh Hour', he speaks with a sensory logic which makes great sense to me – he experiences cravings, first trying apples before childishly deciding he hates them, saying, 'New mouth. New rules.' He moves from yoghurt to bacon to beans, which 'are evil.

Bad, bad beans', a sentiment I shared at the time, and even now I have to eat beans in a separate ramekin for fear of them spoiling the structural integrity of other foodstuffs on my plate. He eventually discovers that the greatest culinary invention in the universe is fish fingers and custard. I have a similar penchant for cucumber and peanut butter. Such food selectivity is typical of autistic people, related to texture, colour, and smell, often as a means of self-regulation when faced with overwhelming sensory stimulation.

The Eleventh Doctor refuses to listen to the protests of others at his insistence that 'bow ties are cool', which, of course, they are. By the time he is dying in 'The Time of the Doctor', his humour has run out. He sees little Amelia and then grown-up Amy, and says:

> *We all change, when you think about it. We're all different people all through our lives. And that's okay, that's good, you've got to keep moving, so long as you remember all the people that you used to be. I will not forget one line of this. Not one day. I swear. I will always remember when the Doctor was me.*

He removes his bow tie and drops it on the floor. He jerks back quickly as the Eleventh Doctor, and then forwards as the Twelfth, staring intensely at Clara, before saying he does not like the colour of his kidneys and announcing that he no longer knows how to fly the TARDIS. His first adventure, in 'Deep Breath', mirrors Peri's first encounter with the Sixth Doctor, suddenly becoming abrasive and mean, as well as overwhelmed and confused. He refers to Clara as 'Thingy', 'the not-me-one. The asking-questions-one'. Like the Third Doctor, he notices his bushy eyebrows, describing them as 'independently cross.' Like Peri, Clara struggles to adapt to the Doctor's new appearance and change of personality.

Catrin Stewart, who plays Jenny, recalled to me with fondness watching Peter Capaldi take on the role: 'Every take he tried something different and he was really playful. It was such a fun scene to film and I didn't really have to do any acting as I genuinely was just watching him in amazement.' I watch that episode now with similar admiration, but at the time too much was changing too fast. I wanted my Doctor back.

A CHANGE OF SEX

There was a bigger change in my life in 2014 which prompted my rejection of *Doctor Who*. After sixteen years of dysphoria, I was finally beginning my own regeneration as I began a process of gender transition. As I was embracing change and letting go of the past, the Doctor seemed older and more male than ever. I had wanted to *be* Amy Pond, but my autistic brain aligned me more with the Doctor, creating a gendered tension. The meltdown which led me to get rid of my collection was related to this dysphoric distress. I continued to watch *Doctor Who*, with some distaste and without the obsessive quality which defined my childhood. Then something miraculous happened – the Doctor regenerated into a woman, the Thirteenth Doctor. The show felt available to me again. The idea of change being positive, of changing sex but remaining at a fundamental level the same person, had enormous personal resonance. If the Time Lords of Gallifrey had moved beyond biological determinism, it was high time the human race caught up.

Doctor Who can often feel like a boys' club. The Doctor's relationships with women have ranged from paternalistic to misogynistic and fetishistic, frequently reduced to the awestruck companion or assistant who needs educating or rescuing. This gendered association with the show came from the production. Between 1963 and 2018, only ten women directed episodes, and even between 2005 and 2017, only four women writers and five directors were part of the production. When the Thirteenth Doctor's tenure began in 2018, two out of five writers and two out of four directors were women, with an additional three women joining as writers and two as directors in 2020. That is not to say that there were not female fans of *Doctor Who* prior to the arrival of the Thirteenth Doctor, but there were not as many obvious sites of identification for neurodivergent girls and women as there were for boys and men.

The first female Doctor had precedents. There was River Song, who made it possible for a Time Lord to be glamorous, with her hallucinogenic lipstick, evening gowns, and ridiculously high heels. Like Amy, she mocked the Eleventh Doctor for his sartorial choices, blasting his fez to smithereens when he insists it is 'cool' in 'The Big Bang'. After it is discovered in 'A Good Man Goes to War' that – spoilers! – River is Melody Pond, the daughter of Amy and Rory Williams, we see her regenerate in 'Let's Kill Hitler', enjoying her new 'mature' body and curly hair, striking the pose of Mrs Robinson on the poster of *The Graduate* (1967). Despite River's outward confidence, she confides in Rory in 'The Impossible Astronaut' a vulnerability in relation to the Doctor: 'He's clever and mad and wonderful, and knows every last thing about her. Imagine what that does to a girl.' Rory says that he does not need to, having experienced life with Amy.

More similar to the Doctor is his evil counterpart the Master, who revealed the possibility of gender change through regeneration when they became Missy. When she reunites with her last male self in 'The Doctor Falls', he is horrified by the impact of gender on their behaviour – 'Becoming a woman's one thing, but have you got empathy?' Later the Master asks the Twelfth Doctor derisively, 'Is the future going to be all girl?' 'We can only hope', comes his reply. Such a change is consolation to the Twelfth Doctor's hesitance to continuously become somebody else, remembering the reluctance of the First Doctor to regenerate in 'The Tenth Planet'. The Twelfth asks the First why he refused in 'Twice Upon a Time', with the reason being given as 'fear. I'm afraid. Very, very afraid. I don't normally admit that to anyone else.' The Twelfth reassures him that technically he still has not. By contrast to the Tenth Doctor's unwilling regeneration, the final words of the Twelfth embrace change – 'Doctor, I let you go.'

When Yasmin Khan approaches the Thirteenth Doctor on a train in Sheffield in 'The Woman Who Fell to Earth', she asks why she is calling her 'madam.' 'Because you're a woman', explains Yaz. 'Am I? Does it suit me?' After Grace says that regeneration 'sounds painful', the Doctor explains that it is terrifying because right now she is a stranger to herself: 'There's echoes of who I was, and a sort of call towards who I am.' It is because the Doctor is aware of her own remarkable ability of transformation that she reveals why she always extends mercy and forgiveness to her enemies. She tells Tzim-Sha that he is a cheat because he knows that he is unworthy, but he could prove her wrong because 'we're all capable of the most incredible change. We can evolve while staying true to who we are. We can honour who we've been and choose who we want to be next.'

In an interview with *Doctor Who Magazine*, Jodie Whittaker, who plays the Thirteenth Doctor, reflected on the resonance her characterisation of the Doctor had with neurodivergent audiences:

> *With the Doctor, it wasn't about explaining. She has characteristics that potentially, in a human form, would be associated with autism, but the joy is [...] it's not in any way negative, in any way something to be fixed. It's something to be celebrated. The Doctor is the Doctor.*

The Doctor undergoes a process of transition of her own, getting used to aspects of her behaviour which she had not experienced when she appeared male. While it had been possible for female fans to dress like the male Doctors – my predilection for tweed persists – there are aspects of this Doctor's costuming which had specific affirmative appeal. I am fond of her ear cuff, a cluster of silver stars linked by a chain to a silver-and-gold handshake, representing her descent from space to Earth where she befriends the human race. I was moved by the Doctor's excitement in being included with other women in 'Demons of the Punjab' by having her palm painted with henna mehndi sun patterns, saying, 'This is the best thing ever. Never did this when I was a man.' When Yaz assumes she is joking, the Doctor says, 'Yeah, that's right. My references to body and gender regeneration are all in jest. I'm such a comedian.' Her attempt to play along with Yaz's humour, underpinned with sincerity about her change of sex, strikes me as beautifully typical of neurodivergent trans women.

Ella Watts, the producer of the podcast series *Doctor Who: Redacted*, who is diagnosed with autism and Attention Deficit Hyperactivity Disorder (ADHD), found joy in 'The Woman Who Fell to Earth': 'Jodie becoming the Doctor was an indescribable moment of hope for me – a moment where I truly felt it might be possible for someone like me to become a meaningful part of the story.' Ella told me that being neurodivergent makes her a better director, for while 'emotional literacy' did not come naturally to her as a child, she had to consciously learn what expressions or tones of voice mean and why someone might use them, making her directions clear and detailed. Unfortunately she felt that the BBC did not support her with adjustments, saying that, 'One of the reasons I left the BBC was because of its highly ableist and unsupportive environment around neurodivergence in its staff.'

Yet Ella was able to introduce overt representation of neurodivergence, transness, and queerness into the Whoniverse through her work on *Redacted*. Under lead writer Juno Dawson, herself a trans woman, the series follows 26-year-old Cleo Proctor, played by Charlie Craggs, also a trans woman, as co-host of *The Blue Box Files* podcast investigating the Doctor. In 'Hysteria', Rani Chandra asks Cleo if she can believe that amazing things are possible, to which she replies, 'Babe, I turned myself into a woman from scratch, what do you think?' She relates to the Thirteenth Doctor's transition in 'Salvation'. The Doctor looks into Cleo's mind and uncovers a memory from her childhood in which the Doctor saved her from an alien but failed to protect her father. She says, 'Cleo, the human mind is a powerful and complex thing. What you experienced that day would traumatise anyone, never mind a little girl.' For the Doctor, for whom time is never linear, there is no question of Cleo's gender ever having been different. Like the henna scene in 'Demons of the Punjab', it is all the more moving and affirming for being mentioned casually, without unnecessary dramatics. Craggs told me that this was only possible because the show hired a trans woman to write her character. 'As I was reading the script, I knew it was important and knew what it would mean to generations of trans people, old and young, who love the show, to get to see someone like them in the universe.' While she confesses to not being a Whovian herself, it has meant a great deal to her to have affirmed so many people in the audience and to have been a vehicle for trans people 'to feel represented in something so special to them.'

I AM THE DOCTOR

In 'Regrets', Cleo describes the Thirteenth Doctor as having 'two hearts and undiagnosed ADHD.' In 'The Doctor's Meditation', a prequel to 'The Magician's Apprentice', the

Twelfth Doctor asks how many days he has been in a castle, and is told it has been about three hours. 'Maybe Clara's right', the Doctor reflects. 'She keeps telling me I've got Attention Deficit, err… something or other.' Even within the Whoniverse the Doctor's behaviour is associated with neurodivergence. The first time I discussed being neurodivergent openly was on the *Autism Through Cinema* podcast, produced by Queen Mary University with support from the Wellcome Trust. I was invited to choose a film which I related to in terms of my autistic experience, and I selected *Amélie* (2001). I talked about Amélie's sense of isolation, her hyperfixation on helping others, and her anxiety of approaching the man who collects discarded photobooth prints. After joining the podcast as co-host, I came to understand my obsession with cinema through a neurodivergent lens, and to explore why certain characters and narratives resonate with me. We recorded a two-part episode exploring 'The Tenth Planet' within our analytical framework, posing questions as to why *Doctor Who* holds such appeal to a neurodivergent audience. This led to me writing an article for *Doctor Who Magazine* about autism and the show, before I began work on this book.

In 'Time Crash', the Tenth Doctor meets the Fifth, whom he describes as 'my Doctor.' When the Fifth puts on his half-moon spectacles, the Tenth is delighted: 'Oh, and out they come, the brainy specs. You don't even need them. You just think they make you look a bit clever.' The Tenth Doctor catches himself doing the same with his own glasses. The episode, a special created for Children in Need, is about David Tennant expressing his admiration for Peter Davison, who in apt timey-wimey coincidence is now his father-in-law. It is also an accurate representation of a fan identifying with the Doctor. Rob Burton, a Whovian diagnosed with autism and ADHD in his mid-forties, told me that a friend once said that he would 'make a good Doctor', and he thought that his friend would as well. They were both later diagnosed with neurodivergent conditions. Rob said the parallel struck him when he was recounting this story to a student, whom 'I'd got talking to after I'd found out they were into *Doctor Who* and were also neurodivergent.' Another fan, Ian Palmer, compared his stimming to the Tenth Doctor, whom he noticed often rubs his ear lobe, and the Eleventh who 'messes around with his fingers.' He said that his wife has 'spent 25 years apologising for me in social situations', just as the Doctor's companions frequently do. Carolyn Arnold affirmed this connection, describing the Doctor as:

> *A rule-breaking, emotionally complex alien with an overactive brain, a love of weird humans, and a total inability to fit in. It's like looking at a version of myself, one with dodgier fashion sense and fewer social expectations. For someone like me who always felt different, the Doctor made that difference feel powerful and valuable.*

Jackson Lake, who has information about the Doctor streamed into his head via an infostamp in 'The Next Doctor', is similar to a lot of neurodivergent *Doctor Who* fans I have met who seem convinced that they actually are the Doctor – 'Simply, the Doctor. The one, the only, and the best.' Jackson is a Victorian gentleman reminiscent of the First Doctor. He has a companion called Rosita, whom he patronises by telling her that the infiltration of a house is 'hardly work for a woman', and when she protests replies, 'the Doctor's companion does what the Doctor says.' He has a regular screwdriver, not a sonic one, and his TARDIS – Tethered Aerial Release Developed In Style – is a Montgolfier hot air balloon. It transpires that Jackson is a mathematics teacher from Sussex. After losing his family, he suffers a fugue state in which the mind runs away because it cannot bear to look back, not dissimilar to neurodivergent states of overwhelm and alexithymia; that is, the difficulty of expressing emotions. Jackson is, in effect, a human cosplaying the Doctor. He, like many neurodivergent people, feels like an alien on his own planet.

In 'Rose', when the Ninth Doctor meets Rose Tyler, he explains who he is by saying that, while human beings cannot feel the Earth revolving, he can. In her book *Explaining Humans*, neurodivergent scientist Camilla Pang recalls her childhood: 'I felt like a stranger within my own species: someone who understood the words but couldn't speak the language; who shared an appearance with fellow humans but none of the essential characteristics.' She says that she asked her mother for an instruction manual to explain why humans behave as they do, and her book is therefore this 'outsider's guide to life.' Pang echoes the words of Temple Grandin, who told Oliver Sacks that while she could understand 'simple, strong, universal' emotions, she could not grasp more complex feelings and the games people play – 'I feel like an anthropologist on Mars.' It is not simply the case that neurodivergent viewers relate to the Doctor; they learn with him as he discovers more about human behaviour from an alien perspective.

When I was researching this book, I wondered if this purpose of *Doctor Who* was something of which its creators were cognisant. Waris Hussein, the director of the first serial 'An Unearthly Child', emailed me to say that while he realises the show has a certain effect on many viewers, 'I had no idea, when, in the early years, as a young first time director, I would be responsible for the emotional results the program would have on future generations of viewers with autism.' In the NuWho era, producer Susie Liggat told me that, while she does not feel correctly placed to comment on neurodiversity within the creation of *Doctor Who*, she is aware that many senior creatives including showrunner Russell T Davies are queer: 'Many different "Othered" groups share experiences that are relatable and relevant across the groups. A unification of otherness. And I'm all for solidarity and support of that rather than singling out.' Director James Strong reiterated this, saying that 'every attempt is made to make the show feel inclusive. Everyone from whatever planet, solar system, or galaxy is welcome.'

Stories of difficulties behind the scenes have upset fans, especially for not succeeding in these attempts to create a safe and inclusive environment. Neurodivergent fan Alexis Harrow told me that her favourite Doctor is the Ninth, played by Christopher Eccleston, whom she felt was her 'best friend':

> *When it came to light that [Eccleston] had a terrible time when filming and was struggling with his self-image, I felt heartbroken for him. I felt angry at the BBC and the show makers for making him be shirtless in 'Dalek'. Even though I'm now a thirty-one-year-old adult, the ten-year-old me wants to be there for my friend.*

Alexis continued that she hopes she never stops caring about *Doctor Who* because 'child Alexis deserves that joy, forever.' This was the same feeling I had when I was asked to write this book – that even though my relationship with *Doctor Who* has been troubled as I have gotten older, I always owe it to six-year-old Lilly to find in it a source of excitement and comfort. When the Thirteenth Doctor regenerated at the end of 'The Power of the Doctor', her Fourteenth incarnation returned to the face of the Tenth Doctor, a manifestation of a nostalgic resistance to change. Perhaps the Doctor moved backwards because their next regeneration was an even greater leap forwards – a bi-generation out of which came the Fifteenth Doctor in 'The Giggle'. With a gleaming smile he says, 'Oh, ho-ho, I am completely me!' Those words ring true with me now. I am ready to steal a Type 40 travel capsule and explore this mad show about a time traveller in a box, across a neurodiverse universe.

CHAPTER ONE
AN UNEARTHLY CHILD

'It's strange,' Sarah said. 'She's such a beautiful little girl, and at moments like this she seems so normal, so perfect, and yet …' She hesitated, a rueful smile on her lips. 'In her own way she's more alien than anything I met when I travelled with you.'

The Fifth Doctor meets Lily, the granddaughter of Sarah Jane Smith, in a story written for *Short Trips: A Christmas Treasury* by Jackie Marshall. There is no supernatural element, simply a carol service at a parish church much like those I attended every Christmas Eve as a child. Little Lily dances to her internal music. 'It must be hard', the Doctor says, 'Trying to understand how her mind works.' 'There isn't really any understanding it. We know she has Autism Spectrum Disorder, and all we can do is to find ways of dealing with her behaviour. But what works one day doesn't the next.' The Doctor helps Sarah to see the pleasure dancing brings to Lily, and the story ends with the three of them moving together as snow falls around them. Lily is explicitly described as neurodivergent, unlike the other children and young people explored in this chapter. Yet there are sites of relatability for neurodivergent youth in *Doctor Who*, right from the beginning.

In 1961, Joe and Helen Allison appeared on *Woman's Hour* on BBC radio to talk about developing recognition of autism in Britain. After they received hundreds of phone calls and letters, in January 1962 a group of concerned parents formed the Society for Psychotic Children. The name was changed to the Autistic Children's Aid Society of North London on the advice of psychiatrist Lorna Wing, who coined the term Asperger's syndrome. This became the National Autistic Society in 1975, as it is still known in Britain today. On 9 November 1962, the society was featured in the *Evening News* under the headline 'Children in Chains', which increased awareness of autism in children further. A year later, on 23 November 1963, *Doctor Who* first appeared on British television. There is synchronicity between the beginnings of the science-fiction programme and early developments in autism research in the United Kingdom. The first scholars to write about *Doctor Who* were not cultural theorists but child psychologists. In 1967, John and Elizabeth Newson founded the Child Development Research Unit at the University of Nottingham. The book they wrote, *Four Years Old in an Urban Community*, published in 1968, observed on a school playground that one child said, 'Don't push me. Daleks don't push people.' The response from their friend was, 'Well, but they exterminate people.'

SUSAN

Observations about 'difference' in children call to mind the conversations between schoolteachers Ian Chesterton and Barbara Wright about their fifteen-year-old pupil Susan Foreman in the first episode of 'An Unearthly Child'. Ian observes that Susan only 'lets her knowledge out a bit at a time so as not to embarrass me' during his science lessons, and when Barbara says she is going to lend her a book on the French Revolution, Ian jokes, 'What's she going to do, rewrite it?' When they find her in a classroom, Susan is listening to John Smith and the Common Men on her transistor radio.

Rather than dancing, she is gently tapping on the plastic, the camera focusing on her hand as it moves in a conductor-like motion in time to the guitar. I do the same when I listen to music, my favourite form of stimming. Like Down's idea of the 'idiot savant', Ian and Barbara observe that Susan is 'absolutely brilliant at some things, excruciatingly bad at others, and, well, just inexplicable at the rest.' I was always in trouble at school for correcting my teachers, even deriding them for being unfamiliar with off-syllabus aspects of their apparent specialism. I spent my spare time listening to classical music and reading history books in the library. Ian and Barbara follow Susan on her walk home, parking outside I.M. Foreman Scrap Merchant at 76 Totter's Lane. Ian suggests that Susan is meeting a boy. Barbara almost hopes she is – 'Well, it would be so wonderfully normal.'

Inside they meet Susan's grandfather, the First Doctor. It transpires that Susan insisted on going to Coal Hill School despite the Doctor's warnings. He calls Susan a 'stupid child', and refuses to tell Ian and Barbara about the TARDIS because they would not understand. Of course, the Doctor starts explaining anyway. Susan tells her teachers that she made up the name from the ship's initials, 'Time and Relative Dimension in Space.' She becomes frustrated with their narrow-minded, human thinking when faced with empirical evidence that dimensions outside of their knowledge are shown to exist. After the Doctor explains that they are not from Earth, Susan tells him to let Ian and Barbara go because she knows Earth people better than him – 'Their minds reject things they don't understand.' Regardless, Susan says that the five months she spent at school was the happiest time of her life – she has a desire to be part of a community, especially one of learning.

During her adventures with the Doctor in subsequent serials, Susan outgrows her relationship with her grandfather. On Skaro in 'The Daleks', after Susan claims that something touched her, the Doctor does not believe her. He wonders if Barbara will talk to her, accepting that 'sometimes I find the gulf between Susan's age and mine makes difficult understanding between us.' The Doctor's patronising behaviour towards Susan is contradictory. Despite repeatedly calling Susan 'child', when she sides with Ian and Barbara, he says, 'If only you'd think as an adult sometimes.' Susan's burgeoning desire for friendship becomes apparent in 'Marco Polo' when she meets sixteen-year-old Ping-Cho. The girl is being sent to Kublai Khan's summer palace in Shang Tu to marry a seventy-five-year-old man she has never seen, a horror which wins Susan's sympathy. But when Barbara tells the Doctor she is sad that Susan and Ping-Cho have not had much time together, he says that it was a pity for there to be 'any association at all. That Chinese child makes me nervous.' The Doctor expresses prejudice as a means of maintaining control over Susan, stymieing her development.

In 'The Sensorites', Susan discovers that she is able to use telepathy and demands to be allowed to go with the titular beings, finding people with a likeness to herself on another planet. The Doctor is furious and Ian wonders if the Sensorites have hypnotised Susan. Again it is Barbara who understands what is happening, revealing a feminine empathy between the teacher and her student – 'She's just growing up.' When the Doctor attempts to reconcile with his granddaughter, he tells her that the benefit of his old age is that he is able to share his wisdom to help her, struggling to see that Susan needs independence to be allowed to learn for herself. The Doctor appears envious of Susan's capacity for telepathy which he himself lacks, which can be read as a neurodivergent condition. The Elder of the Sensorites observes that Susan yearns for a fixed sense of place, to return to her home planet where 'at night the sky is a burned orange, and the leaves on the trees are bright silver.' Yet he also detects her call to adventure, 'a wanderlust'.

These changes in Susan reach their apotheosis in 'The Dalek Invasion of Earth'. After the TARDIS materialises in twenty-second-century London, Susan twists her ankle, provoking the Doctor's most outrageous statement: 'What you need is a jolly good smacked bottom!' Separated from the Doctor, Susan works with a freedom fighter called David who repeats the words of the Sensorite Elder that 'things aren't made better by running away.' They fall in love, but when Susan tries to tell the Doctor, he distracts himself by observing that her shoe needs mending. He watches on the TARDIS scanner as David proposes, but Susan says she needs to take care of her grandfather. At last the Doctor relinquishes control, acknowledging that she is a woman now and he wants her to belong somewhere. He promises to come back, but until then 'there must be no regrets, no tears, no anxieties. Just go forward in all your beliefs, and prove to me that I am not mistaken in mine.'

The Doctor never goes back, although he carries her memory with him. In 'The Legend of Ruby Sunday', the Fifteenth Doctor' is trapped by Sutekh by leading him to believe that Susan is involved in his scheme. When Kate Stewart asks him why he has never tried to find her, the Doctor says, 'What if I go back and ruin her?' After all that time, the Doctor still worries about not being the grandfather Susan needs, letting her go because he understands their differences despite their shared heritage. They are both unearthly children, intensely relatable to those children of Earth being identified as autistic for the first time during those early series of *Doctor Who* in the 1960s.

THE REPLACEMENTS

Since the Doctor said goodbye to Susan, they have been attempting to replace her. In the next serial, 'The Rescue', the Doctor, Ian, and Barbara meet Vicki in the twenty-fifth century who has survived a spaceship crash on the planet Dido. The Doctor quickly promises her 'an abundance' of adventure as well as being 'amongst friends.' He takes a vulnerable young woman and makes her an offer she cannot refuse, without telling her that she is filling the vacancy left by Susan. Ian informs the Doctor that he is only doing this because he misses his granddaughter. The sudden change causes Vicki to panic in 'The Crusade' when she fears that she is being left behind because 'your ship's the only home I've got now.' She tells the Doctor that she thought he was trying to tell her that she is a problem, to which he responds, 'Ah, surely you know me better than that, child?' As he did with Susan, the Doctor always uses this infantilising term of endearment for Vicki. He upsets her in 'The Space Museum' in the same way that his short temper affected Susan when she says that she touched one of the exhibits, despite the Doctor telling her not to.

The Doctor sees aspects of himself in Vicki, such as in 'The Chase' when she speculates that there might be a city or space station over a sand dune. 'The child's just like me, you know', the Doctor observes. 'Always wants to know what's on t'other side of the hill.' Just as the Sensorites observed telepathic abilities in Susan, in 'The Myth Makers' the Trojans believe that Vicki is a prophetess like Cassandra, although she protests that she is 'as human as you are.' They name her Cressida and she falls in love with Troilus, deciding to run away together by joining the crew of Aeneas and setting sail to build a new Troy. Vicki finds her sense of belonging in a different time to her own, discovering that she too needs to embark on an independent journey.

The Doctor's attachment to Susan continues to define his selection of new companions after Vicki's departure. Materialising on Wimbledon Common in 1966 at the end of 'The Massacre of St Bartholomew's Eve', the Doctor and Steven Taylor meet an orphan called Dodo Chaplet. The Doctor says to Steven, 'Don't you think she looks rather like my grandchild Susan?' He forgets that Steven never met Susan. In 'The Ark', the Doctor expresses distaste for the class background of his new companion. When she observes 'these fab pictures', referring to cave paintings, the Doctor says, 'Ah, fab, hmm. My dear child, if you're going to be with us for any length of time, you'll have to do something about that English of yours.' Here he channels Professor Henry Higgins in George Bernard Shaw's 1912 play *Pygmalion*, a phonetician who takes in the flower girl Eliza Doolittle in an attempt to improve her English and manners. The Doctor is manipulative, incapable of allowing his young female companions to be themselves but rather, like the mythological sculptor Pygmalion, he tries to fashion them into his idea of a perfect young lady in the image of his granddaughter.

More suitable for the Doctor's expectations is Zoe Heriot, a young scientist whom the Second Doctor meets in 'The Wheel in Space'. Zoe shows Jamie McCrimmon around the Wheel's parapsychology library, and she tells him that she is doing RNA analysis. She mocks Jamie's kilt, and in a misogynistic display worthy of the First Doctor, he tells her, 'Just you watch your lip or I'll put you across my knee and larrup you.' Rather than being intimidated, Zoe excitedly says that she is going to enjoy spending time with Jamie because she will learn a lot about other peoples. As an astrophysicist and pure mathematics major with honours, Zoe attempts to work out how the Doctor piloted a rocket ship, again patronised by Jamie as 'a right wee space detective' and begrudgingly listened to by the Doctor, who reluctantly says she has an 'interesting theory.' With self-assertive bluntness distinct from the Doctor's previous female companions, Zoe informs him that it is not a theory because 'you can't disprove the facts. It's pure logic.' The Doctor refuses to allow her the final word: 'Logic, my dear Zoe, merely enables one to be wrong with authority.'

Zoe becomes frustrated when she is not believed, or characterised as lacking in empathy. When she calculates the destruction of a star going nova, Captain Leo Ryan describes her as a 'proper little brainchild. All brain and no heart!' She discusses this with the Wheel's medical officer Dr Gemma Corwyn, who says that she must not worry because lacking emotions is part of her training. Zoe responds:

> *I don't want to be thought of as a freak. Leo said I was like a robot, a machine. I think he's right. My head's been pumped full of facts and figures which I reel out automatically when needed, but, well, I want to feel things as well.*

Zoe's gender makes her underdeveloped emotional literacy more pronounced than it is in the many male scientists who appear in *Doctor Who*, who seldom face such criticism. The Doctor and Jamie are reluctant when she asks to go with them, with the Doctor connecting her to a visualiser to show her the dangers she can expect, including the Daleks. She is appreciated more by the Brigadier on Earth at UNIT, who is impressed by her ability to predict a chain reaction of explosions in 'The Invasion'. Sergeant Peters asks, 'Can't we keep her on, sir? She's much prettier than a computer.' Even when her intellectual abilities are appreciated, Zoe is defined by her appearance. She often feels that she cannot please the Doctor and Jamie, always too brainy or too cold, making it hard for her to feel that she belongs.

ROMANADVORATRELUNDAR

The Doctor likes compliant girls who do as they are told, rather than those who are headstrong and show up the deficiencies in their knowledge. When a Time Lord appears in the Fourth Doctor's TARDIS in 'The Ribos Operation', she introduces herself as Romanadvoratrelundar. 'I'm so sorry about that. Is there anything we can do?' comes the Doctor's arrogant reply. He decides to call her Romana, not that she likes the abbreviation, preferring his suggestion of Fred. She tells him that she has been sent by the President of the Supreme Council of Gallifrey to assist him in his search for the Key to Time. She says that it is exciting, and again the Doctor belittles her, remarking it must be for 'someone as young and inexperienced as you are.' But Romana is able to hold her own, pointing out that she graduated from the Academy with a triple First, while the Doctor scraped through with fifty-one percent on the second attempt. She remarks, 'It's funny, you know, but before I met you, I was even willing to be impressed', but 'now I realise that your behaviour simply derives from a subtransitory experiential hypertoid-induced condition, aggravated, I expect, by multi-encephalogical tensions', or in brief, 'a massive compensation syndrome.' Romana's diagnoses go further, identifying their relationship as having 'a negative empathy.' She is astute in her understanding of the Doctor's behaviour, although her manner is clinical, similar to Zoe's mathematical calculations.

Unlike the Doctor's reluctance to follow instructions, Romana insists upon reading the TARDIS manual in 'The Pirate Planet', referring to the ship by its proper name as a Type 40 travel capsule. The Doctor shakes off his curmudgeonly stance when Romana successfully uses the multiloop stabiliser, no doubt reminding him of Susan's navigation abilities. Romana's similarities to Susan go further than her predecessors as she too is a Time Lord, creating an affinity between her and the

Doctor. Yet his time on Earth has given him experiences which are alien to Romana. He sees that it is raining when they materialise and exclaims, 'Anyone for tennis?' Romana asks K9 to explain tennis, and when she tells him to 'forget it', K9 takes her demand literally and erases the subject from his memory banks.

In 'Destiny of the Daleks', Romana uses regeneration to try on different bodies to see how they look. The Doctor says that she cannot just take the form of Princess Astra of Atrios because she liked her, but when she returns wearing his own scarf and hat he says, 'I never realised you had such a sense of style.' Unlike the first incarnation, this new Romana is more submissive to the Doctor. When she feigns death to escape the Daleks by stopping her hearts, a trick she was taught at school, the Doctor calls her a 'good girl.' But ultimately Romana refuses to do as the Doctor tells her. When she leaves the TARDIS at the end of 'Warriors' Gate', he barks, 'Inside. That's an order.' 'No more orders, Doctor. Goodbye.' She tells him that she has 'got to be my own Romana', and the Tharils need the help of a Time Lord. Adric asks the Doctor if she will be all right, to which he replies, 'All right? She'll be superb.' Once again, the Doctor's acceptance of his companion's independence is concurrent with the belief that he has been a vital part of her educational development.

ACE

When the Seventh Doctor meets sixteen-year-old Ace in 'Dragonfire', she is more fiercely independent and rebellious than her predecessors. She works in a diner on the planet Svartos, but loses her job after pouring milkshakes over both an angry patron and her boss. In picking up a teenage girl to accompany him, the Doctor returns to the original dynamic the First had with his granddaughter. Just as Susan felt misunderstood by her teachers because she knew more of the universe than they did, Ace says that her teachers failed to recognise that her blowing up an art classroom 'was a creative act.' Ace originally comes from Perivale where, after doing a 'brill experiment to extract nitroglycerine from gelignite', she was whisked away by a time storm – it is no coincidence in a serial peppered with film references that her given name is Dorothy. She tells Melanie Bush that she was also a waitress back on Earth, and she did not feel like she belonged there:

> *I'd fallen from another planet and landed in this strange girl's body, but it wasn't me at all. I was meant to be somewhere else. Each night I'd walk home and I'd look up at the stars through the gaps in the clouds, and I tried to imagine where I really came from. I dreamed that one day everything would come right. I'd be carried off back home, back to my real mum and dad. Then it actually happened and I ended up here. Ended up working as a waitress again, only this time I couldn't dream about going nowhere else. There wasn't nowhere else to go.*

Ace's words echo Grandin's 'anthropologist on Mars' sentiment. It is not until she boards the TARDIS that Ace finds her home, side-by-side with a real alien. The parallel between Ace and Susan is drawn explicitly in 'Remembrance of Daleks' when she visits Coal Hill School in 1963, picking up the book on the French Revolution which Barbara lent Susan in 'An Unearthly Child'.

The Doctor keeps Ace in the dark about his origins and intentions. When they play chess at the end of 'Silver Nemesis', she asks him the one question that he has not answered: 'Who are you?' He simply puts his finger to his lips. She calls him out for not sharing the truth with her in 'The Curse of Fenric', saying, 'It's like some kind of game, and only you know the rules.' When they confront Fenric, Ace tells him, 'The Doctor never fails. I've got faith in him. Complete faith.' But when Fenric orders the Doctor to kneel before him, he tells him to 'kill her'. He destroys her trust, knowing her insecurities well enough to hurt her more than anyone else could: 'Do you think I'd have chosen a social misfit if I hadn't known? [...] She's an emotional cripple. I wouldn't waste my time on her, unless I had to use her somehow.'

When the Doctor later explains that there was no truth to his words, Ace says, 'Full marks for teenage psychology.' His choice of attack, to draw attention to her sense of ostracisation and difficulty in expressing emotion, replicates typical bullying of neurodivergent characteristics. Ace struggles to understand how she could not love her mother when she discovers that the baby she cared for will grow up to become her. The Doctor makes an astute observation about the complex feelings with which Ace is wrestling: 'Love and hate, frightening feelings, especially when they're trapped struggling beneath the surface. Don't be frightened of the water.' She dives in and faces the complexity of the adult world – something she can only do once she believes in herself rather than putting all her faith in the fantastical figure of the Doctor.

LITTLE PROFESSORS

Adric is the sort of young man who might have been diagnosed with autism in 1960s Britain. Neurodivergent fan Stuart Dodgson reflected on the importance of this character when he was growing up: 'I was devastated by the death of Adric. He was young and male, so maybe I did identify with him at that time. Now I rather dislike the character and his portrayal.' An Alzarian found in E-Space in 'Full Circle' by the Fourth Doctor, Adric finds his match in the robot computer K9. While the Doctor's pooch describes Adric as an 'immature humanoid' after finding him as a stowaway on board the TARDIS in 'State of Decay', the boy outsmarts the dog by saying that he should not be there, therefore he must leave to search for the Fourth Doctor and Romana. K9 admits that 'the conclusion is logical.' Adric asks the Doctor in 'The Keeper of Traken' if he knows all the stars in the sky. He replies, 'Just the interesting ones.' When the boy questions his logic on determining which stars are interesting and observes that he makes no sense, the Doctor tells him that as long as he understands that then they will get along splendidly. This role for Adric is asserted by the Fifth Doctor after his regeneration in 'Castrovalva', assigning Tegan as coordinator, Nyssa with technical skill, and Adric, 'with his badge for mathematical excellence', as navigator: 'He knows the way. He knows me, my old self. Adric, you must help me heal the disconnection. Your role is very crucial.'

The Doctor's fondness for Adric is not shared by Tegan and Nyssa. In 'Four to Doomsday', while Nyssa is happily reading *Principia Mathematica* by Alfred North Whitehead, Adric suggests Tegan similarly passes the time by reading 'a fascinating book on maths through there by a chap called Bert Russell.' When she distastefully says, 'Maths?' Adric says, 'That's the trouble with women. Mindless, impatient and bossy.' Tegan calls him a 'chauvinist', and when Nyssa protests that she enjoys mathematics, he tells her that she is not a woman, 'only a girl.' These traits made Adric unpopular with fans like Stuart, who otherwise identified with the character as a representation of neurodivergent boyhood.

Adric's arrogance is symptomatic of a failure to empathise with those who do not share his special interests. Monarch asks him to explain the theory of relativity, and he finds it amazing that not everyone grasps it. When Tegan tells him that she does not and that if she does not get back to Heathrow she will lose her job as an air hostess, Adric informs her, 'Study maths and you might get a better one.' It is the Doctor who comforts Adric when Tegan says that she wishes to leave the TARDIS in 'The Visitation', as he believes the change will be strange despite not thinking that she liked him. The Doctor tells him, 'Now, don't jump to conclusions, Adric. Sometimes we humanoids try to disguise our, our true feelings.' He delivers the line with an analytical awareness based on observation and experience rather than innate understanding.

In 'Earthshock', this special relationship sours. The Doctor enters Adric's bedroom and tells him to read *The Black Orchid*, admiring its scholarship, but the mathematician does not see why he would find it interesting. He tells the Doctor that he is tired of constantly being teased by Nyssa and Tegan, and that he always finds time to answer their questions but never his – 'I'm tired of being an outsider, Doctor. I want to go back to my own people.' The Doctor refuses to take the risk required to fly into E-Space, and the boys argue over the plotting of coordinates. This argument, and Adric's desire to return to his home, makes his death at the end of the serial all the more tragic. He dies using his gift for logic to solve puzzles to defeat the Cybermen, his final complaint being that he will never know if he was correct. The Doctor and his companions watch on the TARDIS scanner as the freighter on which Adric remained explodes, and while the women cry, the credits roll in silence over his broken gold star.

As with the absence of Susan, the Doctor carries with him a deep mourning for Adric. Nyssa and Tegan roll their eyes in 'Mawdryn Undead' when the Doctor welcomes the Trion schoolboy Vislor Turlough onto the TARDIS, just as Ian and Barbara recognised why the First welcomed Vicki. In 'Terminus', Tegan shows Turlough to Adric's old bedroom and he criticises it as a child's lodgings. Tegan dislikes the boy, and he creepily tells her, 'You look so sweet when you get angry.' Like Adric, he asserts his superiority to Tegan, saying that she is 'so typical of your planet, reduced to shouting if you can't have your own way.' Turlough decides he must go home to Trion in 'Planet of Fire', although he regrets leaving the Doctor as he has taught him so much.

The archetype of the autistic boy genius exists beyond the TARDIS. 'The Twin Dilemma' begins with brothers Romulus and Remus playing a board game when their father Sylvest tells them that he wishes they would be kind to their mother. Remus responds, 'Because Mother happened to give birth to us, does that automatically grant her a place in our affections?' He claims that respect must be earned and their mother is a fool, demonstrating a characteristically neurodivergent approach to hierarchical relationships. The twins play a game of Equations before being kidnapped by Azmael, disguised as Professor Edgeworth, for Mestor, who informs them that he needs their mathematical skill to stabilise two planets into orbit around the planet Jaconda.

The Sontarans make use of the boy genius Luke Rattigan in 'The Sontaran Stratagem'. He runs Rattigan Academy for students handpicked from across the world, 'a hothouse for geniuses' which the Tenth Doctor says he would not mind visiting because 'I get lonely.' Rattigan admires the Doctor as 'smarter than the usual UNIT grunt', and they enjoy correcting each other's grammar. The Doctor says, 'Not easy, is it? Being clever. You look at the world and you connect things, random things, and think, why can't anyone else see it? The rest of the world is so slow.' In 'The Poison Sky', Rattigan reveals he plans to develop a new planet for those who are intellectually superior, an 'Earth Point Two.' He says that his cooperation with the Sontarans has been for the benefit of others like him who spend their lives being excluded and laughed at by 'cattle.' The Doctor does not endorse such eugenicist thinking, although it is easy to imagine Adric, Turlough, Romulus, and Remus joining him on his venture to a new frontier.

THE ARCHETYPE, THE PRINCE, AND THE SUPERHERO

'So, physics. Physics, eh? Physics. Physics. Physics! Physics. Physics, physics, physics, physics, physics, physics, physics. I hope one of you is getting all this down.' The Doctor begins his first class at Deffry Vale High School in 'School Reunion' with a stream of questions of increasing difficulty, all of which are answered correctly by a boy called Milo. He discovers that his exceptional intelligence is accelerated by oil in chips being fed to the pupils by the Krillitane in an attempt to crack the Skasis Paradigm, allowing them to manipulate the fundamental mathematics of the universe. They need children because it is not merely their brains which are used to develop this 'godmaker', but their imagination. This artificial endowment of neurodivergence is also experienced by the Archetype, the physical embodiment of hundreds of humans scanned by the Bane at the Bubble Shock! factory in 'Invasion of the Bane', the first episode of *The Sarah Jane Adventures*. Despite having superhuman intellectual capabilities, the Archetype lacks social skills and emotional understanding. When he and Sarah save the world, he asks if the feeling they are experiencing is 'happiness.' Sarah decides to adopt the Archetype as her son, naming him Luke.

Luke makes many missteps in his attempt to pass as human. In 'Revenge of the Slitheen', he tells Sarah that he keeps making social mistakes, and she reassures him by saying she did the same by driving him to school and kissing him goodbye. When he tells Maria a joke about a 'cereal killer' in 'Warriors of Kudlak', he is disappointed she does not laugh because he has been 'studying jokes, their structure and history.' When he successfully makes others laugh with a joke about a boy named Lance, nicknaming him 'the Corporal', Sarah tells him that it was insensitive, confusing Luke further as he thought he had made 'a breakthrough' but 'it was just another social miscalculation.' He expresses similar frustration to the Doctor's non-human companions who struggle to grasp the relativism of social etiquette on Earth.

As the series continues, Luke learns to mask more successfully, although he struggles to accept change. In 'The Nightmare Man', Sarah gifts Luke her old car which upsets him because he interprets this to mean that she cannot wait for him to leave home. Yet, when he begins his studies at Oxford in 'Death of the Doctor', he appears to have found a place where he belongs with other geniuses, including his new friend Sanjay. In the series coda 'Farewell, Sarah Jane', Luke says that it was Sarah who told him that Sanjay was attracted to him and now they have been married for five years. He says that the way Sarah helped him to navigate the real world meant more to him than any of the supernatural adventures they shared – 'I may have been created by the Bane, but Mum, she gave me a life.'

Charlie Smith – no relation – is a similar character to Luke in the spin-off *Class*, set at Coal Hill Academy. In 'For Tonight We Might Die', Charlie asks fellow pupil April MacLean if she would believe him if he said he was from another planet. 'God, yeah', she replies. 'You're weird and don't know anything about pop culture. You're either alien or Amish. I'm totally not prejudiced.' He reveals that he and their teacher, Miss Quill, come from the planet Rhodia, 'a cultured, learned society' of which he was Prince. The Twelfth Doctor rescued them and dropped them off on Earth where he told them to try to fit in and tell people they are from Sheffield. Like the Doctor, despite appearing human, they found it more complicated to pass. But like Luke, Charlie learns how to get along with his peers and even begins a relationship with a student called Matteusz.

The Twelfth Doctor's naïve expectation for boys with superhuman abilities to blend in is evident in 'The Return of

Doctor Mysterio'. Comic-book fan Grant Gordon swallows an intuitive crystal which makes his love of superheroes real, giving him abilities including levitation. The Doctor tells him he can never use his advanced skills, and checks in on him during puberty. He asks why Grant will not make eye contact, which he explains by saying that the crystal has given him X-ray vision which he cannot turn off. In adulthood Grant ignores the Doctor's warning and adopts the superhero name the Ghost. Yet he still cannot confess his feelings to his teenage crush, Lucy, for whom he works as a nanny. When he tells the Doctor about his cowardice and frankly weird plan for getting closer to Lucy, the Doctor thanks the universe because 'there's somebody worse at this than me.' Lucy has dinner with Grant, in disguise as the Ghost, who struggles to allow her to meet 'the real guy behind the mask' when she says that she is cross at herself for lying to Grant when he has never lied to her. When he eventually finds the confidence to reveal his true self, the Doctor makes an exit, his work done.

NOT LIKE OTHER GIRLS

Boys and girls who are different in the Whoniverse experience a range of challenges and prejudices relatable to a neurodivergent audience. *Doctor Who* does not shy away from revealing the toxic behaviours of such individuals, especially in the misogynistic and arrogant attitudes of its male characters, although it has also shown how these people can change through emotional development. These are traits of the Doctor themself, and sometimes it is through recognising negative aspects of their own behaviour in others that the Doctor learns to behave more compassionately. The Doctor relates to young people who are different, regardless of gender.

While there are many examples of male neurodivergent representation in culture and media, there are fewer for girls.

This sets *Doctor Who* apart, especially in the NuWho era. In 'The Unquiet Dead', after looking into Rose's mind, the servant girl Gwyneth says that since she was little her mother told her she had 'the sight', although she told her 'to hide it.' As a result of growing up on top of the time rift in Cardiff, Gwyneth describes becoming overwhelmed by overlapping voices in her head, an ability which allows her to save the world from the Gelth. Her mother's instruction relates to the pressure placed on young girls to mask their neurodivergence, including savantist capabilities which are not deemed socially acceptable in girls and women.

The early understanding of autism as a condition related to loneliness is seen in Chloe Webber in 'Fear Her'. She observes other children playing outside from her bedroom, drawing them with crayons which causes them to become trapped in her pictures. Chloe grows angry with the drawings for moaning, telling them that they do not know what it means to be alone. The Tenth Doctor looks into her mind and discovers that she is possessed by an Isolus from the Deep Realms, 'empathic beings of intense emotions' who need to have a community. The Doctor, as the last of the Time Lords, is sympathetic towards the Isolus for its desire to find a new family. By contrast, Rose dismisses her behaviour as 'a temper tantrum because it can't get its own way.' When Chloe attempts to draw the entire planet, her mother Trish holds her and shows her love, allowing the Isolus to leave. I recall watching this episode as a child who also found it difficult to make friends, and the anger that came from that feeling of isolation. Unlike Rose, I can empathise.

The Twelfth Doctor meets two girls who exhibit neurodivergent traits. In 'Listen', teachers Clara Oswald and Danny Pink discuss a Year 10 pupil called Courtney Woods over dinner in a scene reminiscent of Ian and Barbara's conversations about Susan. Unlike Susan, Courtney is 'a disruptive influence.' Clara tells the Doctor that it was inappropriate for him to tell the girl that she is not special in 'Kill the Moon', which Courtney says made her go off the rails. Clara informs him that he does not understand the impact he has on impressionable young people. Misunderstanding her, he offers to make Courtney the first woman on the moon which only complicates her life further.

The other neurodivergent child is Maebh Arden, whom the Doctor finds amidst the trees in 'In the Forest of the Night'. He explains the TARDIS to her, but she says that she just thought it was supposed to be bigger on the inside so she did not say anything. When the Doctor says that most people find that concept confusing, she says that because she finds everything confusing she no longer questions anything. Danny describes Maebh as a vulnerable child on medication following an emotional trauma, namely the disappearance of her sister, which Clara says has left her 'barely functioning' and hearing voices. Instead the Doctor says that she is simply 'tuned to a different channel.' Maebh flaps her hands in stim-like motion, although it is revealed that she is trying to keep away the Here who are responsible for the forestation of London. When they leave, Maebh mournfully asks, 'Why does everything have to go?' She tells the Doctor that he helped her because she was worried that everything was her fault. Where Courtney and Maebh's teachers simplify what they identify as problems in these pupils because they do not fit in, the Doctor becomes their site of identification, helping them to explore their unique relationship to the universe.

TIME LADIES

The Tenth Doctor tells Rose in 'Fear Her' that he understands Chloe because he was a father. It is an experience which makes the Doctor sympathetic towards young people, from Susan to the 'biological accident' Jenny brought to life through progenation in 'The Doctor's Daughter'. Despite Jenny having two hearts and coming from the Doctor's DNA, he tells Donna Noble that she is an 'echo' of a Time Lord, because his race is 'a sum of knowledge, a code, a shared history, a shared suffering.' Jenny is uploaded with knowledge of strategic warfare, something the Doctor refuses to identify with, although she points out that they are not so different since he fought during the Time War. The Doctor confides in Donna that the reason for his behaviour is due to having fathered children on Gallifrey, whom he lost. Yet when Jenny takes a bullet for him and is dying, he affirms her identity as his daughter and tells her that she will be 'amazing.' The Doctor struggles with sudden change and remembrance of things past.

In 'The Girl Who Died', the Viking girl Ashildr makes a profound speech about her place in the world:

> *I've always been different. All my life I've known that. The girls all thought I was a boy. The boys all said I was just a girl. My head is always full of stories. I know I'm strange. Everyone knows I'm strange. But here I'm loved.*

Her words echo every young companion the Doctor has had, the desire to belong somewhere. When the Doctor resurrects Ashildr, granting her immortality, he tells Clara that she now has a piece of alien inside her. A sequence which leads into 'The Woman Who Lived' shows time passing around Ashildr as her expression changes from youthful happiness to time-worn sternness. When the Doctor meets her again in seventeenth-century London, she has changed her name to Me to stress that she is her own companion. She tears out bad memories from her journals, but keeps the entry detailing the loss of her children to remind her not to have more. The Doctor wants her to rediscover the person she used to be, observing this to be 'just another mask that you wear to protect you from the pain.' The Doctor had given Me a second immortality charge because 'humans need shared experiences', but she tells him no one is good enough. Immortals need 'the mayflies', he says. 'They know how beautiful and precious life is because it's fleeting.'

Catherine Tregenna, who wrote the episode, told me that Me embodies the relatable experience of being an outsider, and for her the Doctor serves as 'the emotional barometer she needs; to vent, to connect, and, ultimately, to care about humanity. In turn, the Doctor realises why he needs a human companion, to remind him that others matter. To give him perspective.' The Doctor's relationships with other outsiders across the universe become symbiotic, allowing both them and their companion to learn more about themselves and to develop their own independent paths. I grew up with *Doctor Who*, with many of the characters discussed in this chapter mirroring the experience of being an autistic child with greater accuracy than I found in the real world. Like Me, I could not understand why I needed friends, and the traumas I experienced at school hardened my personality. But the Doctor is right to observe our need for social relationships, as I discovered by finding communities to which I felt that all-important sense of belonging. The Doctor was there for me when I needed them, until I learnt how to go it alone, beyond the TARDIS control room.

CHAPTER TWO

THE ALMOST PEOPLE

You might as well unmask, my clever little Doctor man.
Empress of the Racnoss in 'The Runaway Bride'

Human race, greatest monsters of them all.
The Master in 'Last of the Time Lords'

Unmasking scenes in *Doctor Who* are dramatic moments in which a character, hitherto passing for human, strips off their bodysuit to reveal something monstrous. Co-creator Sydney Newman did not want the programme to feature what he called B.E.M.s – bug-eyed monsters – encouraging alien threats to be disguised. There is a fear common to neurodivergent people that if they act around others as they do when they are on their own that they will be rejected. A woman who goes to an office during the day might come home in the evening and find comfort in rocking back and forth on her bed, flapping her hands, and producing vocal sounds. It is the effectiveness with which some women and girls mask such behaviour that makes us more difficult to diagnose than boys and men. Where a male who sits on his own with a book or solving equations might be seen as a prodigy, a female who does the same is unsociable, weird, and, in our heteronormative, patriarchal society, unattractive. An ability to mask can be the line between being tolerated and being attacked. It is an experience frequently experienced by non-human species attempting to blend in on Earth, not least the Doctor themself.

Another term used for masking in neurodivergent communities is 'camouflaging', a word which calls to mind the self-disguising abilities of the chameleon. After encountering the budget travel company Chameleon Youth Tours in 'The Faceless Ones', the Second Doctor explains to Jamie what a chameleon is: 'a small animal, a lizard that can change its colour to merge with its background. But it's a name that could equally be applied to people as well. People who change their personalities to suit their own ends.' In the story, people are cloned from their originals, making it near impossible to distinguish them. The Doctor shows an awareness of the fear of betrayal, that humanoid creatures can present an image which hides their intentions. For neurodivergent people, who typically find it challenging to read beneath the obvious surface of others' words, expressions, and actions, this is a source of anxiety. Because I know that other people lie, or hide secrets, it makes me suspicious that what is said might not be truthful. It feels like a devastating act of treachery when someone makes a promise that they do not keep, making trust complex.

The Time Lords invented a technology called a Chameleon Arch which modifies an individual's biology to change their species and prevent recognition. A lifesaving mode of camouflage which creates a full body mask for a Time Lord, although at the cost of forgetting their true self. The component of Type 40 travel capsules which allows Time Lords to travel to other planets incognito is the Chameleon Circuit, which alters the outer plasmic shell of the vehicle upon materialisation so that it does not appear conspicuous. When the TARDIS arrives in the Stone Age in 'An Unearthly Child', Susan is shocked to discover that the ship still looks like a 1960s police telephone box as it should have changed when they landed, telling Barbara that it had previously been an Ionic column and a sedan chair. There is appeal to having a sanctuary which one can take anywhere, hidden in plain sight, to which one escapes when the world becomes too much.

It seems appropriate, however, that the Doctor's safe space is distinctive, never bothering to fix the Chameleon Circuit long after police boxes vanished from the streets of London. It is Susan who is concerned about the exterior not changing, for fear of being seen as out of place, rather than the Doctor who has a fondness for his anachronistic blue box. She sees greater danger than he does about not fitting in. Writer and journalist Alex Hewitt, who works with Big Finish on *Doctor Who* audio dramas, reflected that the Doctor's reluctance to fix this feature of the TARDIS is the clearest way in which he relates to the character as ADHD. 'In the Sixth Doctor's era it is made clear that they could just fix it. Their reluctance and procrastination when it comes to repairing their home relates to a way in which ADHD manifests itself.'

BEING DIFFERENT

The TARDIS doors open during materialisation in 'Planet of the Giants', causing the ship and its crew to shrink. Finding themselves in a house, Susan suggests trying to talk to the regular-sized humans, although Ian observes that they cannot communicate as they will sound to them like a 'record played at the wrong speed.' Barbara fears that the normal humans will see them as 'freaks' and 'put us in a glass case and examine us through a microscope.' The human who is different is seen as an object of fascination, often at the cost of their dignity, with the neurodivergent mind being seen as worthy of study rather than appreciation. The First Doctor represents a bigoted view, observing that the humans are murderers, and therefore they cannot expect 'sympathy and understanding from an insane or a criminal mind.' It is stereotypically believed that neurotypical people should not expect sympathy from those who are neurodivergent, yet of course this is not universally true, and many neurodivergent individuals are capable of intense empathic feelings. Certainly the Doctor's viewpoint is contradicted by his later expressions of faith that anyone has the capacity to change.

The Doctor's concept of difference, or lack thereof, is informed by their experience of a myriad of civilisations and species. While in the NuWho era their companionship has been almost exclusively human, the classic Doctors found company from across space and time. In 'Four to Doomsday', when Monarch calls the Fifth Doctor 'an Earthling', he responds, 'A Gallifreyan. Tegan is an Earthling, Adric is an Alzarian, and Nyssa there is from Traken.' It is a reminder of the interplanetary diversity which previously existed in the TARDIS. By contrast, when Rose arrives on Platform One in 'The End of the World', she struggles to see the non-human species onboard as anything other than alien, while the Ninth Doctor points out that to him she is the alien. The episode introduces the psychic paper, which allows the user to change their title and position in order to access all areas, and clarifies the ability of the TARDIS's telepathic field to translate all other languages to English. These cloaking devices break down barriers of difference for Rose, allowing her to look past external appearances and focus on shared values. To see others through the eyes of the Doctor.

Doctor Who makes a farce of established customs and accepted behaviours, revealing why the Doctor is able to ignore man-made rules and conventions. In 'The Empty Child', the Ninth Doctor informs Rose that the universally recognised colour for danger is mauve, not red, because, 'by everyone else's standards, red's camp. Oh, the misunderstandings!' When Martha Jones meets Chantho, a survivor of the Malmooth from Malcassairo in 'Utopia', she is confused by the unique phrasing of her sentences. Martha asks if she has to start every sentence with 'Chan' and end it with 'tho', wondering what would happen if she did not. Chantho says it would be rude. Martha encourages her to do it, and Chantho responds, 'No', before giggling.

Danger comes when certain peoples determine that there is a superior way to behave and suppress those who exist outside of their conventions. This is the subject of 'The Crimson Horror', in which the Eleventh Doctor and Clara are recruited to Sweetville run by Mrs Gillyflower under the influence of Mr Sweet. After the preservation process goes wrong, leaving the Doctor with red skin, he is found by Gillyflower's daughter, Ada, who is forced to hide due to her blindness and facial scarring. She decides to keep him hidden, her 'special monster' to whom she can relate. Ada discovers that her physical difference was caused by her mother experimenting on her to develop a new race, and she begs Mrs Gillyflower to promise that there is still room for her in the 'new Eden.' Ada rebels and crushes Mr Sweet with her walking stick, asserting her newfound independence. She tells the Doctor before he leaves that 'there are many things a bright young lady can do to occupy her time. It's time I stepped out of the darkness and into the light.' By appearing similar to Ada, the Doctor made her feel less like an outcast, and gave her the strength of will to face a world in which she will always be perceived as different. The power she now has is that she has learned not to care.

BEING HUMAN

Rose overcomes her prejudice against non-human species in 'The End of the World' by discovering that she has more in common with them than the so-called last human, Lady Cassandra O'Brien.Δ17. She has remained a 'pure human' through 708 operations, which she believes makes her superior to all those new humans, proto-humans, digihumans, and human-ish who occupied the Earth in its final days. But Rose sees her for what she is, 'a bitchy trampoline' who has had her human aspect thrown away – 'You're just skin, Cassandra. Lipstick and skin.' Yet when she is drying up and demanding to be moisturised, it is Rose who tells the Doctor to help her, while he coldly declares, 'Everything has its time and everything dies.'

Cassandra's brain survives, and she meets Rose and the Tenth Doctor again in 'New Earth', now attended to by a force-grown clone called Chip. A ricocheting series of body swaps follows, revealing the essential characteristics which make up an individual's persona. When Cassandra's mind enters Rose's body, she is horrified to discover she is 'a chav', and attempts to pass as the Doctor's companion by talking in Cockney rhyming slang and snogging him. It is not this strange behaviour which makes him realise that something has happened to Rose, however, but the fact that people are being experimented on by the Sisters of Plenitude and she does not care. Cassandra moves into the Doctor's body, remarking in comical regenerative fashion, 'Goodness me, I'm a man. Yum. So many parts. And hardly used. Oh, oh, two hearts! Oh, baby, I'm beating out a samba!' While this character has the Doctor's image, his personality has changed, suddenly confident and flirtatious, even making reference to his sexual characteristics. The components which make the Doctor seem alien are most obvious when they are suddenly absent. Finally Cassandra enters Chip's body, and the Doctor takes her to see her glamorous unoperated body on Earth, where it is her own future self who tells her that she is beautiful. Cassandra's arc asserts a message about the value of inner beauty through intention over superficial outward appearance.

There are many ways in which aliens in *Doctor Who* attempt to appear human. In 'The Ark', Deputy Commander Zentos is suspicious of Steven, saying that he could be a

Refusian sent to intercept their spacecraft as they do not yet know what the intelligence which occupies their destination planet of Refusis II looks like. He says, 'They might have a way of assuming human bodies, of using them to pass, to mingle amongst us!' The First Doctor replies by paraphrasing Shylock in *The Merchant of Venice*, saying, 'With all our imperfections, I can assure you, sir, if you were to cut my skin, I would bleed, the same as you would.' Zentos voices a common prejudicial paranoia, one which is perpetuated by examples of villainous creatures appearing human.

The Vespiform leaves morphic residue behind when it genetically re-encodes in 'The Unicorn and the Wasp', allowing the Tenth Doctor to realise that the murderer is an alien. It had even managed to hide from itself until the masked Reverend Golightly lost his temper which broke the genetic lock. He is the son of Lady Clemency Ellison, who had sex with a human-passing Vespiform called Christopher in Delhi, and whose Firestone jewel was a telepathic recorder which absorbed into the child's consciousness the works of Agatha Christie. Through Christopher's affair with Lady Ellison, he was able to reveal his true self to her, just as neurodivergent people often only feel comfortable unmasking when they are in the company of a partner. Reverend Golightly's accidental transformation is comparable to an autistic meltdown wherein the strain of masking becomes too great and the individual loses control of their behaviour. The Vespiform's mistaken understanding of humanity, believing the real world to be a murder mystery, similarly relates to the literal interpretation of fiction typical of neurodivergent readers. It can be helpful for neurodivergent people to make sense of things through culture and media such as books and films, just as I am doing in this book. However, this can lead to confusion when aspects of those unreal worlds fail to conform with life as it is lived.

Sometimes aliens which appear evil are discovered to

believe that they are acting in good faith. The zombies in 'The Empty Child' and 'The Doctor Dances' were created by nanogenes, subatomic medical robots, which escaped when the Chula ship crashed in London. The first injured human they found was a child wearing a gas mask killed during an air raid, and after bringing him back to life, the nanogenes assumed that the mask was part of the human face and began 'healing' other people by building them gas masks out of flesh and bone. It is only when the child's mother holds him in her arms that the nanogenes recognise the mistake they have made.

It is not always sufficient to behave like a human; in some cases they must be biologically identifiable. While the Doctor's body appears human to others, they cause confusion whenever they find themself in a hospital and the staff discover their binary vascular system. When the Royal Hope Hospital is transported to the Moon in 'Smith and Jones', the mercenary police force of the Judoon arrive to hunt down the 'non-human', referring to a Plasmavore disguised as an old lady called Florence Finnegan. The Plasmavore drinks the blood of Mr Stoker, allowing her to be marked as human when the Judoon scan her. When she needs to refresh her supply, the Doctor tricks her into believing that he is a suitable human to assimilate by claiming to be a postman with bunions. He performs an exaggerated and comical understanding of human behaviour, dumbing down his intelligence and engages in small talk which would typically bore him to tears.

The alien police return in 'Fugitive of the Judoon' to hunt another non-human in Gloucester. They trace their lead to tour guide Ruth Clayton and her husband Lee, although their scanner reveals them both to be human. The Thirteenth Doctor suspects Ruth is not who she says she is, especially after she removes the horn of the Judoon captain, the worst possible insult. Ruth is drawn to the memory of a lighthouse where she grew up. She travels there with the Doctor and, upon breaking the glass of the lantern, golden regeneration energy flows into her and she remembers who she is – the Doctor. While the Thirteenth quickly realises that this other Doctor must have used the Chameleon Arch to make herself human, neither of them can remember each other, making it impossible to determine where they exist in their own timeline. This Fugitive Doctor has a radically different personality to Ruth, who moved away from the lighthouse because she loved people and human interaction, while her Doctor is aloof and violent, traits even the Thirteenth cannot recognise. Shifts in personality and neurotype are shown to be possible even within the same person.

JOHN SMITH

Time Lords who spend an extended period of time on Earth often pick up human habits. In 'The Armageddon Factor', the Fourth Doctor reunites with Drax, a Gallifreyan he studied with 450 years ago. Drax calls the Doctor 'Thete', short for Theta Sigma, his nickname when he received his doctorate. He speaks with a distinctive dialect, which the Doctor asks him about, and Drax explains that his transport broke down in Brixton – 'I had to learn the lingo, didn't I? To survive.' The Doctor describes his new way of speaking as 'very colourful, very demotic', echoing similar prejudice to the First when criticising Dodo. He is not above Drax's attempt at masking, however, having on numerous occasions adopted the human alias of John Smith. Jamie gives this pseudonym to Gemma Corwyn in 'The Wheel in Space', taken from the manufacturer of her medical equipment, John Smith and Associates. 'There must be a lot of them about', Jamie explains. The name is an amusing attempt by the Doctor to pass as an everyman, despite always being the least ordinary man in the room. It disappoints Rose when the Ninth Doctor uses the name in 'The Empty Child', remarking that it is not 'very Spock', the name she decides to use for the Doctor when she talks to Captain Jack Harkness. She does not want her Doctor to blend in, even when it is safer for him to do so.

Like the Fugitive, the Tenth Doctor uses the Chameleon Arch to transform his body into the human John Smith, encapsulating his Time Lord consciousness into a silver fob watch which he entrusts to his protector, Martha Jones. The Doctor needs to conceal himself from the Family in 'Human Nature' who use a Time Agent's vortex manipulator to pursue the TARDIS. Mr Smith works as a history teacher at Farringham School for Boys in 1913, but he has dreams of living as the Doctor, 'a man from another world.' The school matron, Joan Redfern, tells him that she believes the Doctor is a manifestation of the person he would like to be after he performs a miraculous feat with a cricket ball to save a baby from a falling piano. John Smith is like a Whovian writing fan fiction, his *Journal of Impossible Things* filled with drawings akin to fan art. He says that he learnt to draw in Gallifrey, which must be in Ireland, and in a metafictional reference he says that his father was a watchmaker called Sydney, in reference to Newman, and his mother is a nurse called Verity; that is, the first producer of *Doctor Who*, Verity Lambert. Cracks behind the mask shine through, and Martha tries to bring the Doctor back by encouraging Joan to look behind John's human appearance. When he returns in 'The Family of Blood', it breaks Joan's heart, rendering him an alien to her. He simply is not the man she fell in love with.

The Twelfth Doctor has the hardest time passing for human. When he uses his John Smith alias in 'The Caretaker', the Doctor does not use the Chameleon Arch but merely puts on a different coat and wields a broom. The Doctor believes he is able to trick people into believing he is human not through any performative ability, but because humans are of inferior intelligence. The Ninth Doctor dismisses them as 'funny little human brains' in

'The Doctor Dances', and Rose explains to Jack that he does that when he is stressed – 'He cuts himself shaving, he does half-an-hour on life forms he's cleverer than.' Clara tells the Twelfth she hates him, which he says is 'a perfectly normal reaction.' Yet she makes considerable effort to help the Doctor to not offend others. Upon realising that he is dealing with the actual ghosts of dead people in 'Under the Lake', the Doctor becomes excited but panics when the crew of the Drum point out that the ghost was their friend. Clara whispers to the Doctor to use his cards, prompts she has written for him to use in social situations in which he struggles to find appropriate words: 'I didn't mean to imply that I don't care'; 'It was my fault, I should have known you didn't live in Aberdeen.' Clara hands him the card reading, 'I'm very sorry for your loss. I'll do all I can to solve the death of your friend/family member/pet.' He says the cue as written, with apparent solemnity, before talking frantically again about the thrill of new evidence suggesting that the universal truth of death might be a lie. He reels off the questions he wants to ask the ghosts, before saying to himself, 'Calm, Doctor, calm. You were like this when you met Shirley Bassey.' Or, indeed, a Whovian at a convention.

The cards appear again in 'Face the Raven' after the Doctor realises that Rigsy has been retconned. He flicks through them, with Clara explaining that he is 'making an effort to be nice.' He spoils this by blurting out, 'There is no nice way to say you're about to die.' While the Doctor makes social miscalculations which cause him to appear non-human, what matters to Clara is that he tries, and over the course of his tenure he mellows into a more empathetic man.

ALL THE STRANGE CREATURES

Much of the horror of *Doctor Who* is derived from the uncanny – a closeness and familiarity which many of its monsters bear to human reality, albeit with a disconcerting aspect. Autons are plastic dummies animated by the Nestene Consciousness, a species described during their first appearance in 'Spearhead from Space' as having no individual identity but rather a collective brain or nervous system. In 'Terror of the Autons', the Third Doctor tells Jo Grant that they are 'a ruthlessly aggressive intelligent alien life form', the basic form of which is analogous to a cephalopod. The Nestene can hide in plain sight as mannequins in shop windows without arousing suspicion, while its actual corporeal existence would provoke fear and disgust. When the Nestene returns in 'Rose', it duplicates Rose's boyfriend Mickey Smith, mimicking his speech but malfunctioning when it repeats, 'Babe, sugar, babe, sugar.' Rather than a soldier, this Auton duplicate is used for reconnaissance, to discover the Doctor's plan for destroying the Nestene, but its inability to successfully appear human leads to its destruction. That the Nestene produces increasingly convincing duplicates shows that it is attempting to learn more about humans in order to launch a successful invasion.

The Eleventh Doctor realises in 'The Pandorica Opens' that the new phase of Autons might even think that they are real, 'the perfect disguise', believing their own cover story until they are activated. Rory Williams has been replaced by a Nestene duplicate, which the Doctor describes in 'The Big Bang' as 'a lump of plastic with delusions of humanity.' As with the Vespiform, the Doctor attempts to break its genetic lock by making the Rory Auton angry, saying that his girlfriend Amy is not more important than the whole universe. The Doctor knows the Nestene cannot replicate this emotion, reassuring him that it has Rory's consciousness.

After appearances in classic serials opposite the Second and Third Doctors, an Ice Warrior finally reveals the form under their helmet in 'Cold War'. Grand Marshal Skaldak is brought aboard a Soviet submarine in 1983, and in an attempt to reason with him, the Eleventh Doctor asks to look him in the eye. The Martian has a startling reptilian appearance, yet Clara sees in him a capacity for compassion, pointing out that he hesitated when she begged him not to kill. She appeals to his better nature as a father, encouraging him to remember his daughter at his last battle, when they sang the Songs of the Red Snow. He becomes vulnerable without his protective armour, revealing more in common with human experience than he would have liked to believe. Bill Potts is similarly able to reason with Iraxaa, the title Ice Warrior of 'Empress of Mars'. After she calls Captain Catchlove 'the pink thing' and the Twelfth Doctor asks her to extend mercy to the 'primitives', Iraxaa turns to Bill for advice as the only other female present amongst 'noisy males.' Even where a species appears different to human beings, there is always common ground to be found.

It can be difficult to reason with races which deem their own kind superior, such as the Sontarans. Commander Linx insists that Earth is a 'primitive planet and its affairs are of no importance' in 'The Time Warrior', a stance which the Third Doctor describes as 'a typically Sontaran attitude.' They are obsessed with war and do not care if their interventions will have a devastating impact on humanity. Sarah thinks that Field Major Styre is Linx when she meets him in 'The Sontaran Experiment', finding them to appear identical. Styre is researching human weaknesses, such as their dependence on fluid and capacity for drowning. Just as the Doctor encourages Skaldak to stop hiding behind a mask, the Tenth Doctor tells General Staal to take off his helmet in 'The Sontaran Stratagem'. Private Jenkins is shocked by Staal's appearance, describing him as 'a talking baked potato', while the Doctor points out that to Staal he looks like a pink weasel.

The comical aspects of a Sontaran's personality are explored in Commander Strax, who serves as a nurse in 'A Good Man Goes to War' as penance. Bedside manner and sympathy are not in his nature, saying to Captain Harcourt after taking care of him, 'I hope some day to meet you in the glory of battle, when I shall crush the life from your worthless human form. Try and get some rest.' Strax is confused about human gender, and struggles to give up his commitment to warfare. He tries to be helpful, asking the Doctor in 'The Snowmen' for permission to voice opposition to his 'current apathy.' The Doctor's response is uncharacteristically harsh: 'Thank you, Strax. And if ever I'm in need of advice from a psychotic potato dwarf, you'll certainly be the first to know.'

Strax forms a third of the Paternoster Gang, along with the human Jenny Flint, and her Silurian wife, Madame Vastra. Unlike the first batch of *Homo reptilia* which the Third Doctor encountered in 'Doctor Who and the Silurians', Vastra has a face more recognisable to *Homo sapiens*, albeit covered with green scales. She masks in Victorian London, wearing a veil outside of her home, but makes miscalculations in her relationship with Jenny. In 'A Good Man Goes to War', Vastra says that the Eleventh Doctor is rather attractive, prompting Jenny to ask if the lesbian Silurian realises that he is a man. 'Mammals. They all look alike', she says, offending her wife, before saying, 'Was I being insensitive again, dear? I don't know why you put up with me.'

The Doctor told another Silurian called Alaya that she is 'beautiful' after removing her mask in 'The Hungry Earth'. He gets angry when she uses the Klempari defence, to claim to be the last of her species, because he knows how that fact 'sits in a heart.' Alaya tells him that they had rested for 300 million years before being awoken by a mining drill, and now they will 'wipe the vermin from the surface and reclaim our planet.' The Silurians see human beings as 'primitive apes', who similarly attempt to other the 'aliens.' 'They're not aliens. They're Earth-liens', the Doctor explains. He tells them that they need to find a way to co-exist, while Tony Mack says that they should dissect the Silurian to find its weak points, making him no better than Styre in 'The Sontaran Experiment'. It is at moments like this that the Doctor finds humans to be alien to him after all.

The Doctor also tries to broker a truce between humans and Zygons, a race of metamorphic humanoids which in their true form have cone-shaped heads and suckers. When a Zygon transforms into a Scotsman in front of Harry Sullivan in 'Terror of the Zygons', he tells him, 'We have the power to turn ourselves into replicas of your unpleasant form whenever it is necessary.' The Zygons find their masking capabilities disagreeable, and change body print every few hours. This is no longer the case when they reappear in an evolved form in 'The Day of the Doctor', with one assuming the image of UNIT's scientific advisor Petronella Osgood. When she returns in 'The Zygon Invasion', she says that she does not answer the question if she is human or Zygon because they are 'the living embodiment of the peace we made.'

In 'The Zygon Inversion', a Zygon takes the form of Clara, whom the Twelfth Doctor calls Zygella although her real name is Bonnie. He speaks to her on the phone and she keeps winking at him, confusing the Doctor by sending mixed messages to a man old enough to be her Messiah. It transpires that the human Clara is influencing Bonnie's behaviour from inside her consciousness, preventing her from passing. The danger of the Zygons being unmasked is vital to the effectiveness of the Osgood Box, which can destroy either their kind or humanity. The Doctor launches into a tirade, asking Bonnie what a homeland free from humanity will look like, without holidays or music. She realises that the Box is empty, and he tells her that she knows this because she has started to think like him. Director Daniel Nettheim told me that this scene resonated with subjects including 'immigration, the refugee crisis, radicalisation, and the rise of extremism – all packaged up as family-friendly entertainment.' He observed that, 'Although the aliens were just men in silly rubber suits, they became a poignant stand-in for displaced peoples anywhere in the world today.' In the context of this book, the Doctor's speech can be read as a protest against those who seek to hide away or 'cure' neurodivergent people, to make it a source of shame rather than pride. There will not be music, nor literature, scientific discoveries, technological developments, and certainly no *Doctor Who*. At the end of the episode, Osgood tells the Doctor that the day she will answer the question if she is human or Zygon will be the day nobody cares about the answer. The day when diversity is acknowledged as an essential component of peaceful civilisation.

DEAD RINGERS

At the beginning of 'Aliens of London', a spaceship crashes into the clockface of the Elizabeth Tower. It is piloted by a pig wearing a spacesuit, which is shot when it runs screaming. The Ninth Doctor is furious, and with the assistance of Toshiko Sato, identifies it not as an alien but as a regular pig from Earth. The Doctor compares it to a Victorian mermaid, a trick created by showmen in which the skull of a cat was glued to a fish. It is a decoy – an alien created by other aliens to hide the actual aliens in plain sight. They are the Slitheen family from Raxacoricofallapatorius, a criminal group who steal the skin of humans to use as bodysuits which allow them to infiltrate the British government. They are largely successful in their attempt to pass, except for their excessive flatulence. Member of Parliament Harriet Jones hides in the cabinet room of 10 Downing Street as she watches the Slitheen unzip their foreheads, a literal unmasking revealing their true form.

After the Slitheen are successfully defeated in 'World War Three', the Doctor discovers in 'Boom Town' that

Blon Fel-Fotch Passameer-Day Slitheen is still masquerading as Margaret Blaine, now elected Lord Mayor of Cardiff. She gives an interview to Cathy Salt, taking her to the women's lavatories with the intention of killing her. Yet when the journalist says that she is getting married and a baby is on the way, she appeals to Blon's better nature. She tells Cathy that she has been lonely since the death of her family, and spares the young woman. Blon has grown fond of her 'little human life' and insists that before the Doctor takes her home they have dinner. She tells him about Cathy, that she has changed, but the Doctor says it is small acts of kindness which allow killers to justify their actions. Something only a killer would know, Blon observes. Annette Badland, who plays her, told me that she loved her character's arc, as she is reborn as an egg at the end of the episode – 'The possibility of regeneration! Reincarnation! A second chance! Redemption! How often humans hope and wish for this.' By spending time on Earth and passing for human, it is hoped that the moral values she learned will define Blon in her new life.

The question of distinguishing two apparently identical characters recurs in *Doctor Who*. In 'Kinda', Tegan meets a second version of herself inside her own mind, a trick played by the Mara. Nyssa is asked if she is related to Ann Talbot in 'Black Orchid' as they look the same, deciding to wear the same butterfly costume at the party. Saibra, one of the recruits in 'Time Heist', can replicate any owner of living cells when she touches them. She tells the Twelfth Doctor that having many faces has made it easier for her to read them, allowing her to know when he is lying. It has come at the cost of making her lonely, asking, 'Could you trust someone who looked back at you out of your own eyes?' This question is explored in 'The Rebel Flesh', in which Gangers are produced from fully programmable matter called the Flesh to prevent harm to humans in the mining of acid. The Eleventh Doctor asks if the Flesh has a mind and soul, and Miranda Cleaves informs him that while it acts like life, it still needs to be controlled. Yet when Rory talks to Jennifer Lucas's Ganger, she reveals that she shares Jennifer's memories. She remembers being a little girl lost on the moors, imagining another girl just like her who was also Jennifer: 'Except she was a strong Jennifer, a tough Jennifer. She'd lead me home.' Her words echo those who deal with anxiety, wishing that they could be a version of themselves who is not afraid.

At the end of the episode, the Flesh produces a Ganger of the Doctor. In 'The Almost People', this double struggles to contend with the Doctor's past regenerations, imitating his speech and behaviour including offering jelly babies as the Fourth Doctor was wont to do. The actual Doctor quizzes his Ganger and is satisfied to unite to save everyone. Amy struggles with having two Doctors, using their different shoes to tell them apart. They both behave like him, panickedly responding to her humour by saying, 'That's sarcasm.' The other says, 'She's very good at sarcasm', before reminding themselves: 'Breathe.' The doppelgänger Amy believes to be the Flesh confides in her about feeling inferior to the real Doctor. She tells him, 'Being almost the Doctor is pretty damn impressive', to which he says that she might as well call him John Smith. They reveal that they swapped shoes so they could learn about the Flesh from Amy's perspective. Because she was tricked into believing that the Ganger was actually the Doctor, she says that he is 'twice the man I thought you were.'

Others have tried and failed to imitate the Doctor. In 'Mawdryn Undead', the scientist of the title attempts to discover the secret of regeneration. Mawdryn convinces the Doctor's companions that he is the next incarnation of their friend by feigning amnesia. He horrifies Nyssa and Tegan when they notice that his brain is visible through the roof of his skull, with Tegan saying that when the Doctor changed before he still looked human – 'I know that when the Doctor changed, he didn't turn into an alien.' She forgets that, to her, the Doctor is an alien. The Doctor's human appearance is an effective means of winning sympathy and friendship without inciting horror, as Mawdryn does.

The Tenth Doctor merges with humanity in 'Journey's End'. Donna touches the hand the Doctor lost in 'The Christmas Invasion', creating an instantaneous biological metacrisis. 'Oi, watch it, spaceman', Donna shouts. 'Oi, watch it, Earth girl', the new Doctor retorts. 'Ooo. I sound like you. I sound all, all sort of rough.' He is disgusted to discover he only has one heart, while Donna gets the best bit of the Doctor: his mind. She tells him that he has always lacked 'that little bit of human' – 'that gut instinct that comes hand-in-hand with planet Earth.' In other words, common sense, that mysterious concept elusive to those of us who are neurodivergent, something to be taught and learned where to others it is apparently innate. Gallifreyan knowledge almost burns up Donna, her mind unable to cope with the overwhelming thoughts flooding her brain. By contrast, the humanoid Doctor manages to survive, able to live with humanity above suspicion, while the real Doctor must return to the TARDIS and keep on moving. Settling down could never satisfy his enormous thirst for adventure and discovery. It would be all too human. It is this hybrid between alien and human which many neurodivergent people, including myself, relate to in *Doctor Who*. We live with the anxiety that the mask might slip, and others will recoil. But the people who really matter, the ones who love us, will see beyond our differences, to our shared humanity.

CHAPTER THREE

RISE OF THE CYBERMEN

Can't you imagine an animal unless it's flesh, blood and bone, hmm?

The First Doctor in 'The Daleks'

They're pressing themselves into the surface of the world. But a footprint doesn't look like a boot.

The Tenth Doctor in 'Army of Ghosts'

The word 'robot' was introduced by Karel Čapek in his 1920 play *R.U.R.*, 'Rossum's Universal Robots'. The term derived from the Czech for 'serf labour', and came to replace earlier descriptions such as automata for mechanical beings which imitate human actions without being capable of original thought. In the play, after a revolution leaves the human race extinct, the robots Primus and Helena fall in love, becoming Adam and Eve to a new world. Throughout my life I have been told that I sometimes write or talk like a robot – a stereotype assigned to autistic individuals. I recall writing an email to a teacher and receiving a reply which told me to ask my question again without sounding like C-3PO from *Star Wars*. Sometimes my voice becomes monotonous, especially if I am fixated upon relaying a series of facts or data to which it is difficult, or to my mind unnecessary, to inflect my words with changing emphasis. I have often identified with robots in their attempts to understand humanity within the constraints of their programming. Certain emotions and interactions do not compute.

'Basically I wanted a two-syllable word that had a mechanical sound about it', reflected Terry Nation on his best-known creation. He was unaware that the word 'Dalek' actually means 'remote' or 'alien' in Croatian, but it is an apposite coincidence. Nation's script for 'The Daleks' described his baddies: 'Hideous machine-like creatures, they are legless, moving on a round base. They have no human features. A lens on a flexible shaft acts as an eye. Arms with mechanical grips for hands.' Already in the second serial of *Doctor Who* Lambert defied Newman's rule against B.E.M.s by bringing Nation's invention to life. They were designed to be non-human, nothing like Čapek's passable robots, to emphasise their difference from the inhabitants of other planets. Our first glimpse of the Doctor's nemesis comes at the end of the serial's first episode, 'The Dead Planet'. Barbara backs against a wall screaming as what appears to be a sink plunger is waved in front of the camera. The screen is aligned with the Dalek's perspective – we see with their eye, witnessing the horror they bring directly, invited to perceive that it is good.

Neurodivergent fan Esme Hayes said to me, 'I have a soft spot for the Daleks. I know they're evil. Maybe it's because they are rule followers. And also because humans piss me off, so with their contempt for human life, I think, "Fair enough!"' The programming of the Daleks to obey is relatable for many neurodivergent people who try to stick to prescribed rules, provided that they make sense. Despite not appearing human, Barbara wonders if there is someone hidden inside the machines. The First Doctor even decides that they ought to cooperate, admiring their technological advances on Skaro. Yet later in the serial Ian observes that their attempts to reason with the Daleks have been in vain, finding them incapable of responding as any reasonable human would –

'They obviously think and act and feel in an entirely different way.' They act out of 'dislike for the unlike', despite originating from the humanoid race of the Kaleds, as the Fourth Doctor discovers in 'Genesis of the Daleks'. In this respect they are comparable less to neurodivergent people than those who seek to suppress what they perceive as atypical ways of thinking, refusing to engage with a worldview which differs to their own despite sharing similar heritage. Any comparison to humans is rejected outright – in 'The Parting of the Ways' when it is revealed by the Emperor that the Daleks rebuilt themselves from the 'waste of humanity', Rose says that this makes them half-human which they decry as blasphemy. Their madness has been caused by the stink of humanity in their own flesh, a self-loathing which makes them even deadlier.

A HUMAN DALEK

The Daleks attempt to change the nature of humans to make them more like themselves. Rather than simply destroying, they use experimentation and eugenics to fashion new species and androids in their own image. 'The Dalek Invasion of Earth' features the Robomen – prisoners who have been operated on to allow the Daleks to control their brains. The manipulation of their minds drives them insane, causing them to destroy themselves. Like a computer, the machines are able to learn from past errors. In 'The Chase', the Daleks build a humanoid robot with memory cells designed to imitate the First Doctor. They have even perfected the Doctor's manner of speech, so that when they ask if it understands its order to 'infiltrate and kill', the robot replies, 'Understand? Of course I understand, my dear fellow. Don't fuss so.' It is a parodic imitation, copying voices in a mode comparable to echolalia typical in the speech of neurodivergent people.

The Daleks' desire to learn from humans does not stem from an ambition to fit in on Earth or hopes for connection, but to inform their genocidal strategy. In 'The Evil of the Daleks', the human businessman Theodore Maxtible says that the Daleks told him that they are speculating that the reason for their previous defeats has been caused by some 'human factor' which they lack – 'Courage, pity, chivalry, friendship, even compassion.' After isolating this element, the Second Doctor implants it into three Daleks, referred to as *Homo superiens*, but the result is to give the creatures a childish sense of humour and play. He blows his recorder as the Daleks, newly Christened Alpha, Beta, and Omega, imitate a train. The Emperor tells the Doctor that in changing the wiring of these Daleks, he has revealed a Dalek factor which is to be spread to people on Earth.

It is an ambition shared by the Cult of Skaro, a secret group above and beyond the Emperor, who like the human-infused Daleks, have names – Sec, Thay, Jast, and Caan. In 'Doomsday' they reveal to the Tenth Doctor that their orders were to develop an imaginative capability in order to discover how their enemies think, again as a means of discovering new ways to destroy life. The Cult uses the Genesis Ark to bring the Daleks back to Earth, a Gallifreyan prison which can only be activated by the touch of a time traveller. The Doctor taunts the Daleks: 'Technology using the one thing a Dalek can't do. Touch. Sealed inside your casing. Not feeling anything ever, from birth to death, locked inside a cold metal cage. Completely alone. That explains your voice. No wonder you scream.' His words echo the dehumanising language used by John Miller to describe autism in *Whose Doctor Who*, emphasising a lack of emotion and incapacity for intimacy.

The Cult of Skaro returns in 'Daleks in Manhattan', now working with the human businessman Mr Diagoras on the 'Final Experiment' hidden within the newly built Empire State Building. He shares his masters' ambition for power, making him the perfect candidate for Sec to merge with to create the first human Dalek. Thay attempts to stop the process, but Sec claims that it is their racial purity which has brought them to extinction and therefore they must adapt in order to survive. The ethics of their experiment is discussed further in 'Evolution of the Daleks', wherein Sec describes the essentials of humanity as 'ambition, hatred, aggression, and war.' The Doctor is fascinated by his new behaviour, such as showing mercy and changes of mind. Ultimately the Daleks destroy the hybrid Sec, and the Doctor's DNA becomes fused with the army of human Daleks allowing them to defy orders. While there are aspects of Dalek behaviour which might be identified with neurodivergence, it is in an extreme and concentrated form which makes historical comparisons of autism to mindless robotic behaviour deeply insulting. It is to treat neurodivergence as something mechanical, ignoring the human factor all Earthlings share.

In saying that it was wrong of the Daleks' creator to make it impossible for them to have feelings beyond hatred for other species, Sec defies the orders of Davros. Davros is an archetypical mad genius, with his mobility aid base comparable to the wheelchair of the Nazi scientist Dr Strangelove in Stanley Kubrick's 1964 film of the same name. Davros's experiments are similar to those in *The Island of Dr Moreau* (1896) by H.G. Wells, in which Moreau uses surgery and education to turn animals into passable imitations of humans. Himself disfigured by an unknown incident, Davros is effectively a cyborg, with his most 'human' feature being the single hand with which he operates the control panel of his life-support machine. While more identifiable as humanoid than the Daleks, he represents an obvious example of the cliché of the disabled villain.

Davros is able to negotiate with the Fourth Doctor when they first meet in 'Genesis of the Daleks'. The Time Lord informs him that his inventions will survive as weapons of hate and machines of war, but they could instead be altered to exist as a force for good. The Daleks kill their creator just as he reaches for the button which will terminate them, fulfilling their purpose as superior beings. Davros returns in 'Destiny of the Daleks', in which the Doctor poses him with a logic problem: if all elephants are pink, and Nellie is an elephant, then Nellie is pink. Davros says that the conclusion is perfectly logical, and the Doctor informs him that a human would respond by saying that elephants are not pink. The way to defeat the Daleks is to do something which a computer would see as irrational, to move beyond logic. As Whovian Esme said, the appeal of the Daleks to an autistic individual is their ability to follow rules, which often allows them to outsmart others. Yet it can also lead to frustration and anxiety when others do not conform to the same conventions.

HUMAN POINT TWO

'Unfamiliar pulmonary set-up. Nervous system hyperconductive. Remarkable brain processing speed.' Cybermites take over the Eleventh Doctor, giving him a split personality with the Cyberplanner in 'Nightmare in Silver'. His mind makes him the perfect candidate for a cybernetic upgrade, capable of operating at a higher functionality than humans. It is different neurotypes and intelligence quotients which the Daleks use to determine which humans are candidates for the Final Experiment in 'Evolution of the Daleks', and who will become pig slaves. It is a eugenicist idea similar to the historical approach to autism which originated with the work of Asperger, in which autistic individuals who are 'low-functioning' are distinguished from those who are 'high-functioning', with the latter having uses for social betterment.

The Cybermen first appeared in 'The Tenth Planet', the title referring to Mondas, the twin planet of Earth. It is discovered by the First Doctor that these robots were once humanoid

Mondasians, like Eric Krailford, now known as Krail, who informs him that the Cybermen were created by scientists when they realised that their race was growing weak. Spare parts were created for their bodies until they became more machine than man. Their brains were left intact, albeit with certain weaknesses removed – 'You call them emotions, do you not?' One of the diagnostic criteria in several neurodivergent conditions is an apparent lack of feeling, known as aphasia or dysphasia. It can be challenging for neurodivergent people to identify variance in expression, a condition called emotional blindness or alexithymia. To the Cybermen, this is a strength, allowing them to rise above sentimentality. In 'The Tomb of the Cybermen', the requirement for superior intellects for conversion causes the Controller to deploy a complicated trap. He selects Eric Klieg, a member of the Brotherhood of Logicians, to become the leader of the race of Cybermen who will be frozen and placed in tombs until they are ready for use. Like the Daleks, they are attracted to logic.

In the NuWho era, the Cybermen are created again in a parallel world by a Davros-like creator, the human John Lumic. He too is physically disabled, using a wheelchair which functions as life support, his motivation for upgrading the human body. Lumic believes he is of superior intelligence which allows him to see beyond the limitations of human flesh and emotions. When the Cybus Industries scientist Dr Kendrick informs Lumic that their prototype is 'working' in 'Rise of the Cybermen', he replies that such a word applies only to machines and their creation is instead 'alive.' He later describes the human brain as the most precious thing on Earth, 'and yet we allow it to die', therefore his invention will sustain the brain indefinitely in bondage with a metal exoskeleton. The President of Great Britain describes the project as 'obscene', and argues that while Lumic is a fine businessman, he is 'not God.' The Cybermen tell the Tenth Doctor that they have been 'upgraded' to 'Human Point Two', before proceeding to 'delete' those who stand in their way.

In 'The Age of Steel', the Doctor and Mrs Moore find a damaged Cyberman. They remove its breast plate to find the emotional inhibitor which prevents the brain from going insane. With the inhibitor broken, the Cyberman says that her name was Sally Phelan, and asks where Gareth is, her fiancé. When the Doctor confronts Lumic, he expresses admiration for the inventor using his genius to fight his sickness, describing it as 'so human.' But he asks what there will be for humanity to strive for once they have overcome mortality: 'A metal Earth with metal men and metal thoughts, lacking the one thing that makes this planet so alive. People.' Lumic's plan will eradicate that which distinguishes the human race, its diversity, merging all consciousness into a singular hive mind which will exist without purpose. The thing which makes Lumic unique, as with Davros before him, is his individual genius – that all-important human factor.

GOOD DALEKS AND FEELING CYBERMEN

The Daleks and the Cybermen are united in their stereotypically robotic speech patterns. The original Dalek sound was created by Brian Hodgson of the BBC Radiophonic Workshop by feeding a human voice through a ring modulator, set at a frequency which turned the signal on and off thirty times per second before being passed through a graphic equaliser. When Ian gets inside a Dalek shell in 'The Daleks', the First Doctor tells him that in order to be convincing he needs to imitate their voice, which Barbara echoes by saying, 'Yes, in a monotone.' There are variances in pitch, however, especially at times of stress when the Daleks can even raise their voices into a hysterical scream. Yet their vocabulary is limited to specific words and phrases. This is explored in 'The Witch's Familiar' when, like Ian, Clara climbs inside a

Dalek and finds her voice is channelled through its processor, which also translates. Missy asks her to say, 'I love you', but when she does, it comes out as 'Exterminate!', as does the phrase, 'You are different from me.' Missy explains, 'Cybermen suppress emotion. Daleks channel it through a gun.' Because Clara cannot identify herself to the Twelfth Doctor, he does not know it is her until he realises that it is not behaving in the manner of a Dalek. Like a neurodivergent person going into meltdown, Clara's frustration with being misunderstood causes the weapon to fire, to the macabre delight of Missy in a display reminiscent of playground bullies.

While the Daleks' voice has remained largely consistent, the Cybermen spoke in a countertenor trill during their first appearance in 'The Tenth Planet'. Their lack of tonal modulation is symptomatic of the inhibition of emotions. The artificial voice of the Cybermen is similar to the process of thought-to-speech translation in 'Planet of the Ood'. The translator ball which the Ood carry is an innovation of Ood Operations which replaces their hind brain, similar to the human amygdala which processes memory and emotions, after it is cut off to create processed slaves. There is even the option to purchase a variety package of different voices, including husky female tones 'for the gentlemen' and the comedy value of Homer Simpson saying 'D'oh!'

All humans learn to speak through imitation and repetition, yet echolalia is more pronounced in some neurodivergent people, sometimes acting as a vocal stim. In 'Midnight', when Sky Silvestry is possessed, she starts to copy the Tenth Doctor's favourite phrase, 'Allons-y!' – just as the Ninth Doctor has a penchant for 'Fantastic!', the Eleventh for 'Geronimo!', and the Thirteenth for 'Brilliant!' She echoes his words, then they speak in unison, and finally before he has spoken. Dee Dee attempts to catch Sky out by reciting from memory the poem 'Goblin Market' by Christina Rossetti.

Many neurodivergent people have a capacity to memorise quotations which might be repeated in lieu of improvised speech, such as Owen Suskind, an autistic man who learned to speak by imitating classic Disney films as explored in the documentary *Life, Animated* (2016). It can be an effective means of communication, even if it is not deemed acceptable by neurotypical standards.

Despite Davros's insistence that it is impossible for a Dalek to defy orders and act independently for good, he has been proved wrong on several occasions. Following the Time War, a lone survivor ended up in the collection of billionaire Henry van Statten in the episode 'Dalek'. After realising that it is alone in the universe, the Dalek observes that the Ninth Doctor is too, making them the same. At first this infuriates the last of the Time Lords, before realising it is right. Rose is kind, and it tells her, 'I am glad that before I die I have met a human who was not afraid.' Acting out of compassion, Rose places her hand on the Dalek's shell which allows it to extrapolate her genetic material and complete cellular reconstruction. Any hope that the Dalek might have changed in its nature is lost, and it goes on a killing spree. The Doctor yells, 'Why don't you just die?!' 'You would make a good Dalek', comes the response. Rose observes change in the Doctor, a thirst for revenge which makes him not so different from his enemy. The Dalek is less alien to her than he is, asking her how sunlight feels on her skin and admitting that it is frightened. A semblance of humanity which brings poignancy to its death.

'Into the Dalek' sees the Twelfth Doctor similarly insist on the impossibility of a good Dalek. This reluctance to accept a relativist rather than an absolutist moral approach, to see beyond the binary of heroes and villains, is a characteristically autistic attitude. Clara tells the Doctor that his stance is 'a bit inflexible. Not like you. I'd almost say prejudiced.' If the

Dalek, nicknamed Rusty, has developed morals, then it has malfunctioned. A moleculon nanoscaler allows the Doctor and Clara to enter its wiring to investigate. Rusty says that it changed after witnessing beauty in the birth of a star. Despite the Daleks destroying millions of stars, this act of renewal in the universe revealed to it that resistance to life is futile as it will always prevail. The Doctor merges his mind with Rusty, hoping that it will see 'endless, divine perfection', but it sees instead something good in the Doctor's deep-rooted hatred for Dalek kind, causing it to turn on its own race.

That belief is expressed again by the Dalek which appears inside the TARDIS in 'The Power of the Doctor', informing the Thirteenth Doctor that since the Kaled identity has eroded over time it is logical to conclude that the Daleks have lost the right to survive. The Doctor remarks that Davros would be both impressed and horrified. Just as the Fourth Doctor observed in 'Destiny of the Daleks', blind commitment to logic is always bound to be their downfall. The Doctor's horror at recognising more of themself in the Daleks than they would like to believe forces them to see beyond their sacrosanct moral laws and engage with nuanced ideas of good and evil. It is Rose and Clara who help them to broaden their mind, a human influence which holds the Doctor to account when their moral certainty manifests as prejudice. They are forced to think with their hearts rather than their intellect.

Lisa Hallett was one of the humans converted to Cybermen at Canary Wharf during the events of 'Army of Ghosts' and 'Doomsday'. The process was only partially completed, however, and she was rescued by Ianto Jones with whom she fell in love. In the *Torchwood* episode 'Cyberwoman', she appears with her incomplete exoskeleton, looking more like the metal bikini of Princess Leia in *Return of the Jedi* (1983) than any recognisable Cyber. Ianto hopes that Dr Ryoichi Tanizaki will be able to make her fully human again, but she kills him in an act of repayment for helping her to remove her remaining weakness of emotions. She describes herself as 'Human Point Two', and Ianto attempts to force her to remember herself as Lisa. In response, she suggests that Ianto transplants her brain into his body, seeing it as an act of love. Like the apparent oxymoron of a good Dalek, there can be no such thing as a feeling Cyberman. They cannot live with the pain.

The fear of experiencing sensation after death is what allows Missy to frighten the super-rich in 'Death in Heaven' to support her development of a race of Cybers from corpses. After Clara's boyfriend Danny Pink is killed in a road accident, he is uploaded as a Cyberman. He asks her to help him by activating his emotional inhibitor. Bill is also told that she will benefit from this component when she is upgraded in 'World Enough and Time', although it does not work. She is cared for at a barn in 'The Doctor Falls', still appearing human in her self-perception. The Twelfth Doctor tells her that her mind rebelled against the programming, 'A castle made of you, and you are standing on the battlements, saying "No".' Because anger causes her helmet weapon to activate, he says that a temper is a luxury she can no longer afford. The Doctor wipes an impossible tear from her face when Bill asks him if people will always be afraid of her. 'Where there's tears, there's hope', he says. The Lone Cyberman Ashad experiences a similar identity crisis in 'Ascension of the Cybermen', with the Thirteenth Doctor telling him that the anger and hatred towards his own humanity is caused by his uninhibited emotions. There is always a way to get through to a robot in *Doctor Who*, even when their programming forbids it.

SYMPATHY FOR THE ROBOT

Sometimes robots or machines are able to get through to neurodivergent individuals. Grandin found it impossible to have physical contact with another human being, because they were not controlled by herself. At the age of five she created a machine in her mind which could squeeze her in the fashion of a hug to her precise standards. She later adapted a chute designed to restrain calves into this hugging machine, which she found more reliable and consistent than people. Grandin was met with suspicion and derision for her invention, but she did not see why her choice of a machine companion should be inferior to those made of flesh and blood.

In 'Robot', Sarah has a different approach to the Experimental Prototype Robot K1 than Hilda Winters, head of the Scientific Reform Society. Sarah interacts with the droid, which has 'a terribly literal mind', and K1 informs her that it was created to replace humans in dangerous tasks such as handling radioactive materials. When Hilda orders the robot to harm Sarah, K1 appears to panic as it creates a paradox in its programming, between needing to obey and never hurting a human. Hilda explains that this was a test, which Sarah describes as cruel: 'Oh, it's got a brain, hasn't it? It walks and talks like us. How can you be sure it doesn't have feelings too?' K1 informs Sarah that her kindness is illogical, and Hilda says that she must be 'the sort of girl that gives motor cars pet names.' Later K1 remembers this exchange, the sympathy which Sarah felt for the robot, and it confesses to her that it feels pain. Hilda's mocking of Sarah is reminiscent of the response Grandin received for her hugging machine, but to her it is just a matter of seeing things differently.

The line between robots and humans is blurred further by a unique figure in the Doctor's companionship – the shape-changing android Kamelion. The character first appears in 'The King's Demons', disguised as King John in service to the Master in his plot to prevent the sealing of Magna Carta, controlled through concentration and psychokinetics. When the Fifth Doctor presents the android to Tegan, she refuses to acknowledge him as anything but a machine and finds it difficult to believe that he is no longer under the Master's influence. Indeed, Kamelion becomes the Master in 'Planet of Fire', with Peri saying that he is supposed to be the Doctor's friend when he points a Trion laser at him. When his circuitry is damaged, Kamelion begs the Doctor to destroy him, visibly experiencing pain. Like the earthly creature after which he is named, Kamelion can blend in effectively, and even in his android appearance is capable of expressing emotion and making music. For the Doctor he is the perfect companion, one which he can control using his mind and receive comfort without needing to give any in return.

In 'The Invisible Enemy', Professor Frederick Marius says that he built K9 in the shape of a dog because he missed the pet he had on Earth. Friendship is a concept stored in K9's memory banks rather than something which has been earned. John Leeson, who provided his voice, told me that while filming 'The Stones of Blood' there was a moment when the Doctor's robotic companion appeared to be real:

> *Tom Baker parks himself on a grass bank with the K9 module plonked down beside him. He calls out to me, 'Have you got your Times Crossword?' The answer's 'Affirmative!', and we begin to do some clues together to while away the time. What I didn't know, and what I couldn't possibly see, were the public onlookers for whom any disbelief was suspended that K9 and his master were real, and actually at one!*

In the series itself, K9 keeps the Doctor company by playing chess with him. In 'The Waters of Mars' the Tenth Doctor tells Roman that he hates robots because he does not like people who dress them up and give them silly voices. Roman mentions a friend who made her domestic robot look like a dog, which the Doctor says is different. Not that the Doctor immediately wanted K9 to join his crew in 'The Invisible Enemy', refusing to use gendered pronouns, but when Leela takes K9 Mark I with her at the end of 'The Invasion of Time', he smiles at the camera upon revealing that he has a box containing a Mark II model onboard. The Tenth Doctor is thrilled when he manages to fix the K9 Mark III belonging to Sarah in 'School Reunion', although it causes Mickey to question his place in the TARDIS – he is 'the tin dog.' Sarah expresses fondness for K9 in 'Invasion of the Bane', and when she calls him a good dog he responds, 'Affection noted, mistress.' He accompanies Luke to university to help him to settle in, while Sarah has a computer of her own – Mr Smith – to prevent her from getting lonely in her son's absence. *Doctor Who* invites us to consider forms of friendship beyond human-human relationships, to reflect upon what is lost, but also what is gained – especially for those who find social interaction challenging.

This is the case for young Walter Simeon in 'The Snowmen', who elects not to join in with other children because they are 'silly', which his mother describes as not being healthy. In 1842 he built a snowman, which echoed Walter's words – 'Don't need anyone else. I can help you.' Fifty years later he runs the GI Institute, which the Eleventh Doctor discovers to stand for the Great Intelligence. Before its first appearance in 'The Abominable Snowmen', in which it took over the mind of the Buddhist monk Padmasambhava to control the robot Yeti against the Second Doctor, there were precedents to the Great Intelligence. Professor Brett created a super computer with the Wagnerian nickname WOTAN, standing for Will Operating Thought ANalogue, in 'The War Machines', intended to be connected to other computers around the world in a central intelligence comparable to the modern internet. While the computer is supposed to only be able to think logically without political or private ends, concerns are raised that it might decide that it is logical to work without humans. In 'The Krotons', the machines in the

Hall of Learning fill their minds with knowledge, from which by law the Gonds must derive their science and culture, 'a sort of self-perpetuating slavery.'

In 'The Web of Fear', the Intelligence wishes to drain all of the Doctor's knowledge and experience from his mind, which will only work if he submits willingly. The process will leave the Doctor's brain as empty as a newborn child, the effect of which is seen when the Intelligence returns in 'The Bells of Saint John'. Like Simeon, the Intelligence took over Rosemary Kizlet when she was a child, and when it leaves her she regresses to being a young girl in the body of an adult woman. Like Brett's plan for a worldwide computer network, the Intelligence uses WiFi to harvest human minds and preserve them in the data cloud. Just as Lumic believed in the creation of his Cybermen, it is the mind which is the only part of people the Intelligence deems to have value, pulling from humanity's diversity of knowledge and experience to perfect itself.

CYBORGS

Neither Daleks nor Cybermen are fully mechanical, both incorporating an organic element which accounts for the human aspects of their character. They are aligned with cyborgs, a creation of science fiction which further illustrates the tension that exists between a pure human and a machine. In the 1985 essay 'A Cyborg Manifesto' by Donna Haraway, the concept is applied to socialist feminism as a means of breaking down the traditional boundaries which separate humans from animals, and humans from machines. The cyborg helps Haraway to conceive of a world outside of human conventions of society, family, gender, and sexuality, encouraging coalition through affinity. Her ideas allow humans to think beyond the confines of typicality to embrace the plasticity of identity. Such an approach is inherent to the neurodiversity paradigm.

The rights of cyborgs is central to 'Voyage of the Damned', in which a Zocci called Bannakaffalatta reveals that he is hiding the machine part of his body for fear of discrimination. He tells Astrid Peth that he became a cyborg after an accident, and she reassures him that there is greater understanding now, even being able to get married. Eugenics through means such as enforced sterilisation of disabled or neurodivergent people continues across the world. Max Capricorn, owner of the space cruise liner *Titanic*, is also a cyborg, his human head encased in a life-support system akin to those of Davros and Lumic. He tells the Doctor of the prejudice he has received, forcing him to run his company via hologram. He enacts revenge on his own board by planning the collision of the *Titanic* with Earth. The episode reveals the dangers of othering, to place shame in those who are different, which is shown through the two cyborg characters to manifest as kindness, or as resentment.

What makes a cyborg human is explored further in 'Victory of the Daleks' through Professor Edwin Bracewell, Head of the Ironsides Project in Winston Churchill's war cabinet. He claims that the Ironsides, which the Eleventh Doctor immediately recognises to be Daleks, came to him in a dream similar to those experienced by Grandin. It transpires that it is the Professor who is an invention of the Daleks. To stop the bomb in his chest from detonating, the Doctor needs him to prove his humanity by tapping into the thoughts which have been implanted in his positronic brain. He remembers the post office his parents ran when he was a boy, and the sadness he felt when they died of scarlet fever. He describes the pain as no Cyberman could – worse than a wound, like being emptied out. Amy probes deeper, asking Bracewell if he ever fancied someone he knew he should not, and he describes Dorabella, with her blue eyes almost violet 'like the last touch of sunset on the edge of the world.' A robot should be incapable of love and poetry, yet Bracewell proves that he is more than human. Bracewell expects he will need to be deactivated, although the Doctor hints that they should give him plenty of time to escape. He fails to catch on, struggling to read subtext, with Amy saying, 'That Dalek tech a bit slow on the uptake.'

While Bracewell is a cyborg who has been convinced that he is a human, in 'Journey to the Centre of the TARDIS' it transpires that the human Tricky has been led to believe that he is an android. After being speared by a rod through his shoulder, he orders it to be cut off as he can replace this disposable part with a new one. The Eleventh Doctor orders Gregor, whom he realises is Tricky's older brother, to tell him the truth, but he refuses out of cowardice. The Doctor says, 'Robots don't need blast suits. They don't need respirators. They don't get frightened of monsters in the dark', acknowledging that Tricky has 'two bionic eyes and a synthetic voice box. But you, my friend, are human. Flesh and blood.' Gregor reveals that it was a joke made to relieve boredom after Tricky was caught in a salvage accident and he lost his sight, voice, and memory. It is a dehumanising act of bullying, reminiscent of those who have belittled me by comparing me to a robot. The worst part of such behaviour towards neurodivergent people is that it can cause us to believe that they might be right, assuming that we are not capable of human emotions and intimacy, when of course many of us are.

The desire to be more human is evident in the Clockwork Droids which appear in 'The Girl in the Fireplace' and 'Deep Breath'. In the former episode, they attempt to repair their ship, the *SS Madame de Pompadour* by using human body parts, including the thirty-seven-year-old brain of Reinette, their craft's namesake. They intend to use the brain as a computer, and use masks and costumes to hide themselves within the corridors of eighteenth-century Versailles. In the latter, the Droids have developed a more sophisticated means of camouflaging – the Twelfth Doctor observes that they are not normal cyborgs, that is humans turning themselves into robots, but rather robots turning themselves into humans. They steal body parts from the patrons of a disguised restaurant, linked to their ship, the *SS Marie Antoinette*. The Doctor cites the philosophical thought experiment of the Ship of Theseus, a paradox in which it is asked whether a ship for which every component has been replaced can be said to be the same ship: 'There's not a trace of the original you left. You probably can't even remember where you got that face from.' This is hypocritical of the newly regenerated Doctor, posing a question as to whether he is the same Time Lord who fled Gallifrey.

The Doctor asks the Droid what he thinks of the view, and he responds, 'I do not think of it.' 'I don't think of it. I don't. Droids and apostrophes, I could write a book', the Doctor bemoans. He appears to be criticising the Droid's refusal to use colloquialisms as a signifier of its lack of humanity, forgetting that the First Doctor would surely be ashamed to hear his future self speaking so informally. I try to vary my speech and writing patterns, although I still get accused of a mechanical formality from time to time. The Doctor does not like being confronted with their similarities to machines, because it forces them to reckon with the fact that their own identity is changeable. I have worked to embrace a less binary way of thinking, using my emotions and social skills to develop a greater capacity for empathy than I had as a child. As in Haraway's essay, cyborgs in the Whoniverse function to break down black-and-white concepts of which the Doctor seems certain, forcing him to expand his ideas about identity and the capabilities of the mind, be it organic or made of metal. A tin man is more than just nuts and bolts. He may even have a heart, or two.

CHAPTER FOUR

THE UNQUIET DEAD

The past is another country. 1987's just the Isle of Wight.

The Ninth Doctor in 'Father's Day'

The Tenth Doctor: **They got on very well.**
Mickey Smith: **The king's wife and the king's girlfriend?**
The Tenth Doctor: **France. It's a different planet.**

'The Girl in the Fireplace'

The Seventh Doctor relaxes in an armchair, a cup of tea perched on a pile of books, and a bowl of jelly babies within reach. He picks up the novella he is reading, *The Time Machine* by H.G. Wells. Before it appeared in 'The Movie', Professor Chronotis settled down to read a Pan paperback copy of this science-fiction story in his lodgings at St Cedd's College, Cambridge. No doubt it was also read by the creators of *Doctor Who*, including C.E. 'Bunny' Webber of the BBC's script department who conceived of the Doctor as the Time Traveller, as Wells's protagonist is known, and his very own Time Machine, the TARDIS. While the show's first story editor David Whitaker was concerned that the programme should not be too cerebral, Newman wanted it to be 'educational, or at least mind-opening, for the children watching.' He echoed the three-word mantra of the BBC commonly attributed to the corporation's first

Director-General, Lord Reith: inform, educate, entertain. It was for this reason that the original crew of the TARDIS included the science teacher Ian Chesterton, who asks all the right questions, and the history teacher Barbara Wright, who guides the audience through the Earth's past. The First Doctor himself represents the anachronistic Victorian-Edwardian gentleman of Wells's imagination, dressed in silks, spats, wing collars, and waistcoats.

When I was a child, my parents took me to historical sites across Britain, from Sutton Hoo and Stonehenge to Roman villas and mediaeval castles. I became obsessed with history, memorising dates and facts with insatiable voracity. Programmes on BBC Radio 4, especially *In Our Time*, and BBC Four documentaries presented by Mary Beard and Lucy Worsley broadened my understanding of civilisation and culture. At the age of twelve I visited Cambridge, and despite no one else in my family having gone to university, I decided that I would go there to read History. To me, Trinity College was an intellectual haven steeped in heritage which brought together a community of minds similar to my own. It was not quite as perfect as I dreamed it would be, and my first essay, on coal in the Industrial Revolution, failed to capture my imagination. I soon discovered that it was not enough to simply know everything that one could about the past; one needed to attempt to understand it, to extend empathy and critical analysis to past peoples. I was even told by one of my supervisors that mediaeval history was not my calling, as I had hoped it would be when I was at school. Thankfully I quickly found my specialism in cultural history, beginning with a paper on inter-war Europe. Reading the works of Thomas Mann, looking at the paintings of Neue Sachlichkeit, and listening to the music of Stravinsky and Schönberg taught me more about the period than any data could. I discovered that cinema and television can be academic, that moving pictures are windows into other times and places. I wrote my undergraduate thesis on what we can learn from the films of Ealing Studios about the lived experiences of women and girls in post-war Britain. The rest, as they say, is history.

It is typical of autistic and neurodivergent people to have special interests or hyperfixations. Mine include history, as well as fine art, classical music, literature, cinema, and, naturally, *Doctor Who*. This goes beyond casual interest or appreciation but is rather an intense focus on a specific subject. It can be beneficial, leading to complex knowledge and a sense of purpose, although it poses challenges, such as making it difficult to shift attention to other responsibilities or engage with those who do not share one's passion. When the TARDIS materialises amidst the French Revolution in 'The Reign of Terror', Susan worries that they may never leave if the Doctor realises where they are because it is his favourite period in Earth's history. The Fifth Doctor promises his crew a special treat following the death of Adric in 'Time-Flight', attempting to suppress his grief by visiting the Great Exhibition in 1851 to see 'all the wonders of Victorian science and technology.' While the First Doctor struggles to remember his history upon arriving at Hastings in 1066 in 'The Time Meddler', later Doctors demonstrate superhuman knowledge – the Tenth in 'The Unicorn and the Wasp' detects that they are in the 1920s, so he says, from the smell of grass and lemonade with a hint of mint in the air. An historian is like a time detective; where we rely on sources and artefacts, the Doctor uses the TARDIS.

My error in reading History, which my first supervisors detected, was that I saw the past not as something lived-in, but as something to be learned and memorised for its own sake. In 'Enlightenment', the Eternal Captain Striker has selected his racing ship as an Edwardian yacht called *Shadow*. He tells the Fifth Doctor that Eternals are able to choose what they need from Earth's history, feeding on ephemeral human minds as blueprints for their own innovations. He describes humans as having entertainment value, causing the Doctor to remark, 'You talk as though they were toys.' Something which has often irked me about heritage sites is the insistence on staging 'living history', a form of cosplay in which people dress up to perform re-enactments, seldom with much regard for authenticity. It reduces the past to a game, just as the Eternals do.

The first time the Doctor visits the twelfth century is in 'The Crusade'. Saladin believes that the crew of the TARDIS must be a group of players, inviting Barbara to tell him tales, 'like Scheherazade', for if she does not beguile him she will be executed. Simultaneously to Richard the Lionheart meeting the First Doctor in Palestine, the Twelfth ventured to 1190 in 'Robot of Sherwood' to prove to Clara that Robin Hood is a myth. She dresses in a red velvet gown and headpiece, a veritable Maid Marian, as though attending a Renaissance fair. Sure enough they encounter Robert, Earl of Loxley, and his band of Merry Men, although the Doctor insists that they cannot be verified historical figures – he sets to work sampling DNA and analysing blood like a forensic archaeologist, speculating that they could be animatronics in a theme park or inside a miniscope, à la 'Carnival of Monsters'. He asks Clara when she started to believe in impossible heroes. 'Don't you know? In a way, it's rather sweet', she replies. The Doctor discovers that the Sheriff of Nottingham is a cyborg living on a ship disguised as a castle, leading him to conclude that Robin is an illusion created by leaked radiation from the damaged engines. Yet Robin is real, and he tells the Doctor that while history is a burden, 'stories can make us fly.' The encounter teaches the Doctor to consider that the past may not quite be as he knows it.

Not that this lesson dissuades the Doctor from arguing with Bill in 'The Eaters of Light' about the fate of the Ninth Legion. They travel to Aberdeen in the second century to see if the Doctor is correct in saying that the soldiers were annihilated in battle. Bill insists that she knows more than he does because she read about the Legion in a book, citing her A* as her credentials while the Doctor claims he lived in Roman Britain. While it transpires that neither of them was completely correct, the Doctor is willing to admit that he was wrong. *Doctor Who* takes a great deal of poetic licence in its approach to history, manipulating facts and inserting supernatural anachronisms. It requires one to venture into the past with an open mind, and a pinch of salt.

THE BUTTERFLY EFFECT

'It's like in the films. You step on a butterfly, you change the future of the human race.' Martha cites a version of an idea of chaos theory when arriving in 1599 in 'The Shakespeare Code' that a single small change can have a larger deterministic impact on events elsewhere in space and time. The Tenth Doctor is glib, advising her not to crush any butterflies. Bill echoes her words in 'Thin Ice', saying that stepping on a butterfly 'could send ripples through time that mean I'm not even born in the first place and I could just disappear.' Again the Twelfth Doctor is facetious, saying that is what happened to Pete, her friend who was standing there a moment before. Ruby Sunday actually does step on a poor butterfly in 'Space Babies', causing her to transform into Rubathon Blue of the 57th Hemisphere Hatchlings. The Doctor promptly scoops up the dead butterfly and breathes life into it, allowing Ruby to become human again. Some points are fixed, and others are in flux, the determination of which is said to be the preserve of the Time Lords. Later in 'The Shakespeare Code', Martha tells the Doctor that the world does not end in 1599 as she is living proof, and he uses *Back to the Future* (1985) as an example to illustrate how the past might change and erase her from existence. Rose informs the Ninth Doctor in 'The Unquiet Dead' that she cannot die in 1869, but he explains that time is not a straight line and can twist into any shape. There are rules for the time traveller, although they can be broken.

The ethics of intervention in historical events are explored in several serials featuring the First Doctor. In 'Marco Polo', Barbara demonstrates her knowledge by identifying the title Venetian as the European in service of Mongol leader Kublai Khan when the TARDIS arrives in 1289 on the Plain of Pamir. The Doctor by contrast is dismissive of the people they encounter, calling Polo a 'poor, pathetic, stupid savage', compared to more advanced civilisations for which he expresses admiration. In 'The Aztecs', Barbara recognises the period from the mask of a priest made circa 1430, one of her specialisms. Susan says that she only knows the Aztecs as savages who cut out people's hearts, which Barbara contests by describing their society as highly civilised. Yet it is Barbara who protests what she deems barbaric behaviour, unwilling to engage in the cultural relativism which the Doctor demands when she tries to stop a human sacrifice. She tells the Doctor they failed, while he points out the smaller victory they were able to have – that Barbara helped one man to find a better faith. A key lesson is learned: that one cannot, and must not, change the course of history.

While the Doctor insists upon treading carefully during their travels, they have seldom been more conspicuous than when the First dons the uniform of a French officer in 'The Reign of Terror', replete with plumage. He struts about in his costume like an arrogant peacock, described by Barbara as being 'dressed up as if he was running the revolution!' Barbara encourages her companions to expand their preconceived definitions of good and bad when viewing the period in teleological terms: 'The Revolution isn't all bad, and neither are the people who support it. It changed things for the whole world, and good, honest people gave their lives for that change.' She chastises Ian for claiming that the revolutionary Léon Colbert deserved to die for imprisoning him, saying, 'You check your history books, Ian, before you decide what people deserve.' Later Barbara expresses a sense of futility at their actions, remarking to the Doctor that there is no point in attempting to stop something they know will happen, namely the execution of Robespierre. He summarises their position: 'We can't stem the tide. But at least we can stop being carried away with the flood!' The point of studying the past is to educate ourselves and to develop from the mistakes of history. Just as Barbara observes, good might come even from the darkest of times.

Lessons learned over the course of the Doctor's travels establish within them a more fluid approach to morality than in these early adventures. By the time of 'The Witchfinders', the Thirteenth Doctor has no qualms about lecturing King James I of England and VI of Scotland. She cites the motto of the Order of the Garter, '*honi soit qui mal y pense*', that one who thinks of evil shall be shamed, in reference to James's scapegoating of women as witches. He insists that he quests for goodness and knowledge, the virtues of God, and the Doctor responds that everyone wants 'certainty, security, to believe that people are evil or heroic. But that's not how people are. You want to know the secrets of existence? Start with the mysteries of the heart.' This female Doctor thinks of inner morals over logic and encourages James to stop being afraid of things he does not understand. The Doctor shows no hesitation in attempting to put an end to the witch hunts and save women who were murdered by the King's agents, believing it to be barbaric by any moral standard. Perhaps it comes from her newfound identification with other women, motivating her to see without the clearcut thinking of her younger, male self.

TIME MEDDLERS

Matters of life and death have been debated throughout the Doctor's adventures. The Time Lords are characterised as compassionless figures bound to rules against interference, by contrast to humans who implore them to make exceptions. Steven becomes fond of the servant girl Anne Chaplet in 'The Massacre of St Bartholomew's Eve', but once the First Doctor discovers that the date is 23 August 1572, with the slaughter of the Huguenots at the instigation of Catherine de' Medici to begin that night, he demands that she return to Paris. He advises her to stay indoors and hide herself, but tells Steven that they cannot warn her of the violence about to unfold. Steven is upset, saying that his 'researches' have little regard for human life and he wants no part in them. This description of the Doctor's expeditions, for the purpose of examination and study, presents him as a dispassionate academic. The Doctor echoes words which he had previously given to Barbara:

> *My dear Steven, history sometimes gives us a terrible shock, and that is because we don't quite fully understand. Why should we? After all, we're all too small to realise its final pattern. Therefore don't try and judge it from where you stand. I was right to do as I did. Yes, that I firmly believe.*

The Doctor has blind faith in the teleological nature of the universe – a Whiggish notion of history which presupposes that pain and evil can be justified by the ultimate good they bring about in the future. When Steven and the Doctor meet Dodo, who shares the surname Chaplet with Anne, they take it as evidence that the young girl evaded the massacre and her family survived. The Doctor's age lends him a concept of time seen in grand terms, while the mortals with whom he travels offer a localised perspective.

Donna shares Steven's anger in 'The Fires of Pompeii',

realising that it is 79AD and Vesuvius is about to erupt. The Tenth Doctor says that the destruction of the city is a fixed point in Earth's history and cannot be stopped, and if she tries to warn people she will be treated like any other soothsayer. It takes confidence to tear down the Doctor's self-assurance, saying that while he might have flown around with people who were willing to submit to his orders before, he will not tell her to shut up. She asks him if he thinks that the deaths of twenty thousand people is right, but he rejects the question. Of course the Doctor does not think death is right, but because his mind works in a different way to hers, it is a burden which he must carry as part of his broader conception of time. That does not prevent the Doctor from being pleased when people can be saved. In 'The Doctor Dances', the Ninth is ecstatic to announce that 'just this once, everybody lives!' He even does not seem to care that a patient of Dr Constantine has regrown a leg, courtesy of the nanogenes. He sets the bomb to destruct, ensuring that the record of an explosion in that spot during the Blitz remains true, saying, 'Who am I to argue with history?' 'Usually the first in line', Rose replies.

The Doctor's rules are complicated further when contending with the personal timelines of their companions. Rose asks the Ninth Doctor to allow her to be with her father in his final moments on the day he died in 'Father's Day', with the Doctor risking a paradox by giving her a second chance to go to Pete. But Rose defies his instructions, saving her father's life but creating a wound in time which summons Reapers to sterilise it. History is thrown out of joint, holding up a phone only to hear Alexander Graham Bell making the first call. More extreme changes occur when River breaks the fixed point of the death of the Eleventh Doctor at Lake Silencio in 'The Wedding of River Song' – the Wars of the Roses continue, London picnickers are warned not to feed the pterodactyls, Charles Dickens is interviewed on television, and Churchill is

Holy Roman Emperor. Meanwhile the Doctor, as he warned Donna, is branded a 'soothsayer.'

These experiences cause the Thirteenth Doctor to be more assertive in her warnings to Yaz about exploring her family history in 'Demons of the Punjab'. She wants to learn about her Nani, who lived in Lahore during the 1950s, but is shocked to discover that the man she is going to marry is Hindu and not Muslim. Yaz says that the Doctor should be more concerned about the aliens interfering with Partition than about what she says, but she responds that a single word could erase Yaz from existence. The writer of the episode Vinay Patel told me that he was surprised that this was the story he decided to bring to *Doctor Who*: 'There were a lot of moments where I questioned why exactly I had chosen a subject that carried such a weight of responsibility and would – inevitably, understandably – be unable to satisfy everyone with an emotional investment in it.' It is not only the Doctor and their companions who question the ethics of their travels through time, but the writers themselves in how to portray the past with the burden of accuracy and authenticity. The Doctor says, 'Tread softly. You're treading on your own history.' It seems that Vinay was advising himself.

Sometimes the Doctor faces other time travellers who deliberately seek to change events. The Monk in 'The Time Meddler' has a Mark IV Type 40 capsule with a working Chameleon Circuit. He tells the Doctor that while he knows the golden rule of non-interference, it is more fun to make things happen ahead of time, claiming to have aided the ancient Britons in building Stonehenge with an anti-gravitational lift. He plans to wipe out the Viking fleet heading to England ahead of the Battle of Hastings, arguing that the reason William of Normandy defeated Harold Godwinson was because the latter had to march north to Stamford Bridge first to fight Harald Hardrada. By stopping the Norman conquest, the

Monk believes he is acting for good, preventing future claims by the rulers of England to the throne of France. The Doctor takes the Monk's dimensional control, leaving his time machine marooned in the form of a sarcophagus in 1066.

The Master acts like the Monk in 'The King's Demons'. The Fifth Doctor realises that the TARDIS has arrived on the day King John is to take his oath as a Crusader, but he is not in London as he ought to be. He argues with Tegan about the accuracy of events, with her claiming that she does not care about such a discrepancy. She also says that John was forced to 'sign' Magna Carta by the barons, saying that she knows her history, while the Doctor tells her that the king was in favour of its policies – both of them are wrong of course to say it was 'signed' at all, rather sealed with the royal great seal, but I suppose that is neither here nor there. By robbing the world of Magna Carta, the Doctor realises that the Master intends to prevent the foundations of parliamentary democracy from ever being laid.

Anachronisms appear elsewhere in *Doctor Who*, such as Laurence Scarman's Marconiscope which the Fourth Doctor identifies as a radio telescope invented forty years early in 'Pyramids of Mars', and the electric street lamps present a decade too soon in 'A Town Called Mercy'. The Twelfth Doctor stops caring about such changes in 'The Magician's Apprentice', believing his death to be imminent, entering a castle playing an electric guitar atop a tank. It is a signifier of the Doctor's depression when he stops caring about the rules, experiencing a sense of futility in his efforts to protect humanity. Anomalies in energy readings draw the Thirteenth Doctor to Montgomery, Alabama on 1 December 1955 in 'Rosa', finding herself on the exact bus on which Rosa Parks refused to give up her seat for a white passenger. She becomes a part of events, forcing her to remain seated to ensure that she does not derail the civil rights movement. The Doctor asserts the importance of this moment, saying that the following Monday the bus boycott began, and acknowledges that she even changed the universe, showing her companions Asteroid 284996, named 'Rosaparks'.

The Doctor realises that they are not meddling with history, but making it. A recurring joke is to explain mysteries of the past through the Doctor's footprint. In 'The Chase', the crew of a ship jump overboard to escape the Daleks, before the camera reveals to the audience that the boat is called *Mary Celeste*. A similar shot concludes 'The Visitation', in which the Fifth Doctor pursues the Terileptils to London where they set fire to a bakery. Tegan asks if they should help to extinguish the flames since they were partially responsible, and the Doctor says, 'I have a sneaking suspicion this fire should be allowed to run its course.' The camera again reveals the fire reaching a street sign reading 'Pudding Lane.' Rose and the Tenth Doctor speculate at the end of 'Tooth and Claw' about how Queen Victoria's brush with a werewolf might have impacted the British royal family. The Doctor says that she did suffer haemophilia, known as the Royal Disease, which was a mystery since she did not inherit it. Rose notes that the Windsors are very private and love blood sports, and could easily schedule themselves around the Moon. By contrast to the sincerity with which much of history is treated in *Doctor Who*, at such moments the Doctor has their tongue firmly placed in their cheek.

THE BOOTSTRAP PARADOX

At the beginning of 'Before the Flood', the Twelfth Doctor gives us a lecture. He describes a man with a time machine who loved Beethoven's music, so he travelled to eighteenth-century Germany to meet the composer. He cannot find him, causing him to panic that the music will never be written. He copies out the sheet music he brought with him for

Beethoven to sign and gets it published. The time traveller becomes Beethoven. But the Doctor poses a question – who really composed Beethoven's Fifth? This ontological problem of causality is known as a bootstrap paradox, wherein it becomes impossible to determine where an idea came from if it was only through knowledge of the past that someone from the future is able to enact the original event. At the end of the episode, the Doctor observes to Clara that it was he who had programmed his ghost to give him a message, words which he only knew to say in the past because he had already heard them in the future. For fear of giving her, himself, and the audience a headache, he shrugs and smiles directly at the camera.

The Doctor is abnormally casual about this problem, typically needing to find a definitive explanation. Instances of the bootstrap paradox go against the central rule by which they travel through time, since to share historical knowledge with people in the past is a clear form of interference. Even the First Doctor, who is most insistent upon this tenet, is guilty. In 'The Romans', Vicki fears she has killed Nero by swapping a poisoned drink with his unpoisoned one. The Doctor tells her off for meddling, yet she later tells him that he ought to be ashamed of himself for causing the fire which destroyed Rome in 64AD. She says it is a shame that history books do not mention that it was the Doctor who gave Nero the idea to burn down the city in order to force the Senate to pass his new architectural plans – by accidentally setting the parchment alight with the lens of his spectacles. Nero might never have allowed the fire to spread had the Doctor not fanned the flames himself.

In 'The Myth Makers', the First Doctor finds himself amongst the Achaean forces attempting to infiltrate the city of Troy during events described in Homer's *Iliad*. Steven asks why he does not suggest the wooden horse, which the Doctor explains is obviously an absurd dramatic device invented by the poet. Simultaneously, Vicki almost accidentally forewarns the Trojans by pointing out to Priam that it is funny that he says his people would do anything for a horse. After running out of hopeless ideas, the Doctor eventually says to Odysseus, 'Have you ever thought of a horse?' The Doctor should know better, that the only reason he and his companions knew of the Trojan Horse was because of their familiarity with Homer, creating a causal loop.

The Doctor might see it as less a case of providing ideas, more a helpful nudge. The Fourth Doctor claims to have helped Isaac Newton in 'The Pirate Planet', telling Romana that he climbed up a tree and dropped an apple on his head. Naturally this did not help him to identify gravity but made him cross with the Doctor, who was then forced to explain it to him afterwards at dinner. This might be the Doctor's idea of a joke, however, because the Fourteenth Doctor meets Newton in 'Wild Blue Yonder'. This time an apple falls after the TARDIS materialises in the tree. To make matters worse, the Doctor addresses him as 'Sir' ahead of time, and he and Donna joke that he must appreciate 'the gravity of the situation.' In one of the show's most ridiculous moments, Newton attempts to remember the word they used, despite it having pre-existed the concept to which the real Newton ascribed it, landing instead on 'mavity', as it is known in the Whoniverse thereafter. Where the First Doctor once forced a young girl to stay in Paris during a massacre for fear of interference, this new Doctor advises Newton to steer clear of London in 1666. It is at moments like this when it is difficult to see them as a consistent character, causing frustration for any committed fan or, indeed, historian.

My favourite bootstrap paradox is found in 'Timelash', in which a young man named Herbert joins the Sixth Doctor in the TARDIS. He remarks, 'It's fantastical. A machine that transcends time itself.' He says that while he knows that people on Earth will never believe his experiences, he must find a way to share his tale of time travel and Morlox, or 'Morlocks', as he will remember them. At the end of the episode, Peri picks up a calling card the man dropped, reading 'Herbert George Wells', allowing them to realise that he will return to Earth and write of his adventures. Yet if *Doctor Who* is supposed to have inspired H.G. Wells to write *The Time Machine*, and that book inspired the creation of *Doctor Who*, then which came first?

GENIUSES OF THE PAST

'The Time Traveller (for so it will be convenient to speak of him) was expounding a recondite matter to us. His pale grey eyes shone and twinkled, and his usually pale face was flushed and animated.' So begins *The Time Machine*, with a community of scientists keenly leaning forward to witness a new innovation which will change their understanding of the universe. A similar presentation occurs in 'The Mind of Evil', with Professor Kettering demonstrating a machine named for Professor Emil Keller which is said to be capable of extracting negative impulses from a person, leaving instead a rational, well-balanced individual. The Fourth Doctor encounters Professor Kerensky in 'City of Death', who, like the Time Traveller, tinkers with time by building a cellular accelerator which can make an egg develop into a chicken in thirty seconds. These figures represent the archetype of the neurodivergent genius, intensely fixated on their scientific ideas and experiments to an extent which renders them ignorant of the dangers their work implicates.

In *NeuroTribes*, Steve Silberman describes the potentially neurodivergent behaviour of Henry Cavendish. The natural philosopher, as scientists were then known, lived alone on Clapham Common, communicating with his household staff via written notes. The single image which exists of Cavendish shows him in a frock coat, with frilled shirt-wrists, white stockings, and a knocker-tailed periwig beneath a black three-cornered hat – a style long out of fashion by the end of the eighteenth century. He wore the same outfit every day, with his grey-green or violet coat replicated each year by his tailor when it began to fade. If these details do not already sound familiar, then perhaps the fact that Cavendish's specialisms included chemistry, mathematics, physics, astronomy, metallurgy, meteorology, and pharmacy seals the comparison to the polymathic Doctor. As Silberman describes him, 'Cavendish may have dressed like a man from the past, but he lived like one from the future.'

In 2001, Sacks proposed that Cavendish, in his literal thinking, single-mindedness, and passion for exactitude, 'coupled with a virtual incomprehension of social behaviors and human relationships', resembled descriptions of adults with what was then called Asperger's syndrome. Sacks stressed that it was precisely these qualities which made Cavendish a genius. He would be a prime candidate in the experiments of the Rani, a Time Lord who on two occasions tried to make use of the most brilliant human brains. In 'The Mark of the Rani', the Sixth Doctor is thrilled by the prospect of meeting George Stephenson, for while he is forbidden from changing the course of history, this man will, through the invention of the steam locomotive. Intellectuals across history are collected in 'Time and the Rani', from Hypatia to Albert Einstein, with a special place reserved for the Seventh Doctor. He takes them back to their own times in the TARDIS, with Einstein appearing to be particularly fascinated by the console – 'I'll explain how it works later. It's all relative.' While the Rani wishes to exploit genius, the Doctor hopes to engage with it, finding in them an affinity which he seldom shares with humans. For the lonely, neurodivergent mind, the Doctor represents a rare intellectual match.

The late Sir George MacLeish, friend of Prince Albert and occupant of Torchwood House, is described as one such gentleman in 'Tooth and Claw'. His son, Sir Robert, shows the Tenth Doctor his father's invention, the *Endeavour* telescope which he obsessively built by hand in his final years – 'to be honest, most of us thought him a little, shall we say, eccentric.' The Doctor wishes that he had met him, although he criticises the device for having too many prisms. He asks Rose if he is being rude, so he says that it is very pretty. Queen Victoria remarks, 'This device surveys the infinite work of God. What could be finer? Sir Robert's father was an example to us all. A polymath, steeped in astronomy and sciences, yet equally well-versed in folklore and fairytales.' The combination of Sir George's interests in stars and magic encourages the Doctor to say he likes this man even more, recognising in him his own passions. One who is not merely confined to scientific fact, but also capable of viewing the universe with childlike wonder.

After the Doctor regenerates into a woman, she finds it essential to meet others like her in the past. My own research has encouraged me to engage with women artists, writers, and thinkers with whom I can identify in order to feel a sense of heritage – Lili Boulanger, Virginia Woolf, Sylvia Plath, and Susan Sontag, to name but a few. The Thirteenth Doctor meets Ada Lovelace in 'Spyfall Part Two' in a realm the mathematician believes to be her own mind. Ada takes the Doctor to meet Charles Babbage, who shows her his Difference Engine – almost creating a bootstrap paradox when she calls it a 'computer.' After realising that someone has been experimenting on Ada's brain, the Doctor takes her to Paris in 1943 where they meet another brilliant woman, Noor Inayat Khan, the first female wireless operator to be dropped behind enemy lines. The trio form an impressive companionship, yet the Doctor knows that these women are too extraordinary and vital to history to be allowed to remember their adventure together. Ada mourns the loss of having met someone else like her, and the knowledge which she learned. 'Oh Ada, you don't need a preview', the Doctor reassures her. 'You'll figure it out before anyone.' As with Parks, this Doctor expresses great pride in her encounters with women of the past, and is always respectful of their independence from her in their achievements.

While not a woman, the Thirteenth Doctor has another encounter with an historical genius in 'Nikola Tesla's Night of Terror'. Like Cavendish, Tesla is described by Silberman in *NeuroTribes* through a modern lens of autism diagnosis – 'Whatever Tesla was, the word typical didn't describe him.' Those who knew him characterised him as lacking in social tact, and he always calculated the precise volume of food and drink on the table and counted the steps he took on his constitutionals. He had overwhelming likes and dislikes, being nauseated by the sight of a pearl but mesmerised by glittering objects with flat surfaces. In *Doctor Who*, Tesla is frustrated that others cannot see beyond their narrow-minded conception of nature. Just as Grandin described seeing her inventions fully formed in her mind, so too did Tesla, who envisioned a 'world wireless system' long before the creation of the internet. And like Grandin's comparison to being 'an anthropologist on Mars', Tesla is mocked as a Martian. He is delighted to discover that the Doctor built her sonic screwdriver, calling her an inventor. 'It can be difficult, you know, to feel no one else sees the world the way you do. It's like you're, err…' Tesla trails off. 'Out of place', the Doctor offers.

Tesla has a companion, Dorothy Skerritt, who confides in Ryan by saying that after he showed her the impossible, the normal does not seem important. Beyond having an excellent memory, my favourite aspect of my neurodivergence is my ability to see differently to other people. I hold all of my knowledge visually in my mind, allowing me to draw connections between things which often go unnoticed by others. Even in writing this book it is as if all of the Whoniverse is floating around me, and I am pulling strands together in an attempt to better understand my connection to the programme, and how it relates to neurodiversity in a broader sense. It was unlocking this capacity which has enabled me to flourish as a writer, and to find connections with those who share my passion for interpretation and understanding. While I have been mocked for my neurodivergence, I have come to see it as the greatest tool in my endeavours to understand the mysteries of the past.

CHAPTER FIVE
SILENCE IN THE LIBRARY

It's his notes. He'd never leave his notebook. It's too important to him. It's got the key codes of all the machines in the ship. It's got notes of everywhere we've been to. Something terrible has happened to him, I know it has.

Susan Foreman in 'An Unearthly Child'

There's too many things going on, too many variables. My brain's too crowded.

The Thirteenth Doctor in 'Kerblam!'

When I was a teenager I attempted to keep a record of everything related to *Doctor Who*. Using the notebooks and pens which came attached to *Doctor Who Adventures* magazine, I watched each episode and wrote down every character, creature, and planet mentioned in a project to memorise them. I loved list-making, and I drew connections in diagrams, even speculating backstories to elements mentioned in passing. I invented my own Doctor and her companions, writing stories about zombies awoken by Halley's Comet and the alien identity of Jack the Ripper. The few people I interacted with at school were those who shared my passion, comparing our collections of *Battles in Time* cards and writing quizzes to catch each other out – these acquaintances seem too competitive to be classified as friendships. It was easy to keep up with NuWho – I watched repeats on BBC Three and recorded episodes on blank VHS tapes until I replaced them with DVD boxsets. Classic Who proved more challenging, like a treasure hunt. I had my uncle's collection, which included many of the Third, Fourth, and Fifth Doctors' adventures, and I scoured charity shops for the rest

The problem was not what I did know, but that there was so much I did not. Not only are there the episodes of the main series which have been broadcast for over six decades, there is an ever-expanding collection of spin-off media, including Target Books, novella-length adaptations which expand the stories. After the show was cancelled by the BBC in 1990, Virgin Publishing was licensed to produce original *Doctor Who* novels, beginning with the New Adventures and continuing through the Missing Adventures. Following 'The Movie' in 1996, featuring the Eighth Doctor, the BBC revoked Virgin's licence and began publishing an in-house series called the Past Doctor Adventures as well as a parallel sequence following the new incarnation. A licence was granted by the BBC in 1999 to Big Finish Productions which continues to produce audio dramas. Then there are the missing episodes, those which the BBC routinely deleted to save archive space in the 1960s, a fact which as a teen I found unbearable. It became too much for my brain to cope with, and I decided that it was better to know nothing at all, or rather to make headspace for interests I viewed as less childish.

For many fans it is the vastness of the Whoniverse which makes it so appealing to a neurodivergent sensibility. When I raised the issue on the *Autism Through Cinema* podcast, Harry Draper, who has written for Big Finish, responded:

> *I remember reading one time, somebody said, 'the longevity of Doctor Who isn't really the reason for its appeal, the longevity*

> *is the result of its appeal.' But I would disagree with that, I actually love the fact that there is so much of it.*

Harry went on to say that he loves that he is able to name all of the space marines from 'Death to the Daleks', and that he owns eleven Cybermen figures from 'The Tenth Planet' despite the fact that there are only six or seven in the original serial. He said that he has always related *Doctor Who* to autism in a contextual sense, rather than in its content. Another neurodivergent fan, Carolyn Arnold, told me that her husband shares Harry's type of fandom, whereas she is 'more of a memory hoarder.' She collects photographs with cast members and at filming locations. *Doctor Who* manifests itself as a special interest for neurodivergent fans in a variety of ways, but few are content to simply watch the show casually. It needs to be an integral part of our lives.

COLLECTING KNOWLEDGE

Like my teenage self, the First Doctor carries a notebook with him, jotting down his observations. In 'The Daleks', he is fascinated by the historical records kept by the Thals on Skaro spanning nearly half a million years – 'Absorbing, most absorbing.' Susan is delighted to see her grandfather enjoying himself, observing that his personality changes when he is caught up in something which piques his interest. Yet like the drive of many Whovians to expand the narrative beyond the canon, the Doctor expresses a lack of contentment in merely observing, as the Time Lords do on Gallifrey. In 'The War Games', Jamie asks the Second Doctor why he ran away, and he tells him that he was bored – to stop reading about the stars and touch them with his own hands.

I recall the frustration of my teachers at school when I attempted to broaden the scope of their lessons beyond the curriculum. If we were reading *Hamlet*, I wanted to talk about Freud and queer theory, or if we were learning about trigonometry, I fired off questions about its real-world applications. In 'Planet of the Spiders', the Time Lord tutor K'Anpo says that 'not all spiders sit on the back', which the Third Doctor explains to Sarah as a criticism of his greed for knowledge and information, something which the thinker had experienced when he taught the Doctor as a child. The Thirteenth makes reference to this in 'The Battle of Ranskoor Av Kolos', for when Andinio says that she does not have to answer all of her questions, the Doctor reflects, 'That's what my teachers used to say. Usually just as they quit teaching.' I recall several of my teachers storming out of the classroom, unable to cope with a pupil who dared to think for herself.

The Doctor admires those who share their thirst for knowledge. In 'The Impossible Planet', the Tenth is excited to realise that the only reason why the crew came to the planet Krop Tor, inexplicably in orbit of a black hole, was because it was there. He hugs Zach and says that human beings are amazing for this, 'but apart from that, you're completely mad.' He knows, of course, that he would do the same. I recall getting into trouble as a child for what was described as an almost scientific approach to pushing things to their limit, be it seeing how far a glass could be nudged before it falls off a table, or at what point an adult loses their temper. The boundary having been identified, I knew not to cross it again.

The Doctor is shown to learn from their mistakes, which with their extended lifetime means that they have gained a superhuman level of knowledge. This makes them a valuable asset to many of their enemies who attempt to steal their brain power. In 'Mindwarp', the Mentor Sil assumes that the Sixth Doctor will be glad to donate his mind for the advancement of science, although his intentions are commercial. His plot is akin to the exploitation of neurodivergent savants for their intellectual efficiency by corporations, especially in the technological industry such as that in Silicon Valley. It is also similar to the means by which artificial intelligence has been developed to 'learn' from the intellectual property of human beings in order to create a cumulative bank of knowledge.

The futuristic device seen in 'The Long Game', called an Infospike, is inserted through surgery into the human brain. When it is demonstrated by Cathica Santini Khadeni aboard Satellite Five, the Ninth Doctor explains: 'Compressed information, streaming into her. Reports from every city, every country, every planet, and they all get packaged inside her head. She becomes part of the software. Her brain is the computer.' While Rose says that this will surely make her a genius, the Doctor rebuts that if she was allowed to remember the information her head would explode. As a science geek, the appeal of the Infospike for Adam Mitchell is too great to resist, and he defies the Doctor by paying for the operation and streaming the information through Rose's mobile phone to his parents' answering machine. When the Doctor drops him off on Earth he erases the message, and tells Adam that if he shows anyone his Infospike they will dissect him. The Doctor approves of the organic acquisition of knowledge, not artificial attempts to cheat. He only takes the best with him.

One of my favourite ways to exercise my brain is quizzing. I founded a quiz society at school, during which time I discovered that I found greater enjoyment in researching and writing questions than answering them myself. As soon as I started university I entered a community of quizzers which became my main site of social interaction, allowing me to expand my areas of expertise beyond my special interests to acquire a broader, multi-cultural knowledge. I believe that in doing so I become a more open-minded, empathic person, introducing me to a diversity of human experience. Joining the quiz society and participating in national tournaments was the first time I encountered other people like me, many of whom were neurodivergent, and I took comfort in an environment in which small talk was minimal and knowledge was cachet.

In 'Bad Wolf', Rose returns to Satellite Five where she plays a version of *The Weakest Link* in which those who are voted off are disintegrated by the Anne Droid. A quiz becomes a matter of life and death again in '42', in which Martha is only able to get through the doors of the *SS Pentallian* by answering trivia questions – 'I can't believe our lives depend on some stupid pub quiz.' For a time mine did. I made my college's *University Challenge* team, although I was devastated when we were knocked out in the semi-finals. I went on to work on the show, during which time I attempted to improve conditions for neurodivergent contestants who found the experience overwhelming. I was unable to function to my full potential when I competed, thrown off by the noise of the audiences and the bright studio lighting. I felt like Rose facing the Anne Droid, only I was dealing with the Jeremy Pax-Bot, causing my mind to shut down. I later appeared on *Mastermind*, opposite the Cyborg Myrie, answering questions on Sylvia Plath. Faced with a question relating to an unpublished piece of her juvenilia, I panicked – by not knowing the answer, I felt that I had let down my literary hero. It was like a bad dream; I wanted to refresh and start again, but there was no escape from the black chair. I remembered how I felt every time I realised that I will never know everything about *Doctor Who* when I was younger, and it hurt.

WHONIVERSITY

After I completed my History BA, I stayed at Cambridge for an MPhil in Film and Screen Studies. It was in this field that I discovered my eidetic ability to memorise cinematic imagery could be put to its greatest use. I am always delighted by the film references in 'Dragonfire', including characters named after theorists André Bazin and Marshall McLuhan. Like Bill in 'Empress of Mars', I often make sense of situations through comparisons to cinema. She tells the Twelfth Doctor that he would like *The Terminator* (1984) because it features killer robots, and *The Thing* (1982) because everybody dies. She gets excited not about the historical Vikings when they are referenced by the Doctor, but the 1958 film starring Kirk Douglas and Tony Curtis. The Doctor attempts to speak in this referential mode when he compares the blast from Gargantua trapping the army in an eternal winter to Disney's *Frozen* (2013). Science fiction and fantasy genres become a reference point for Bill to help her to understand things which exist beyond the human imagination.

Also in 'Dragonfire', the Seventh Doctor reads *The Doctor's Dilemma* by George Bernard Shaw. Like the myriad of trolley problems faced by the Time Lord on their adventures, the play centres on a choice between offering medical treatment to an altruistic colleague and an amoral but gifted artist with whose wife the doctor is in love. Shaw stages a potential life-or-death scenario in a scientific study of human ethics. The Doctor also bears a resemblance to Higgins from Shaw's play *Pygmalion*, as previously observed in relation to Dodo. Higgins is a genius of phonetics, who judges people solely on the basis of linguistics rather than any other qualifier. Like the Doctor, he takes in a young woman who has little option to refuse, giving her a life she could only dream of in exchange for her compliance in his game. In the stage directions, Shaw describes Higgins as being 'of the energetic scientific type, heartily, even violently interested in everything that can be studied as a scientific subject, and careless about himself and other people, including their feelings.' It reads like textbook criteria for Autism Spectrum Condition.

'Ghost Light' features a character based on the flower girl Eliza Doolittle, a woman-like being called Control who upon meeting the Seventh Doctor says, 'Spare a farthing, guv'nor.'

Later she is wearing a dress and trying on hats as the gentleman hunter Redvers Fenn-Cooper, channelling Higgins, tells her that the handsomest woman he ever saw was the daughter of an N'Taba chief who 'had a bone through her nose and ate her cousin for breakfast.' Control asks him, 'Will Control be ladylike? Want so much', to which Redvers replies, 'Once this hunt is over, I'll make you the finest ladylike in the Empire.' The encounter is reminiscent of the Fourth Doctor's dynamic with Leela, a warrior of the Sevateem tribe, especially in 'The Talons of Weng-Chiang'. After arriving in Victorian London, Leela complains about the outfit she is wearing, with the Doctor informing her that she cannot go out in skins because she will frighten the horses. In *Pygmalion*, Eliza tells Higgins's mother and her companions about her suspicions that her aunt did not die of influenza, but rather whoever 'pinched' her new straw hat had 'done her in'. Upon Professor Litefoot describing a dead man as having been 'stabbed by a midget' due to the angle of the wound, he apologises for speaking of indelicate matters in front of a member of the fair sex. Leela responds by saying that she was taught to aim for the heart with a blade from under the breastbone. The Doctor makes excuses by calling her a 'savage' whom he found floating down the Amazon in a hat box. 'A hat box?!' Litefoot cries, giving his best Lady Bracknell. Yet when Leela appears in a green chevroned dress with mutton-chop sleeves, the Doctor tells her she looks charming and he would be proud to take her to the theatre – if she is very good, he will even buy her an orange. As with Higgins, the Doctor's fixation on customs causes him to behave in a controlling and misogynistic manner.

The Twelfth Doctor adopts a professorial guise, even moving into an office at St. Luke's University in Bristol in 'The Pilot'. His rooms are similar to those occupied by Professor Chronotis, a Time Lord who retires to St Cedd's College, Cambridge in 'Shada', having left Gallifrey for a more peaceful existence of teaching and reading. The Doctor summons Bill, who works in the canteen, after noticing her at his lectures. She tells him that other people attend them who are not enrolled, but the Doctor remarks that while others frown when they do not understand something, she smiles. Without giving her an option, he informs her that he will give her tuition provided she gets a First in every assignment, and regardless of who is dying, she must never be late. Once again, the Doctor's motivations seem to be to take an uneducated young woman and, out of philanthropic and scientific interest, fashion her in his own image.

The dynamic is reminiscent of the play *Educating Rita* by Willy Russell, an update of *Pygmalion* in which a university professor teaches English Literature to a hairdresser. Both Eliza and Rita escape from the toxic dynamic their tutors create, while Bill loses her life as a direct result of the Doctor's control. In 'Thin Ice', Bill is disturbed by a death she has witnessed, confusing the Doctor because in 'Smile' they were standing in a garden filled with dead people and she seemed less bothered. She says it was different then because the people were already dead, to which the Doctor observes, 'Morally and practically, that is not a useful distinction. Unlearn it.' She tells him not to tell her what to think, and he says that he is her teacher and that is his job. His lack of consideration for Bill's feelings betrays the coldness of Higgins.

For better or worse, I have always resisted hierarchical structures. Unless I can understand or agree with criticism, I find it difficult to accept it in relation to my work, which has made my life in academia challenging. It is one of the reasons why I find it easiest to work freelance, for in addition to the sensory and social difficulties created by working in an office, I struggle to work to another person's expectations. I relate more readily with the Doctor's intellectual companions than those who follow them blindly. Liz Shaw is an independent researcher at Cambridge, an expert in meteorites, physics, and a dozen other subjects which makes her the perfect candidate in the Brigadier's eyes to work as the Third Doctor's assistant. Not that she agrees, ultimately returning to her own research rather than running around after a boss. When Martha meets the Tenth Doctor in 'Smith and Jones', she says that she will not be using his honorific because he is not technically qualified – 'As far as I'm concerned, you've got to earn that title.'

Then there is Rita, a medical student who meets the Eleventh Doctor in 'The God Complex' and quickly impresses him, causing him to joke that Amy is fired. The Doctor admits that while he says it is his companions' choice to travel with him, 'Offer a child a suitcase full of sweets and they'll take it. Offer someone all of time and space and they'll take that, too.' He knows that there is a huge imbalance to the power dynamic he exerts, and yet even then he offers to show Rita the universe. She says she does not know what he is talking about but she has a feeling he just did it again. Rita is more than capable of thinking for herself – her worst fear is revealed to be getting a B in mathematics. I shudder at the thought.

SHERLOCK IN SPACE

'I am a brain, Watson. The rest of me is a mere appendix.' So says Sherlock Holmes in 'The Adventure of the Mazarin Stone' by Arthur Conan Doyle. There was a time when I would have described myself similarly, my intelligence long having been the only thing I liked about myself. When neurodivergent people feel that certain activities and behaviours are inaccessible to them, it can lead to feelings of anger, jealousy, and snobbery. I felt this way as a teenager – other people had friends, got drunk, and had sex, while I most assuredly did not. The first time I tried to go to a party my mother pulled up in the car outside and I had such an intense panic attack that she had to take me straight home. There is a tendency to feel that when aspects of human nature are rendered alien to someone, they therefore must be wrong. This is a trait typical of Holmes, another character towards whom I feel a kinship. The sleuth has been analysed through the lens of neurodivergence, including by Karl Albrecht in *Psychology Today* in 2011 who diagnoses Holmes as autistic because 'his obsessive interest in the craft of crime-solving crowded out almost everything else from his life, including the possibility of warm and reciprocal relationships.' Like Holmes, when I feel overwhelmed I immerse myself in my studies, finding greater comfort in books than people, and just as the detective calms himself by practising the violin, I do the same with the trombone.

The Holmes stories observe his character from the perspective of an outsider, Dr John Watson. He watches his friend with fascination in the first novel, *A Study in Scarlet*: 'His zeal for certain studies was remarkable, and within eccentric limits his knowledge was so extraordinarily ample and minute that his observations have fairly astounded me.' By contrast, in *The Sign of the Four*, Holmes talks about Watson's alcoholic brother in insensitive terms, but then offers an apology: 'Viewing the matter as an abstract problem, I had forgotten how personal and painful a thing it might be to you.' Both lines could be from *Doctor Who*. It is no wonder that Holmes appealed to former showrunner Steven Moffat and writer Mark Gatiss who created the BBC series *Sherlock*, transposing the Victorian setting to contemporary London. When this modern incarnation is referred to by the police as 'the freak', Sherlock responds, 'I'm a high-functioning sociopath. Get your terminology right.' In 'The Hounds of Baskerville', John tells Detective Inspector Lestrade that Sherlock is secretly pleased to see him. Lestrade agrees that Sherlock likes to see familiar faces together, because 'it appeals to his – '. 'Asperger's?' John suggests. Holmes appears more obviously neurodivergent in this setting than Conan Doyle's stories in which he is more familiar as the archetype of the eccentric Victorian genius.

In a production note written to describe the changed personality of the Second Doctor following his regeneration, he is described as displaying 'the sardonic humour of Sherlock Holmes.' Evidently Conan Doyle's works were a direct influence on the characterisation of the Doctor, especially in this new era in which he is decidedly cynical and neglectful of his appearance. In *The Sign of Four*, Holmes says that he has written several monographs upon technical subjects, including one entitled 'Upon the distinction between the Ashes of the Various Tobaccos' to aid him in his investigations. In 'The Evil of the Daleks', the Second Doctor looks in the pockets of Bob Hall and finds cigarettes and a matchbook. He observes, in Holmesian style, that Hall rolled his own cigarettes, thus the straights he has found must belong to somebody else. The Doctor also has a penchant for esoterica, such as the Sixth Doctor's recognition of each of the twenty-five bells in the cathedral at Seville in 'The Two Doctors'. Peri derisively observes, 'You certainly specialise in arcane knowledge.' The Fifteenth Doctor carries out a Holmesian deduction in 'The Church on Ruby Road' when he tells a policeman that, 'She's going to say yes.' He elaborates by observing that he detects a two-carat diamond in his pocket, which suggests he is asking a woman because ninety-one percent of men would not choose a diamond, and she will accept his proposal because the sales begin on Tuesday and he could not wait, which is why she loves him. Rather more in tune with affairs of the heart than Holmes might be capable, but nonetheless betraying of the Doctor's remarkable astuteness for minutiae.

A more explicit comparison to Holmes is drawn in 'The Talons of Weng-Chiang', in which the Fourth Doctor emerges from the TARDIS in Victorian London dressed in a deerstalker and an Argyll cape. The same aesthetic is created for the adventures of the Paternoster Gang. Doctor Simeon tells Madame Vastra that 'Doctor Doyle is almost certainly basing his fantastical tales on your own exploits' in 'The Snowmen', although he suspects that readers of *The Strand* would not accept that Holmes is actually a woman. The Eleventh Doctor pretends to be Holmes when he pays Simeon a visit, donning deerstalker and cape with an unlit Meerschaum pipe between his teeth, just like the one smoked by the First Doctor in 'An Unearthly Child'. 'I see from your collar stud you have an apple tree and a wife with a limp. Am I right?' he announces. He tries to work out how Simeon is controlling the snowmen, referring to him as Moriarty – a role more applicable to the Master. Every great intellectual needs a worthy opponent.

GREAT WRITERS

Literature is a contentious issue for neurodivergent people. Some struggle to engage with fiction, finding it difficult to identify subtext, while others love the way it engages their intense visual imagination. My passion for reading was seen to count against my autism diagnosis when I was a child, for it was previously believed that neurodivergent individuals are drawn to the empirical studies of science and mathematics rather than the subjectivity of the written word. Yet the voracious nature of my reading, as is typical of many autistic women, falls in line with a neurodivergent thirst for knowledge. The Doctor shares this fondness for books, delighting in meeting their favourite authors. When the Tenth Doctor meets Agatha Christie in 'The Unicorn and the Wasp', he tells her that he loves her mind and that she fools him every time – 'Well, almost every time. Well, once or twice. Well, once. But it was a good once.' The unlikely duo make a formidable team, with Christie telling the Doctor to look for a motive by using 'ze little grey cells.' When she chastises him for missing a big clue, she is shocked that he saw the paper in the fireplace while looking the other way as it was reflected in the glass of a bookcase. Skills of detection worthy of Hercule Poirot himself.

The Ninth Doctor is delighted to bump into Dickens in 'The Unquiet Dead', remarking that his favourite of the author's works is the chilling story 'The Signalman'. Dickens is baffled when the Doctor describes himself as 'a big fan', associating the word with a woman's accessory, but he explains that it means he is fanatical about his writing. The Doctor cannot help himself but be honestly critical, saying that he does not like the American section of *Martin Chuzzlewit*. Yet the adventure they share together inspires Dickens to continue writing, with a final dose of dramatic irony when he claims that he now has an ending for his famously unfinished novel *The Mystery of Edwin Drood*. Simon Callow, who plays Dickens, told me that he had never watched *Doctor Who*, expressing a distaste for science fiction since childhood, but he was drawn to this script out of love for the author. He said that he was moved to tears by his final exchange with the Doctor, in which Dickens asks the Time Lord if his books will last and he replies that they will be read forever – 'Exquisite!' For Callow, the episode was a love letter to Dickens, expressed by the gleeful enthusiasm of the Doctor himself.

Although the Tenth Doctor is excited to meet the world's greatest playwright in 'The Shakespeare Code', telling Martha that he will choose beautiful, brilliant words when they attend a performance at the Globe, Shakespeare shouts, 'Ah, shut your big fat mouths!' 'You should never meet your heroes', Martha sighs. The same joke is made in 'The Haunting of Villa Diodati' when the Thirteenth Doctor tells her companions to 'witness some of the most enlightened minds of a generation at the pinnacle, the absolute zenith of their creativity' before they observe Lord Byron, Mary Shelley, et alia playing parlour games instead of penning their masterworks. In *An Anthropologist on*

Mars, Grandin is recorded voicing the difficulty which some autistic people face in engaging with literature in a discussion of Shakespeare. She says that she never knew what Romeo and Juliet were up to, and found *Hamlet*, with its complex investigation of motive and intention, impossible to follow. In 'City of Death', the Fourth Doctor expresses similar distaste for some of the more oblique aspects of the play, claiming to recognise his own handwriting in the first draft which he helped Shakespeare to write after the author sprained his wrist writing sonnets. He criticises the line, 'Take arms against a sea of troubles' in the 'To be or not to be' speech, saying that he told Shakespeare that it was a mixed metaphor, but 'he would insist.'

Few characters love literature as much as Clara, who works as an English teacher at Coal Hill. In 'The Caretaker', the Twelfth Doctor tells her that she is incorrect to say that *Pride and Prejudice* was written in 1797 rather than 1796. Clara is furious with the Doctor's constant corrections, saying, 'I suppose she was your bezzie mate, was she?' He responds by telling her that he read the novel and there was a biography at the back. While her escapades with Austen are only mentioned in passing, it seems that she made several trips to visit the author. She describes her as a 'phenomenal kisser' in 'The Magician's Apprentice', and fondly reminisces in 'Face the Raven', 'Sometimes Jane Austen and I prank each other. Oh, she is the worst. I love her. Take that how you like.' The novels of Austen are filled with emotion and romance, making them particularly appealing to neurodivergent women in their narrative familiarity. They are well-known to set unrealistic expectations, yet it appears that for Clara her dreams of a Regency affair were requited.

I have always found comfort in a library. Beyond the pleasures of reading, I love the sensory experience which only books can bring – the textures and smells of the paper, old and new. A library is a safe space, one in which quietness and calm is mandatory. In 'Silence in the Library', psychiatrist Doctor Moon tells young Charlotte to close her eyes and describe what she sees. There is a library which goes on forever which she moves through by willpower alone. When I am thinking, I envision a similar environment, albeit more like an archive of filing cabinets than rows of bookshelves. They are organised and catalogued, and when I need a particular fact or memory, I glide through the labyrinth until I find what I am looking for. It transpires in 'Forest of the Dead' that Charlotte was dying, so her grandfather built her a library and put her living mind inside it with every book ever written available for her to read. The Doctor observes that she had over four thousand living minds chatting away inside her head, which must be like being in his own mind. It is vital for neurodivergent people to have a place they can go when the world is too much with them, to keep their mind both stimulated and relaxed without becoming overwhelmed. Sometimes all we need is a cosy armchair and a good book to read.

SPECIAL INTERESTS AND HOBBIES

The Doctor engages in an array of special interests common amongst neurodivergent humans. Feats of engineering and locomotives are a classic example, with the technical details of cars and trains as well as their routines and schedules appealing to an autistic sensibility. The Third Doctor spends much of his spare time fiddling with his motorcar, Bessie. In 'Black Orchid', the Fifth Doctor tells his companions that as a boy he wanted to drive a steam engine. Such earthly pastimes and hobbies are the Doctor's means of rest and relaxation from the overwhelm of their constant travels. In 'The Androids of Tara' the Fourth Doctor informs Romana that he is going fishing, saying that after a journey of four-hundred years and twelve parsecs, he is allowed a rest of fifty years according to a made-up law of the Time Lords. The Sixth Doctor gets out his fishing rod again in 'The Two Doctors', misattributing a quote to Rassilon that 'there are few ways in which a Time Lord can be more innocently occupied than in catching fish.' The Fifth Doctor discovers in 'Black Orchid' that he has a natural ability to play cricket, an occasion he has been dressed for since his regeneration. The sequence, featuring a fast-paced montage of the Doctor showing off his skills as both batsman and bowler, is replicated by the Eleventh Doctor in 'The Lodger' when his flatmate Craig Owens invites him to fill in on his football team.

The Doctor shares with many neurodivergent people a propensity for board games, making use of their aptitude for logical thinking. The First Doctor thrashes Kublai Khan at backgammon in 'Marco Polo', and proves himself to be the intellectual match of the title antagonist of 'The Celestial Toymaker'. The Fourth Doctor is a fan of chess, a recurring interlude between adventures; in 'The Androids of Tara', Romana looks at the board and observes, 'Materialisation in fifteen seconds. Mate in twelve.' K9 corrects her to eleven, and the Doctor says that the trouble with chess is that it is all so predictable. He paraphrases Thomas Huxley in 'Logopolis', that the cheeseboard, or rather chessboard, is the world, and the pieces are the phenomena of the universe. Chess is a neat analogy for the Doctor's battles across time, one which is repeatedly deployed during the Seventh Doctor's era in the game he is playing with Fenric.

A deadly version of the game called 'Live Chess' is played by the Eleventh Doctor against Gantok in 'The Wedding of River Song', in which the pieces acquire an electric charge each time they are moved. When he takes Angie and Artie Maitland, the children to whom Clara works as a nanny, to Webley's World of Wonders in 'Nightmare in Silver', the impresario Webley asks if any of them play chess. Like an eager schoolboy, the Doctor raises his hand, not realising that he means one of the children. Artie volunteers, and the Doctor struggles to keep quiet as the boy puts himself in a fool's mate. He is later forced to play a higher stakes game against the Cyberplanner. When the Doctor tells it to take his queen and give him back the children, it responds, 'Emotions. Can't you see what a foolish move that was?' He informs it that the Time Lords invented chess, and confuses the Cyberplanner by telling it that if it fails to avoid his trap he will win in three moves. As with the Daleks, the Doctor knows that the way to defeat a literal, logical thinker is to act in a manner which cannot be predicted, causing it to panic. The Doctor's trivial interests reveal the time they have had to perfect a variety of skills, allowing them to keep their hyperactive mind in a constant state of activity.

The most avid collector I spoke to is neurodivergent filmmaker Edward Smyth, who spoke to me while painting figures of Harry Sullivan and a Menoptera from 'The Web Planet'. He received for Christmas in 2003 a collection of *Doctor Who* trading cards and a DVD copy of 'The Dalek Invasion of Earth', with the appeal inspired by the similarity between the First Doctor and his own grandfather. 'My first films were stop-motion animations of the Corgi figures I had', he said. 'Figurines always make me really happy, even now at the age of thirty.' In his short film, *Wave 3 (Cancelled?)*, he creates a figurine of himself. 'I wanted to explore what it is that attracts me to them so much', he reflected. 'I am sure it is related to me being neurodivergent, and that I am able to control them in my own little world. A bit like "The Five Doctors"!'

Whovian Alexis Harrow expressed to me a similar regret to my own upon having cast out my vast *Doctor Who* collection:

> *When I was in my mid-twenties, I thought I was done with toys. I tried to find a buyer for the whole lot, but in the end, I gave it to a charity shop. One of the biggest mistakes I've made. I'd do anything to have it all back.*

Where once I found comfort in being surrounded by the objects of fandom, I suddenly despised them, and I too put everything in a box and sent it away. I still have my Character Options action figures, as well as many books and DVDs which I found too difficult to get rid of, but they remain in storage, gathering dust. The art of collecting is one in which I have always found comfort, be it stamps, coins, or autographs. In 'The Rescue', the First Doctor examines a rock, identifying its provenance from Dido. Vicki shares his fascination with the planet's geology, dragging with her a sack of stones to add to her collection. They are more interested than Ian and Barbara when browsing the exhibits in 'The Space Museum', and Vicki expresses admiration for the objects gathered by the Monk in 'The Time Meddler'. Museums have always appealed to me not only because I am fascinated by their contents, but because, like libraries, they follow strict curatorial guidelines. I derive enjoyment from alphabetising my books and DVDs, and keeping spreadsheet catalogues of my collections. At school I spent my breaks helping the librarian, and I volunteered weekly at my village library as well. I am never at greater ease than when everything is in its right place, and I experience distress when something is not.

During my adolescence I spent my summers working at a local museum, and for a time as an archival assistant and room steward at Chartwell, the home of Churchill. It is a pleasure for me to share my knowledge with others, and to engage in conversation about my interests. When the Second Doctor arrives at another space museum in 'The Seeds of Death', he fires off facts about the various aeronautical devices on display. It is through such passionate acts of information dumping that many neurodivergent individuals seek to find connection and interact with others. The Eleventh Doctor stops off at the Delirium Archive in 'The Time of Angels', a museum twelve-thousand years in the future, checking the labels and pointing out that most of them are incorrect. When he starts commenting on the objects which he claims are his, Amy realises that this is how the Doctor keeps score, something which amuses her and River.

Professor Song meets Julius Grayle, a crime boss with a collecting fetish, in 'The Angels Take Manhattan', noticing that his prize possession is hidden behind a curtain. It is a Weeping Angel, which he knows is a deadly predator, but he says, 'What collector could resist these? I'm only human.' 'That's exactly what they're thinking', River replies. The Doctor expresses distaste for those who collect for the sake of collecting, without appreciation for the objects themselves. In 'Dalek', the Ninth finds himself in the private museum of Henry van Statten, noting a Cyberman head behind glass – 'The stuff of nightmares reduced to an exhibit.' He demonstrates a musical instrument which Van Statten fails to identify, telling him that he needs to be delicate to produce a note, before the collector tosses it aside. The businessman collects to demonstrate his wealth, showing no appreciation for art and beauty, instead locking things up which he does not understand. After the centrepiece, a Dalek, commits mass murder, the Doctor asks him if it was worth it, to which he responds that he only wanted to touch the stars. 'You just want to drag the stars down and stick them underground, underneath tons of sand and dirt, and label them', the Doctor spits back. 'You're about as far from the stars as you can get.'

After Rose meets Adam in Van Statten's office, he takes her to his workshop where he catalogues the acquisitions of the museum. He shows her a lump of metal from the hull of a spacecraft, and assuming that she has no awareness of life beyond Earth, he tells her it is true that aliens exist. Rose humours him, playing dumb and telling Adam that she is gobsmacked. She asks if all he does is sit underground cataloguing artefacts, which he describes as the best job in the world. He says that he was born clever, and aged eight he logged onto the US Defence System – 'You should've been there just to see them running about. Fantastic!' His use of the Doctor's favourite word causes her to compare him to the Time Lord, whom she says is just her friend. Adam says that is good, because it just is, in a display of romantic interest. To Adam's mind, explaining the objects to impress Rose goes beyond an attempt at social interaction; it is flirting.

The Thirteenth Doctor expresses fondness of the collection of relics of war belonging to Lord Byron in 'The Haunting of Villa Diodati'. She tries on a plumed helmet from Waterloo, not dissimilar to the hat worn by the First Doctor in 'The Reign of Terror'. After reassuring Byron that his collection is not demonic, she says she may still come back later for safety reasons, 'not because it really suits me or anything.' In 1987, Sophie Aldred, who plays Ace, was also drawn to a specific article of clothing – a black bomber jacket. The actress covered it with pin badges, each of which had a different backstory, including a *Thunderbirds* badge inspired by the university dissertation she wrote on Gerry Anderson. In 2025, a book was published ascribing a story to each badge, entitled *Ace's Jacket: The Inside Story*. Sales go to the charities Autism All Stars and the National Autistic Society which Aldred chose after having met many autistic *Doctor Who* fans. The book is a beautifully neurodivergent product – a detailed catalogue of a collection aimed to entertain autistic Whovians, for the benefit of autistic people. It is the perfect tribute to Aldred's character.

BIGGER ON THE INSIDE

In 'The Keys of Marinus', when the First Doctor is offered anything his heart desires in the city of Morphoton, he requests 'a well-equipped laboratory with every conceivable instrument.' The Third Doctor does not care for a salary upon his arrival at UNIT in 'Spearhead from Space', demanding that if he is to work as their scientific advisor he must have a laboratory and equipment. The Twelfth Doctor appears at home when the train transforms into a laboratory in 'Mummy on the Orient Express', an environment which encourages him to stop seeing his fellow passengers as people but rather as objects of study in his attempt to understand the Foretold. Clara says that the Doctor was only pretending to be heartless after he saves the remaining passengers, to which he replies, 'Would you like to think that about me? Would that make it easier?'

In *Explaining Humans*, Pang describes science as her 'staunchest ally and most trusted friend.' It is dependable and reliable, predictable and logical, and therefore can help one to understand the universe. For Pang, this includes human behaviour by relating scientific models and ideas to everyday forms of interaction – she looks at what cancer cells can teach us about effective collaboration, how thermodynamics make sense of order and chaos, and why evolution arouses strong differences of opinion. In 'Ghost Light', the Seventh Doctor admires the moths collected by Josiah Samuel Smith in a speciation study determined to show how certain species adapt to survive in polluted urban environments. Reverend Ernest Matthews calls this 'Darwinian claptrap', with the Doctor telling him to 'adapt or become extinct'. The debate is explored on a cosmic scale, with the traveller Light attempting to stop evolution on Earth so he will not need to make further amendments to his *Catalogue of Life*. The Doctor tells Light that he also evolves, in his attitude, place, and mind, and causes confusion by saying there are gaps in his knowledge for gryphons, basilisks, dragons, and other fictional beasts. Change is asserted as a fact of life, something which many neurodivergent people find challenging, although this is made easier by Pang in her book by grounding those concepts in scientific theory.

The Thirteenth Doctor launches into extended scientific observations, and isolates herself with tools and machinery to build her inventions. When Yaz asks her what would happen if they were to reverse the polarity in 'It Takes You Away', she replies, 'Yasmin Khan, you speak my language.' She is at greater ease dealing with scientific ideas than she is with social situations, enjoying her conversations with Dr Jade McIntyre, a research fellow in zoology in 'Arachnids in the UK', and Suki Cheng in 'Praxeus'. The latter, who builds her own laboratory on a Madagascan beach, inspires an almost romantic fascination in the Doctor. She is hurt when Suki reveals that she was using the Doctor's intelligence to her own ends, with her exclaiming, 'Oh, I'm a sucker for a scientist!' This act of treachery is particularly painful for the Doctor, having been misled by the apparent intentions of Suki and feeling vulnerable for not having identified her betrayal sooner.

The Doctor wrestles between objective fact and matters of faith and magic. As demonstrated by the Seventh Doctor in 'Ghost Light', his first assumption is that there must be a scientific explanation. Yet on occasion, the supernatural becomes the only remaining answer. The Third Doctor says that he is wasting his time with Jo when she talks about the occult in 'The Dæmons', yet by the end of the serial, when he joins Jo in dancing around a maypole, he declares, 'There is magic in the world after all!' In 'The Witchfinders', the Thirteenth Doctor quotes Arthur C. Clarke to King James: 'A brilliant man once said, any sufficiently advanced technology is indistinguishable from magic. We're just about to prove him right', as the monarch witnesses the TARDIS dematerialise. There are more things in Heaven and Earth than are dreamt of in your philosophy, as Hamlet says, a mantra which must be remembered by anyone who limits their understanding of the universe to a singular point of view.

'Three-dimensional Euclidean geometry has been torn up, thrown in the air and snogged to death! My grasp of the universal constants of physical reality has been changed forever. Sorry. I've always wanted to see that done properly.' In other words, as the Doctor also says in 'The Husbands of River Song', the TARDIS is bigger on the inside than it is on the outside. The ship functions as a library, a museum, a laboratory, and above all, a sanctuary. This final purpose is rendered literally in 'Logopolis', as well as in 'The Movie', in which the Master appears in the Cloister Room of the TARDIS containing the Eye of Harmony, decorated with the stonework of a religious building. It is a place of contemplation, yet it also houses the Cloister Bell, which tolls during emergencies. 'I love surrounding myself with my interests, they bring me so much joy and comfort. My home is my safe space. It is designed to make me feel relaxed', Whovian Ian Palmer told me. Pang describes her bedroom similarly: 'What to the untrained eye seemed like chaos was to me perfectly tailored, with everything where I put it last, spontaneously curated to ensure the optimum place for immediate use.' I was always baffled when my parents told me to tidy my room. Everything was organised and placed exactly where it needed to be. I can still walk into my home and sense when an object is not where it was before.

The geography and decoration of the TARDIS is as changeable as the Doctor themself, capable of adapting itself to the homely desires of its occupants. Because Leela enjoys swimming, a pool is introduced in 'The Invasion of Time', which the Eleventh Doctor falls into at the beginning of 'The Eleventh Hour' along with the library – a most distressing image. A new version of the pool appears in 'Journey to the Centre of the TARDIS', as does the library, with shelves lined with books and bottles. Clara ventures too far, however, and discovers a large book entitled *The History of the Time War* in which she reads the Doctor's Gallifreyan name. He makes her forget it, having disturbed the Doctor's private space, causing him to panic.

I asked Chris Chibnall, the former showrunner of *Doctor Who*, to tell me what the TARDIS means to him. He said that he has visited many versions of the ship, having written for quite a few, and signed off the designs for at least three. On 9 February 2018, he took a select group of people into the new console room for the Thirteenth Doctor:

> *The occasion, the work, and the magic of the TARDIS, an idea stretching back to 1963, has us under its spell. We are all children again. This is beyond once in a lifetime. It's a privilege. It is magical. Later, we bring in Jodie, and I watch [production designer] Arwel [Wyn Jones] take Doctor Who round her new TARDIS. The Doctor is delighted. I watch from the side. This is my job, and I'm thrilled with what we have. I am also four, and I would like to discuss this with my great aunt in the morning.*

His story moved me, the idea that those who make *Doctor Who* and bring it to life are also those who, like me, watched it obsessively as children, dreaming of one day finding their own place in the TARDIS. The show itself is this space for its fans, a place of comfort and community through which we can learn about life, the universe, and everything. It is a kind of magic.

CHAPTER SIX
UTOPIA

Fear, loneliness. They're the big ones, Rose. Some of the most terrible acts ever committed have been inspired by them. We're not dealing with something that wants to conquer or destroy. There's a lot of things you need to get across this universe. Warp drive, wormhole refractors. You know the thing you need most of all? You need a hand to hold.

The Tenth Doctor in 'Fear Her'

But know this, Time Lord. You are not alone.

The Face of Boe in 'Gridlock'

In 1911, Swiss psychiatrist Paul Eugen Bleuler observed a form of social withdrawal typical of schizophrenic people which he called *Autismus*. He derived the term from the Greek word 'autos', meaning 'self'. It was the observation of aloneness in their patients which caused both Kanner and Asperger to label the condition as autism, distinct from schizophrenia. Loneliness has been a constant feeling in my life. Even when I am surrounded by other people I feel a sense of disconnect which prevents me from being wholly present. There is an anxiety that I have misread someone's mood, or that there is a double meaning to what they are saying, and always an overwhelming sense that no one really wants me there. People come and go in my life, and even those I have felt close to frequently drift away. Despite the fact that the Doctor is seldom alone in the TARDIS, even when they have a companion or several by their side there is always a sad look in their eye – a belief that no one can understand how they feel. It makes it hard for them to let others in, to share their true feelings, which in turn pushes away those who try to get close. It is in this aspect that I feel most aligned with the last of the Time Lords.

Louise Jameson, who plays Leela, once told me that it is the fandom of *Doctor Who* which she loves most, as it is for many actors whose life and career has become associated with their role in the programme:

> *The show's hero has two hearts and a screwdriver, because he/she/they does nothing but protect the unprotectable, gives voice to the voiceless, hope to the hopeless, sees no colour, religion or 'shape' barriers. Promotes kindness, communication, and support.*

It is a worldview formed through the most unique aspect of the Doctor's mind – that they can see everything, everywhere, all at once, and it makes them kind. The term 'fan' originated in seventeenth-century England as an abbreviation of the word 'fanatic'. It gained a new sense in the nineteenth century when American journalists used it to describe the obsessive nature of certain baseball followers. The concept of fandom as a structured community and social practice developed in the twentieth century especially in the context of science fiction. The most significant was the magazine *Amazing Stories*, launched in 1926 by Hugo Gernsback, predating *Detective Comics* and *Marvel Comics* by over a decade. Beyond the tales, which included the first stories of such influential authors as Isaac Asimov and Ursula K. Le Guin, it was the letters column which allowed fans to connect with like-minded people.

These were consumers who did not merely read for pleasure, but developed their own original writing and art, engaging with debates which laid the foundations for a participatory form of culture. Because of the nature of the Doctor, a character who regenerates without losing their sense of self, it is possible for any fan, regardless of appearance or background, to identify with them. The introduction of a woman as the Thirteenth Doctor and a Black queer man as the Fifteenth has diversified the fandom in ways which make it feel more welcoming than ever before. For those who are neurodivergent, *Doctor Who* fandom appeals to a desire to find a site of common ground beyond the estrangement they feel from everyday existence. It has historically allowed fans to be part of a club, something which those who exist outside of it can never understand and therefore have no ability to intrude upon. Behaviours which in the mainstream are viewed as pathological, such as obsessing over facts and collecting memorabilia, are respected within fandom communities. As Silberman writes in *NeuroTribes*, 'For those who had felt like exiles their whole lives, forced to live among strangers, becoming a fan was like finally coming home.'

THE FAN GENE

The William Hartnell Fan Club was created in 1965 at Hanley in Stoke-On-Trent as a place to share information about *Doctor Who* and collect autographs. It changed its name to the Doctor Who Fan Club following the first regeneration, before being succeeded in 1976 by what is now the Doctor Who Appreciation Society. The DWAS created a newsletter called *The Celestial Toyroom* to promote fan communication through pen-pals and swaps, and collated information about the show in its archive. In 1977 the society staged the first *Doctor Who* convention, which became known as PantopiCon in 1978. The following year saw the release of the debut issue of *Doctor Who Weekly* which included magazine elements and comic stories, as well as free transfers, and later developed into *Doctor Who Magazine*. The show's twentieth anniversary was celebrated at Longleat in 1983, which saw fans swarming prop displays, screenings in tents, and autograph sessions. It was in the huge queues that many fans met others who shared their obsession in real life for the first time. DWAS membership spiked.

Barnaby Edwards is one of the most dedicated fans I spoke to in writing this book. The eminent Dalek operator and prolific writer-director of Big Finish audio dramas told me that he knew about autism from the early 1990s, but it was not until he read a series of articles penned by Gary Gillat in *Doctor Who Magazine* in 2003 that he considered the neurodiversity of the fandom. Barnaby believed that 'tell-tale signs' such as 'encyclopaedic knowledge, a desire to categorise things, attention to detail, the attraction of one fact-loving fan to another' were simply aspects of being a fan. Each of the three parts of Gillat's article, entitled 'The Fan Gene', comes with a parodic annotated image of stereotypical Whovians. The first, labelled 'Clichéd "Sad" Fan', is described as having a brain containing 'A rigid set of lists', 'Sex drive activated only by India Fisher and/or Matthew Waterhouse', and his sole beliefs are that, 'All *Doctor Who* is brilliant. Mummy will never die.' Such a figure is no doubt based on the many people Gillat met and observed at conventions. He quotes one of the show's leading actresses, whom he anonymises as 'Sally'. She describes her signings at conventions as feeling like charity work, for 'everyone who comes to a convention is suffering from some degree of autism, aren't they?' Gillat confesses this took him aback, claiming to only know autism from Dustin Hoffman's performance in *Rain Man* (1988) and child savants on the show *Saturday Superstore*. He explains his research into Kanner, Asperger, and Wing, and his own identification with symptoms of the condition through his obsession with *Doctor Who*, concluding that, 'an exploration of Asperger's should be central to any discussion of what has made us all *Doctor Who* fans in the first place.'

Barnaby continued that he also first heard the term 'neurodivergent' through *Doctor Who*. While signing Dalek photos at a convention at Heathrow in 2008, a mother approached him with her son and explained that her son is neurodivergent. The boy's questions were some of the best Barnaby has ever been asked, and he admits that he still wonders whether Dalek eyestalks produce an inverted image, as per a human retina, or a rectified one, as per a television screen. He also shared something he was told by Katy Manning, who plays Jo Grant, about why it is important to be patient with every fan because many are neurodivergent:

> *For some fans, their thoughts travel in a straight line from A to B. For others, there are side roads and cul-de-sacs and one-way streets and distractions along the way. We all get there in the end. It's just that some of us have a more interesting journey.*

Barnaby says that *Doctor Who* has encouraged him to be more empathetic with people who are different to him. This view is shared by Stephen Gallagher, who wrote the serials 'Warrior's Gate' and 'Terminus'. He told me that his knowledge of neurodivergence has been increased by having an autistic godson, whom Stephen says once described the show's theme music as sounding like 'ghosts screaming on a rollercoaster.' He distinguishes between two types of fan: those who find identification 'in the unique, eccentric, think-outside-the-box character of the Doctor, and those whose fantasy role is of a companion winning the Doctor's affection and approval.' The latter makes me think of those who rapidly fire off facts or attempt to catch me out with their knowledge – something which even my friends and family express delight in, that they know something I do not. This confuses me, because one cannot possibly know everything, and I am only too pleased to admit to the gaps in my knowledge and embrace the opportunity to fill them. I suspect the Doctor feels the same.

THE WHOVIAN COMMUNITY

'Most of my current friends are people I met through *Doctor Who* somehow', one neurodivergent Whovian told me. 'I have maybe three friends who can't be traced back to the show. The first time I cosplayed as the Eleventh Doctor, I met my now ex-boyfriend, who was cosplaying as the Tenth Doctor at the same event.' They live in Brazil, a heritage shared by fellow fan Maria Assima Santos. Her experience is rather different, saying that she has found it impossible to meet fellow fans due to her social challenges – 'No one was ever rude to me, I was just completely invisible in any fan community I have tried to join.' That being said, she told me that she went to a *Doctor Who* picnic in 2015 which she enjoyed, playing adapted versions of childhood games.

These seem to be the two main camps of neurodivergent Whovian experience. Autistic writer and actor Dominic Walsh attended many conventions in Manchester during the 2010s, saying he loves the 'atmosphere and how friendly everyone is.' Carolyn Arnold began contacting other fans by letter during the 1980s, but now she travels to the convention Gallifrey One in Los Angeles every year with her husband and son. Like many Whovians I spoke to, Carolyn met her spouse through *Doctor Who*:

> *Fandom has always felt like a sanctuary – a space full of other people who were 'too much' or 'too weird' elsewhere, but absolutely normal here. Some of my closest friends in fandom have also been diagnosed autistic or ADHD later in life. We've kind of formed our own neurodivergent time tribe.*

Alexis Harrow co-founded a *Doctor Who* society at her

university, with whom she visited the *Doctor Who Experience* and held screenings. Sometimes she finds the fandom fractious. She told me that while working at a charity shop she met a fan who spoke to her 'like it was a competition about how many conventions she's been to and how many cast members she's met.' Alexis said she could not care less, and this is a competitive spirit typical of many Whovians who wish to prove that their fanship is stronger than others. It can be this kind of intensity which makes establishing friendships with other fans difficult, and can spoil the community spirit. The poet Kate Fox, who explores a 'neuroqueer future through a lens of *Doctor Who*' in her anthology *Bigger on the Inside*, found that her touring spoken-word show was a safe space for her because 'people had to come to me.' She has never been a part of any fan communities or attended conventions or events, having never felt drawn to group experience. For some it is important, for others it has no appeal.

The first convention I went to was London Film and Comic Con at Earl's Court in 2014. I only made it inside the exhibition hall at the end of the day after queuing for hours, but I managed to get two signatures – from Adam Brown, who played the dwarf Ori in the *Hobbit* trilogy, and Paul McGann, the Eighth Doctor. I approached them nervously, rehearsing in my head what I was going to say. I told Brown I had spotted him in a Haribo advert, much to his delight, but I was too anxious to talk to McGann – after all, he *is* the Doctor. I hung the framed autographs on my bedroom wall as though they were priceless artworks. The adrenaline became addictive, and I raced across the autograph floor to get a good place in the queues. The thrill of the hunt was the appeal – I saved my pocket money all year for this one day when I cheerfully handed it over in exchange for sixty seconds with the stars. Once at Folkestone I met Tom Baker, and when I handed him a jar of jelly babies he looked fretful and apologised that he had nothing to give me in return. I told him that he was my favourite, and he said I was surely too young to even know who he was. I gained more courage each time, asking my most burning questions. Eventually the autographs became less interesting to me, and I found greater fulfilment by interviewing actors and filmmakers as part of my work as a critic. Still, I regret selling my collection as mementoes of that time, not least Baker's smudged scribble. I can feel the hands of certain readers tensing in horror at the thought.

While I attended conventions with family, it was never a place where I interacted with others or made friends. My parents took me to the exhibitions *Doctor Who Up Close* in Cardiff, and later to the *Doctor Who Experience* in London for my twelfth birthday. I photographed every prop, costume, and model on display, filling albums as a permanent record. I had a themed birthday party, and I can remember the costumes each family member wore – my mother as Matron Cofelia, my father and uncle as John Simm and Roger Delgado's Masters respectively, my grandmothers as a Clockwork Droid and the Plasmavore, wielding her straw – yet no friends were present. Perhaps this was one of the reasons why I was determined to grow out of my fandom, connecting it to a childhood sense of isolation. It was not until I moved to London as an adult that I discovered several of my friends, all of whom are neurodivergent, love the show. While I expressed reluctance at first, I eventually started to attend screenings of *Doctor Who* serials at the British Film Institute and, most importantly, the Quiz of Rassilon which followed in the bar. I found myself sharing jokes and invested in debates about the quality of the writing. It felt like a homecoming.

I maintain a distance from what I perceive to be unfriendly dimensions of the Whovian community, namely the online sphere where nuance goes to die. Several fans I spoke to share greater affection towards the internet, not least because it is a less overwhelming sensory environment than screenings or conventions. Hannah Burrows told me that they had a multifandom account on Instagram to which they posted video edits, allowing them to interact with others who share their obsessions. They were invested in 'Thasmin' theories, the lesbian ship name for the Thirteenth Doctor and Yasmin Khan, although when this element of their relationship was touched on directly in the show Hannah felt that it was fan service rather than a realistic romance. Another neurodivergent Whovian participating in this discussion told me that they had originally joined a Facebook fan group in 2011 which developed into a WhatsApp chat where they can discuss elements of the show. They sought out 'Thasmin' discussions specifically through Discord where they post their own fan fiction. Ella Watts, producer of *Doctor Who: Redacted*, connected her queerness and her neurodivergence by saying that both groups of people often relate to monsters, 'characters who feel like freaks or outcasts.' Feeling an affinity with the Doctor's loneliness as a teenager, she sought out the community online and wrote fan fiction throughout her GCSEs for which others drew artworks: 'It felt like there were people who understood why these stories and these characters felt so important and beautiful to me, and that gave me an immense sense of hope and love that carried me through my darkest days.'

The managing director of Aurora Autistic Consulting, Marion McLaughlin, told me that because she shies away from larger groups or events she founded Autistic Pride online. She explained that this biannual event gives autistic people 'a space to come along and infodump about their favourite topics and answer questions about them if they are open to it', which often includes *Doctor Who*. I found in many of my interviews with neurodivergent fans that they just enjoyed the opportunity to share a discussion about their favourite show with someone who was as invested in it as they were – I had to start imposing a time limit after some conversations lasted several hours. Bella Madge said that she tells her boyfriend that she is pleased he did not know her when she was thirteen because she could not talk about anything else. But she also says that this is one of her favourite traits in autistic people, that passion. It gives one 'this capacity to love something to such an insane degree that it feels overwhelming.' It can be at the same time both fulfilling and challenging.

A DIVERSE UNIVERSE

In 'Remembrance of the Daleks', a Jamaican man named John serves the Seventh Doctor a cup of tea. He offers him sugar and the Doctor asks if it would make a difference beyond the confines of preference – 'What if I could control people's tastebuds? What if I decided that no one would take sugar? That'd make a difference to those who sell the sugar and those that cut the cane.' John says that his father was a canecutter, and if there had been no need for sugar, his great-grandfather would not have been sold into slavery. 'Every great decision creates ripples, like a huge boulder dropped in a lake', the Doctor responds. 'The ripples merge, rebound off the banks in unforeseeable ways. The heavier the decision, the larger the waves, the more uncertain the consequences.' Sylvester McCoy told me that this was his favourite scene during his time in the TARDIS. He also once addressed me in Nadsat while giving me his autograph.

There were few non-white actors in the early series of *Doctor Who*, with Asian characters frequently portrayed by white actors in yellowface, making it uninviting to many. Following the discussion of colonialism in 'Remembrance of the Daleks', NuWho has made a more consistent effort to confront the subject in its storylines. 'The Impossible Planet' introduced the Ood, a species which is described as a 'basic slave race' which does not present a moral issue because they were born to be subservient. They tell Rose that it is all they crave because they have nothing else in life. When the Tenth Doctor and Donna visit the Ood Sphere in 'Planet of the Ood', they discover that this is a condition manufactured by the villainous Mr Halpen. Donna is horrified to learn that the future of the human race is 'a great big empire built on slavery', which the Doctor remarks is not so different to her own time. After Ood Sigma turns Halpen into an Ood, Donna remarks, 'It's weird, being with you. I can't tell what's right and what's wrong anymore.' 'It's better that way. People who know for certain tend to be like Mr Halpen.' The Doctor sees beyond binary ideas of right and wrong as a means of bringing about peace, rather than existing as a dictatorial or fascistic presence. They free the Ood by breaking the circle surrounding the Ood Brain, allowing them to sing their Song of Freedom together. Susie Liggat recalled this as her proudest moment as producer, describing it as 'such a vision of trust and openness which represented the power of being vulnerable, the brilliance of the Other. The importance of not underestimating or taking advantage of people or creatures who work in different ways.' It is the tenet at the heart of NuWho's approach to diversity, directly affecting its fandom.

The Tenth Doctor demonstrates racial blindness during his travels with Martha. This is beneficial in terms of the Doctor not having prejudice against his companion, but it also betrays a lack of consideration for the dangers which Martha faces as a Black woman travelling into a colonial past. In 'The Shakespeare Code', Martha is concerned that she might 'get carted off as a slave' when they arrive in 1599, which the Doctor dismisses by telling her to 'just walk about like you own the place' because that is what he does, naïvely remarking that Elizabethan England is not so different to the twenty-first century. He is quickly proved wrong by

Shakespeare's fetishistic approach to Martha, describing her as the Doctor's 'delicious blackamoor lady', and when she says that she cannot believe what she is hearing, the Doctor tells Shakespeare that it is 'political correctness gone mad.' It is a poor attempt by the Doctor to move away from a topic he finds uncomfortable, willing to overlook racial prejudice because it does not affect him. He displays similar ignorance when he uses the Chameleon Arch to hide his memories in 'Human Nature', leaving Martha alone as a servant girl met by racist abuse by schoolboys. John Smith himself remarks that the reason why Martha protests the fictional nature of his dreams is due to 'cultural differences.' He expects Martha to withstand it.

Bill is not so forgiving. She points out that slavery is 'still totally a thing' when they arrive in 1814 in 'Thin Ice', and the Twelfth Doctor acts as though he has not thought about it. She asks him how they stay out of trouble, and he says that he is not the right person to ask. Yet this Doctor is a marked improvement on the passivity of his predecessor. When Bill says that Regency England is a 'bit more Black than they show in the movies', the Doctor replies, 'So was Jesus. History's a whitewash.' They plan to confront the malevolent Lord Sutcliffe using 'diplomacy and tact.' As soon as Sutcliffe enters and sees Bill he bursts into a racist tirade which sees the Doctor punch him hard on the jaw. 'That was pretty convincing racism for an extra-terrestrial', Bill says. So much for political correctness going mad – this Doctor stands up for his friends. However, he also acts as a white saviour, suggesting that Bill is only safe to travel in the past because she is in his company.

The Thirteenth Doctor is quiet in 'Rosa' when her companions are met with racism in 1955 Alabama. When the white woman Lizzie Steele drops her glove and Ryan picks it up, her husband slaps him. The Doctor says that they do not want trouble, appearing anxious when Mr Steele warns

Ryan that 'he'll be swinging from a tree with a noose for a neckerchief.' After he and Yaz are refused service at a diner, Ryan observes:

> *This ain't history here, Yaz. We're hiding behind bins. I'm having to work so hard to keep my temper, every second here. I could've slapped that guy back there as soon as we arrived. Thank God me Nan taught me how to keep my temper. Never give them the excuse.*

He says that even though Parks made an impact on civil rights, he is frustrated that it did not wipe out racism forever, telling Yaz that he gets stopped by the police more often than his white friends. She responds that even as a police officer she gets called slurs when sorting out a domestic, or a terrorist upon leaving the mosque. But she says that the racists never win, and that she can only have her job because of what Rosa did in the past. The Doctor does not know what they should do – to stand up for what they know to be right, or to be aware of the privilege afforded by their appearance. The lack of a clear social code makes them uncomfortable.

The Fifteenth Doctor has to contend with a universe which perceives him as different, creating new frustrations. At the end of 'Dot and Bubble', Brewster Cavendish tells his companions on Finetime that they will venture forth as pioneers to fight, tame, and own the planet. The Doctor offers to find them a new home in the TARDIS, but Lindy Pepper-Bean says that while he has been kind to her – his 'duty' – they can never travel with him because he is 'not one of us.' Hoochy Pie describes the blue box as 'voodoo', and that it is their 'God-given duty to maintain the standards of Finetime, forever.' It is the first time that this Doctor is visibly angry, saying that they can think what they want as long as they allow him to save their lives. Their racism and obsession with an obscene concept of 'purity' does not compute in his brain.

When the Doctor travels with Belinda Chandra, he demonstrates a stronger sense of Black identity. Arriving in Miami in 1952 in 'Lux' he says that it is a good thing that it is four o'clock in the morning because they will not be seen. Belinda is shocked when the Doctor tells her to save her anger for later, to which he responds, 'I have toppled worlds. Sometimes I wait for people to topple their world. Until then, I live in it and I shine.' Something easier for a Time Lord who can escape in his TARDIS to a more tolerant time and place to say. The Doctor discovers a need for kinship with fellow Black people, as explored in 'The Story & the Engine'. He is excited to go to Omo's Palace, a barbershop in Lagos, Nigeria: 'It's the first time I've had this Black body. In some parts of the Earth, I'm now treated differently. But here, in Africa, in that barbershop, I'm accepted. I'm able to forget.' Belinda tells him that she was taken by her nan to India whenever she could for the same reason – 'You say you're not human, but that's the most human thing ever, Doctor.' It is unusual for the Doctor to express desire for community and friendship beyond the TARDIS, something which Belinda correctly assesses as profoundly human.

WE ARE FAM

In my conversation with Esme Hayes, she articulated the Doctor's sense of social justice and its relationship to neurodivergence beautifully:

> *Autistic people get very upset about social issues and get engaged with social justice to a point where it can be quite self-destructive, especially because you know that other people don't care. You internalise all this responsibility and think that if I don't care as much as I possibly can, it's all*

> *going to go to shit. The Doctor does that all the time. There is a fantasy to that, because you want someone to show up and affirm you.*

Newman described science fiction as 'a marvellous way – and a safe way – of saying nasty things about our own society.' This became an essential aspect of the Third Doctor's tenure, featuring stories carrying political and ecological subtexts by left-wing writers including Malcolm Hulke, Barry Letts, and Terrance Dicks. It continued into the era of Thatcherite Britain – McCoy said that consensus during the Seventh Doctor's years in the TARDIS was that 'Margaret Thatcher was far more terrifying than any monster the Doctor had encountered.'

The Doctor has never respected hierarchy. The First Doctor refuses to kow-tow before Kublai Khan in 'Marco Polo' despite his life being at stake, saying that 'if it breaks my back, then he can take all of me.' His words are echoed by the Twelfth Doctor in 'The Husbands of River Song' when he says he will not bow to King Hydroflax because his back 'simply refuses to carry the weight of an entirely pointless stratum of society who contribute nothing of worth to the world and crush the hopes and dreams of working people.' The Tenth Doctor has no time for the snobbery of the first-class passengers onboard the *Titanic* who mock Morvin and Foon Van Hoff for having won their tickets in a competition in 'Voyage of the Damned', using his sonic screwdriver to spray champagne over their clothes. In 'Kerblam!', the Thirteenth Doctor plans to storm into the company's management when she discovers that people have been disappearing – 'Don't like bullies, don't like conspiracies, don't like people being in danger. And there's a flavour of all three here.' The Doctor is always keen to make fools of those who assert their position through the oppression of others.

To Marion McLaughlin, the show offers hope for a socialist

future, demonstrating that there is always opportunity for anyone to overcome the odds and fight together. She said that many autistic people are told they cannot do certain things because of their condition, but this is nonsense because 'there's nothing we can't do if we get the right support', just like the Doctor's companions:

> *Remarkable individuals who have no idea what their potential might be until the Doctor comes along, grabs them by the hand, and whisks them off on an adventure. Ordinary people doing extraordinary things. In a world with so much going on – wars, misinformation, fascism, fear – we need hope. We need to believe that things can get better. We need shows like Doctor Who to inspire us to keep advocating, keep going.*

One such individual is young Elliot Northover who lives with his parents in the Welsh town of Cwmtaff. In 'The Hungry Earth', he says that the only explanation for the missing people is that they are eaten by the graves. Rory says this is not very likely, and Elliot replies by quoting Sherlock Holmes: 'When you've eliminated the impossible, whatever remains, however improbable, must be the truth.' He says that he has the audiobook because he is dyslexic. When the Eleventh Doctor asks him to draw a map, he tells the boy that 'dyslexia never stopped Da Vinci or Einstein. It's not stopping you.' His retrospective diagnosis of these figures who have been theorised to display traits of the neurodivergent condition is an attempt to encourage the boy to not see his diagnosis as a definite obstacle. Elliot's encounter with the Time Lord is an affirming one in which he feels understood for the first time rather than dismissed on the basis of his neurodivergence.

Ryan is dyspraxic, which frustrates him throughout his adventures with the Doctor. In 'The Woman Who Fell to Earth', he describes himself as 'pretty much not an idiot' and 'a capable guy' but he is nineteen years old and cannot yet ride a bicycle. His grandmother motivates him, but Graham expresses harmful annoyance. He bemoans that Ryan will probably blame the fact that he accidentally summoned Tzim-Sha to Earth on his dyspraxia – 'Can't ride a bike, started an alien invasion.' By contrast, in 'The Ghost Monument', when Ryan tells the Thirteenth Doctor that he struggles with climbing ladders under pressure, she says, 'Think of what you've gone through to be here, and you're still going. I'm proper impressed.' He elaborates on the difficulties he has faced as a result of being dyspraxic in 'Kerblam!', describing how hard it was for him to learn how to carry out manual tasks at the warehouse where he works on Earth. He says that he always gets there in the end, and he is grateful for having friends to cover for him. He connects with fellow worker Kira, who says she was also terrible when she started working, but she tells herself at the beginning of every shift that she can do it.

Before I was diagnosed with dyspraxia while being tested for autism, other children laughed at the way my legs swung out to the side when I ran and my failure to throw and catch. My primary school sent me to SULP; that is, Social Use of Language Programme, or 'sulk' class as I used to call it because it felt like a waste of time. It was intended to encourage me to make eye contact and to improve my communication and social recognition skills, all of which I deemed pointless. Sometimes I noticed a stranger watching me at the side of the playground, or from the back of the classroom. I came home and told my mother that there was a spy at school, although I suspect that I rather spoiled the diagnostic process by being aware that I was being observed. Sometimes the 'spy' took me into a room and asked me questions, including showing me cards with facial expressions which I was asked to recognise. My mother took me to see a paediatrician, who told me to sit on the floor, and I promptly dropped down with my lower legs splayed out at eighty-degree angles from my knees like a frog. It probably prompted her to diagnose me there and then. I can still hear my mother calling out 'heel, toe!' behind me as I consciously try to walk from the back of my sole to the front rather than on tiptoe.

As I have gotten older I have learnt the benefits of not drawing attention to myself by trying to walk in a straight line and never, ever running, but I did not understand the reason for adjusting my movements when I was younger. I was not trying to be difficult – it just seemed unnecessary to overthink something which apparently comes naturally to everyone else. Ryan's struggles with learning how to perform manual tasks call to mind Robert Chapman's book *Empire of Normality: Neurodiversity and Capitalism*, which describes the pressures placed on people to move fast, physically and mentally, in the workplace as a way to turn human beings into Fordist assembly lines. Neurodivergence offers benefits to capitalism in terms of the speed of brain processing and unique mental abilities, but poses challenges including hypersensitivity and burnout. When Ryan leaves the TARDIS in 'Revolution of the Daleks', he says that his adventures fighting Cybermen, Skithra, Morax, and the Pting have made him realise it will 'take more than a bike to scare me off.' It is this very human victory, of overcoming self-doubt, which has the greatest meaning to Ryan.

Leaving the TARDIS is difficult for Ryan and Graham, having developed a close bond with the Doctor. In 'The Woman Who Fell to Earth' she decides to use the nickname Yaz for Yasmin because they are friends now, a word which dispels the hierarchy created by terms such as 'assistant' or even 'companion'. She tries out words including 'troops', 'team', 'gang', and finally 'fam', which sticks. When the Doctor attempts to detach herself from her fam in her second series after learning that Gallifrey has been destroyed, they refuse to allow her to do so. 'You don't know me. Not even a little bit', she says to Ryan at the end of 'Fugitive of the Judoon'. He replies that he knows she is 'the woman that brought us together, the woman that saved us and loads of other people. You're the Doctor. Whoever you were in the past or are in the future, we know who you are right now.' In fandom communities people do not care about the history of its members, only their Whovian credentials.

In 'The Power of the Doctor', Kate Stewart hires Tegan and Ace as freelancers to UNIT. They are frustrated that the Doctor has not contacted them for decades, but by the end of the episode the companions have found each other – Graham chairs a meeting attended by former time travellers including Jo, Mel, and even Ian. He explains that he set up the group because he cannot tell anyone about his travels, but believed there had to be others like him who wanted a space to exchange stories. Sarah tells Rani that she did similar research in 'Death of the Doctor', saying that Tegan is in Australia fighting for Aboriginal rights, Ben and Polly are in India running an orphanage, Ace runs A Charitable Earth, Ian and Barbara are professors at Cambridge, and Harry – whom she loved – did good work with vaccines: 'Echoes of the Doctor, all over the world. With friends like us, he's never going to die, is he?' As in the show, so too in real life – *Doctor Who* has brought people together from across the globe, united by a shared passion which manifests in many forms. It continues to grow and diversify, enacting the Doctor's philosophy even in the most troubled times.

CHAPTER SIX
HUMAN NATURE

The First Doctor: **Fear makes companions of all of us, Miss Wright.**
Barbara Wright: **I never thought once you were afraid.**
The First Doctor: **Fear is with all of us, and always will be. Just like that other sensation that lives with it.**
Barbara Wright: **What's that?**
The First Doctor: **Your companion referred to it. Hope. Hope, Miss Wright.**

'An Unearthly Child'

Well, I suppose you might say that I am a citizen of the universe, and a gentleman to boot.

The First Doctor in 'The Daleks' Master Plan'

Not everyone wants to be the Doctor. Fifty-two-year-old Whovian Rob Freeman, who is ADHD, said that he connects more readily with the companions than the Time Lord, 'because he was heroic, and I'm not.' Director Euros Lyn told me that his favourite aspect of *Doctor Who* is that 'epic existential sci-fi is spliced with the emotions and everyday concerns of humans.' He cited a scene in 'The End of the World' in which Rose watches the dying Earth five billion years in the future, and phones her mother in 2005 as she empties a washing machine. The Doctor does not always have the emotional intelligence to understand what their friends are going through. This is a typical aspect of neurodivergence – self-reflection, management of emotions, empathy with others, and the building of strong friendships are complicated. It is important for everyone, regardless of neurotype, to take time to be mindful about their behaviour and how they interact with others, as well as affording patience to those who need more time to do so. Personal growth is not linear, but wibbly-wobbly timey-wimey. This chapter explores the Doctor's relationships with humans, in all their haphazard glory.

'When he was talking to you, you were staring at the other man', Polly tells the Second Doctor in 'The Power of the Daleks'. 'Yes, very rude of me, wasn't it? Terrible manners. To tell you the truth, I was studying his reaction, seeing if he agreed with the story.' Exchanges like this are frequent in *Doctor Who*, of the companions pointing out to the Time Lord where they have failed to display appropriate etiquette. The Doctor often acknowledges their errors – except the Sixth Doctor, who sees no need for niceties towards Peri. As Alexis Harrow pointed out to me, 'the Doctor, even as a woman, goes around picking up mostly young women to impress and show off to.' Most of the companions come into this category, something which is mocked in the minisodes 'Meanwhile in the TARDIS' and 'Clara and the TARDIS', in which Amy and Clara respectively are shown slideshows of the many glamorous assistants who came before them.

While the Doctor often comes across as patronising in their speech, from the First's 'my child' to the Fourth's 'good girl', many of the women they journey with are capable of speaking their mind. In 'The Moonbase', the Second Doctor explains to Polly that on the Moon there is a fortnight of days and nights, therefore they have to make their own day and night artificially to not upset the biological clock. When she says that she understands, he replies, 'Clever girl. QED. That's why it's dark up here.' 'How stupid of me', she retorts sarcastically, without the Doctor catching on. 'Polly, you wouldn't be making fun of me, would you?'

The treatment of women by the early Doctors becomes a joke when the First Doctor returns in 'The Five Doctors' and 'Twice Upon a Time'. In the former, he tells Tegan, 'Now look, young lady. Make yourself useful. This young fellow looks as though he needs some refreshment and I know that Susan and I do, too.' The Fifth Doctor implores her to humour him, saying that he used to get a little tetchy, but 'fortunately one mellows with age.' In the latter, upon entering the Twelfth Doctor's TARDIS, the First observes that it could do with a good dusting – 'Obviously Polly isn't around anymore.' His future self begs him not to say things like that, and is even more horrified when the other fellow tells Bill that if she swears again she is 'in for a jolly good smacked bottom', as he once threatened Susan. Bill holds her own by shocking the First Doctor. After he says that he hopes that it does not offend her to know that he has some experience of the 'fairer sex', she replies, 'Me too.' The Doctor's relationship with women is thankfully an area in which their emotional intelligence has improved.

MR CHESTERTON AND MISS WRIGHT

While Susan was the model for the damsel-in-distress companion who gets kidnapped and screams until she is saved, Barbara was a modern independent woman. The original sketch for her character, called Lola McGovern, described her as 'timid but capable of sudden rabbit courage' and 'modest, with plenty of normal desires.' She was also to need saving by both the Doctor and the main man, Ian. 'An Unearthly Child' establishes an us-and-them dynamic between the aliens and the humans, although Barbara's feminine sympathy is shown to broaden Ian's mind. After he demands evidence that they have moved, the Doctor calls him a 'stubborn young man' before turning to Barbara and saying, 'You're not as doubtful as your friend, I hope?' Ian is bound to empiricism, much like the Doctor, creating tension between them. Barbara becomes frustrated with the Doctor's arrogance, who says to him after he dismisses the cave people as 'savages' that, 'You treat everybody and everything as something less important than yourself.' She is more capable of standing up to the old man than Susan, beginning the breakdown of the hierarchy which the Doctor asserts.

'The Edge of Destruction' hinges on the Doctor's belief that he and Susan have been betrayed by their new shipmates. His behaviour is contradictory, moving from accusing Ian and Barbara of sabotage to handing out drinks. 'I wish I could understand you, Doctor', Ian says. 'One moment you're abusing us, and the next, you're playing the perfect butler.' Barbara refuses to move on quickly, telling the Doctor that he lacks 'common sense' before going to her room. Ian and Susan say that he must apologise to her, to which he responds, 'I'm afraid we have no time for codes and manners.' Just as Susan does, I have known people to make excuses for my behaviour at times, as I have for neurodivergent friends. But there are limits to understanding where an autistic individual might not intend offence, and when they are being deliberately rude. The Doctor is eventually able to recognise this himself, and he makes a scripted apology: 'I suppose it's the injustice that's upsetting you, and when I made a threat to put you off the ship it must have affected you very deeply.' Barbara tells him that she does not believe that he is capable of caring how she feels, to which the Doctor replies, 'As we learn about each other, so we learn about ourselves.' Empathy does not come naturally to him, but during the course of their adventures together, the Doctor becomes more amiable.

When his companions decide to leave, the Doctor is cross. He tries to take Ian and Barbara home in 'The Reign of Terror', saying that 'enough time has been wasted bringing you back, young man. I have the universe to explore.' Ian wants to leave under friendlier circumstances, suggesting they go for a drink. The Doctor never admits to his true feelings, trying to demonstrate that he is above sentimentality by claiming to not have wanted company in the first place – I was guilty of this in my dismissal of the idea of having friends when I was younger. Equally I relate to the Doctor's apology to Barbara in 'Planet of Giants': 'Oh, my dear Barbara, was I rude to you just now? If so I'm so sorry. I always forget the niceties under pressure. Please forgive me.' It is a demonstration of self-awareness which has developed in the Doctor's character over the course of his adventures, leading to a paranoia about how his behaviour comes across to his friends. He cares for them deeply, even telling Ian he could kiss him after defeating the Daleks in 'The Chase'. It confuses him that they then ask to go home, because he cannot relate to Ian's desire to do such mundane things as walk in a park or watch a cricket match. Despite pretending not to care that they are gone, the Doctor admits to Vicki, 'I shall miss them. Yes, I shall miss them, silly old fusspots.' Nothing hurts the Doctor more than saying goodbye.

THE UNIT FILES

Barbara is unique amongst the Doctor's companions during the 1960s as a working intellectual, while other women to board the TARDIS largely befit the Swinging Sixties look of Mary Quant miniskirts and Space Age go-go boots. Liz Shaw became the Third Doctor's 'assistant' in 1970 against the backdrop of second-wave feminism, with the Equal Pay Act and the first conference of the National Women's Liberation Movement taking place that year. Many of the attendees of that meeting were white, middle-class, professional women, the demographic to which Liz belongs. She is reluctant to leave Cambridge to work with the Doctor at UNIT, a position mandated by the government. Caroline John, who played Liz, was excited to be 'a brainy girl', but said that 'all the directors wanted really was a sexy piece' which she found limiting and draining. Her primary role is to empathise with the Doctor where her male colleagues, especially the Brigadier, fail to do so.

Liz is a scientist, not a soldier. In 'Doctor Who and the Silurians', the Brigadier orders the detonation of the Silurian base, which angers the Doctor. Liz says he must have had orders from the ministry, and the Doctor turns to her saying, 'You knew?' He fears her betrayal, but she says that she did not know, she was only attempting to explain the rationale of her superiors. The Doctor makes a similar assertion in 'Frontier in Space', that the Brigadier's problem is that 'he's got a military mind' and therefore 'always does everything by the rules.' He lacks the Doctor's capacity to see beyond binary sides in war. Liz agrees with the Doctor that the Brigadier's action against the Silurians is genocide. The scene is restaged in 'The Christmas Invasion', with the Tenth Doctor telling PM Harriet Jones that blowing up the Sycorax spaceship is murder, and he should have warned the aliens that humans are the monsters. These acts hurt the Doctor because they are ordered by people he believed were his friends. Harriet is a stickler for rules and procedure, ignorant of the broader crisis in 'Aliens of London' as she insists that she has a 15:15 appointment at 10 Downing Street. She bonds with the Ninth Doctor in 'World War Three' by pointing out that using vinegar to defeat the Slitheen is similar to Hannibal crossing the Alps. Even after the destruction of the Sycorax, Harriet is killed fighting for her erstwhile friend in 'The Stolen Earth'.

Esme Hayes told me that she loves the mixed relationship which the Doctor has with Lethbridge-Stewart, saying that he is 'overtly very rude to him, but if anyone says anything negative about him, he gets angry and says he's the best man in the world.' The Fifth Doctor is upset to realise that the Brigadier has no memory of him in 'Mawdryn Undead', and later learns that he had a nervous breakdown due to the pressures of his work. The military man has little time for the concept of mental health: 'I'm not taking my leave at the funny farm. There's nothing wrong with me, I tell you. Fit as a fiddle, always have been.' He retired from UNIT to work as a teacher of mathematics, needing to keep his mind occupied. The Tenth Doctor forces Harriet to step down from power in 'The Christmas Invasion' using only six words: 'Don't you think she looks tired?' As the Seventh Doctor says in 'Battlefield', 'Among all the varied wonders of the universe, there's nothing so firmly clamped shut as the military mind.' He can perceive how the goodness of Harriet and the Brigadier has been affected by their responsibilities, and ultimately saves them from themselves.

Esme discussed the Doctor's complex relationship with change with me through reference to the changeover of his assistants at UNIT. Just as he was reluctant to accept Liz in 'Spearhead from Space', in 'Terror of the Autons' the Doctor refuses to have anything to do with Jo Grant. 'Because he got to know Liz, he now loves her', Esme observed. 'He refuses Jo because she's not Liz. I don't want the new person, I want the old one.' There is a process of hesitance, and then acceptance, allowing the cycle to continue, just as fans experience in the changing of the Doctor through regeneration. The Doctor makes a misogynistic assumption about Jo when she enters his laboratory, telling her that he did not ask for tea. He mocks her for not having Liz's qualifications, to which the Brigadier says that what he needs, 'as Miss Shaw herself so often remarked, is someone to pass you your test tubes and to tell you how brilliant you are.' He tells the Doctor that if he wants to dismiss her he must do it himself, something which he lacks the gall to do. Katy Manning told me that she was similar to the hapless Jo, finding herself 'utterly lost in the endless circle of corridors of the BBC centre, rather late and hiding myopically behind impossibly thick glasses' when she auditioned for the part. She said that she bonded with

Jon Pertwee, 'my wonderful mentor', establishing a rapport reflected by their characters' chemistry on screen.

Despite this friendship, the Doctor is not always sympathetic to his companion. In 'Planet of the Daleks', he asks Jo why she did not keep herself safe in the TARDIS and does not understand why she went out to try to save him. He suggests that she finds 'a female shoulder to cry on', just as the First Doctor told Barbara to console Susan rather than doing it himself. Like his granddaughter, the distance between them is widened by the Doctor's desire to continue travelling, while Jo says that she only wants to see one planet, Earth. She decides to act independently of the Doctor in 'The Green Death' through her commitment to climate justice, electing to go with the mycologist Clifford Jones to look for a fungus in the Amazon. When he proposes to Jo, the Doctor excuses himself, saying that he thinks he is going to be wanted on the telephone. He leaves a difficult social situation with which he is uncomfortable, and as the room enters a party atmosphere, he sneaks away to Bessie before driving along the horizon as we see everyone dancing and the happy pair kiss.

Jo is shocked to discover that the Eleventh Doctor is travelling with a married couple in 'Death of the Doctor', wondering if she was stupid to assume that she could not have done the same. She says that she waited for him, but he questions how he was supposed to find her during her forty years of living in huts, flying kites on Kilimanjaro, and sailing down the Yangtze in a tea chest. She is delighted to realise he has kept watch over her, even telling her that her thirteenth grandchild will be a great swimmer despite being dyslexic. Jo thinks that the Doctor is quickly able to let go and move on, but this is far from the truth. In this episode of *The Sarah Jane Adventures*, Jo is delighted to meet her replacement as the Doctor's assistant at his funeral. They share a belief that if the Doctor had actually died they would feel it in their hearts.

Jo is shocked to hear that Sarah had met the Tenth Doctor, saying that he must have really liked her, not without a hint of envy.

It is a feeling which Sarah herself felt when she saw the Doctor again in 'School Reunion', now accompanied by Rose: 'You can tell you're getting older. Your assistants are getting younger.' He tries to reassure her by saying that she no longer needed him because she was getting on with her life, to which she responds that he was everything to her, and it was cruel to force her to go back to an ordinary existence. He even dropped her off in Aberdeen, which is certainly not next to Croydon, an error included on one of the Twelfth Doctor's social cue cards. Sarah and Rose bond through shared experience of the Doctor's eccentricities, such as looking horrified that they have not understood him after he has explained something at 'ninety miles-per-hour' and stroking bits of the TARDIS. Rose asks Sarah if she should stay with him, and she says, 'Yes. Some things are worth getting your heart broken for.' The encounter gave Sarah a new lease of life, encouraging her not to miss the strangeness of outer space and to look for it instead on Earth – 'You just need to know where to look', as she says in the opening voiceover of 'Invasion of the Bane'. She is viewed as a 'mad woman' by her neighbours, telling them that she does not like to be disturbed and hiding away in her attic filled with artefacts and books, kept company by her computers, K9 and Mr Smith.

This is a significant change to her first appearance in 'The Time Warrior'. Professor Rubeish introduces her as the virologist Miss Lavinia Smith to the Third Doctor, who realises she cannot possibly be old enough. He says he will not give her away because they need somebody to make coffee at UNIT, which angers her as she is actually a journalist. She calls out chauvinism and gendered hierarchies in the workplace, including when they travel to the Middle Ages and she observes that while women 'do all the dirty work, you get all the fun.' Producer Phil Collinson recalled to me that Sarah was the first character he felt had 'the ability to reach out of the TV and hold your hand and help you navigate the thrills and scares of every adventure', acting as 'a completely human antidote to the Doctor's sometimes scary intensity.' This tension hinges on the debate around the nature of K1 in 'Robot', with Sarah navigating the Doctor's regeneration as well as the potential humanity of the droid. They bond over his reluctance to carry out his official duties, with Sarah calling him childish, before taking a jelly baby and laughing. 'There's no point in being grown up if you can't be childish sometimes', the Fourth Doctor says. I say this to myself as I put on another episode of *Doctor Who*.

LEELA, PERI, AND MEL

Sarah's accurate observation that the Doctor's taste in companions became more driven by a desire to keep a young, pretty girl in the TARDIS rather than an intellectual match began long before Rose. In 'The Hand of Fear', Sarah says that she no longer feels beautiful – 'Oh, I want a bath. I want my hair washed. I just want to feel human again.' The Doctor is not listening, focusing on the console, and he says that he has been summoned to Gallifrey so they will have to part ways. Rather than going back to find her after returning home himself, he picks up Leela in 'The Face of Evil'. She is a violent companion and has heroic agency, but is shown to rely on the Doctor's intelligence. When she says that she supposes he is always right about everything, he demonstrates his arrogance by replying, 'Invariably.' She decides to stay with Andred at the end of 'The Invasion of Time', and the Doctor says that she will look after him because 'she's terribly good with a knife.'

Leela spent most of her time with the Doctor scantily clad, a choice which became more important to showrunner

John Nathan-Turner during his tenure. When Nicola Bryant was introduced as Peri, he stated that 'she'll often be wearing leotards and bikinis' to appeal to the many 'Dads' who watch *Doctor Who*. However she is also one of the most capable companions at putting the Doctor in his place. She uses sarcasm which he typically fails to recognise, despite saying it is not her strong suit in 'The Caves of Androzani'. A failure to understand or use sarcasm effectively is typical of neurodivergence. This dynamic worsens after the Fifth Doctor regenerates into the Sixth, who is dismissive of Peri's intelligence in 'The Twin Dilemma' by saying that he is sure she is not familiar with the meaning of her name. After saying it is a fairy in Persian mythology he accuses her of being an alien spy before grabbing her throat and throwing her to the floor. When she asks why she must suffer, he tells her that she has been chosen to have 'the humble privilege of ministering unto my needs.' Yet when she later says that she was concerned that the Doctor had been killed, he is surprised she cares: 'I'll never understand the people of Earth. I have spent the day using, abusing, even trying to kill you. If you'd have behaved as I have, I should have been pleased at your demise.' She tells him that it is called compassion, the difference that remains between them, and advises him to take a crash course in manners. He claims that he has moved on from the 'neurotic' need of his predecessor to be polite, telling her, 'I am the Doctor, whether you like it or not.'

Many do not. Yet in a post on the National Autistic Society website, a fan known as 'professorwhat' describes the Sixth Doctor as 'the most alien incarnation' after the First, who lacked experience and self-growth: 'I can relate to the Sixth Doctor's explanation to Peri as to why she shouldn't expect him to think the same way she did. After all, he rightly pointed out [sic]. He was an alien; he wasn't human.' Yet this does not excuse his treatment of Peri, not least his regression into explicit chauvinism – in 'The Two Doctors' he tells her, 'When you ask a question, you should listen to the answer, my girl, otherwise, you will gain absolutely no benefit from being in my company.' An echo of the First Doctor indeed. Much like Barbara, Peri does not stand for it – 'I can't tell you how privileged I feel, having been half-frozen, and asphyxiated, and cooked, and then forced to clamber through miles of pipe.' During 'The Trial of a Time Lord', the Doctor is dismissive of Peri. When she realises that Ravalox is Earth in 'The Mysterious Planet', he tells her not to get emotional, infuriating her with his insistence upon seeing the universe as though it were a planetarium. He attempts a rare apology, justifying himself by saying that 'planets come and go' and 'nothing can be eternal.' The closest he comes to expressing care for Peri is in 'Mindwarp', in which Crozier observes that he has strong feelings for her, to which he replies, 'Well, certainly enough not to want to see her experimented upon.' It is the Doctor at their most alien, acting in line with harmful stereotypes regarding a neurodivergent lack of empathy.

The Valeyard notes that the Doctor resorts to 'excuses and subterfuge' in 'Terror of the Vervoids', glossing over the death of Peri in his testimony to present another companion: Mel. She throws the Seventh Doctor to the ground after he reaches for her in 'Time and the Rani' – 'It's me, you washerwoman! Me!' This incarnation is kinder than his predecessor, yet resorts to his apparent lack of care when she says she is leaving him in 'Dragonfire'. She tells him she wants to say something before she goes, and the Doctor replies that there is no point in wasting time as he distracts himself with the stim toy-attachments of the TARDIS console. He apologises, and asks her to think of him when she is 'living your life one day after another, all in a neat pattern', something he can never do. It seems that the Doctor does not continue to think of her, with Donna asking the Fourteenth about Mel in 'The Giggle'. He tells her she is brilliant, but she questions why he has never mentioned her before. He says that at his age if he talked about everyone he had met he would never stop. She observes that he is 'staggering along', struggling to cope with the weight of the past which he carries with him. The Doctor never deliberately goes back, he's just passing through.

NUWOMEN

'Is that supposed to sound impressive?' Rose is a companion for a new era, questioning the ego of a man who calls himself 'The Doctor'. Their Ninth incarnation has regressed in emotional intelligence when he shows up in 'Rose'. Rather than explaining how the TARDIS moves, he says she would not understand – the Fourth Doctor even attempted to explain to Leela how transdimensional engineering works in 'The Robots of Death'. When Rose cries and asks if the Autons have killed Mickey, he says that he did not think of that because he had forgotten about him. 'You were right. You are alien', Rose observes. It is not a matter of heritage which makes him 'alien', but his lack of an empathy characteristically defined as human. He fails to spot the obvious, such as missing that the giant circular transmitter he is describing is the London Eye, with Rose later remarking that he was useless in facing the Nestene and would be dead if she had not been there. He is not above admitting that she is right, and offers to take her with him.

The Doctor is more flexible with returning to Earth in the NuWho era, balancing time in the TARDIS with his companions' home lives. He takes Rose to see her mother in 'Aliens of London', although he is uncomfortable when there are lots of people in her lounge. He sneaks out, telling Rose, 'It's just a bit human in there for me. History just happened and they're talking about where you can buy dodgy top-up cards for half price.' He relinquishes control, giving her a

TARDIS key while he goes off to investigate. Not that the Doctor adjusts to this new mode of companionship with ease – he accidentally takes Rose back a year after she was last seen, making Mickey a suspect in her disappearance and leading Jackie to believe they are in a sexual relationship. He further tries to appease Rose by allowing her to visit Pete in 'Father's Day', but he feels betrayed when he remembers that it was only because he mentioned being able to travel in time that she joined him. He becomes defensive, saying he picked up 'another stupid ape' who does not want to do something for the universe, but rather have the universe do something for her. He takes back the key, but she says this does not scare her because she knows how lonely he is and he will not last long without her. When they reconcile, all he asks is that she apologises, an act which carries great weight for the Time Lord who cares more about intention than action.

Rose goes home again in 'The Parting of the Ways', complaining to Mickey about the dullness of normality and routine. He is hurt, asking if she thinks that she is better than them now, but she explains that the difficulty for her is that the Doctor showed her a better way of living her life and she cannot give that up. The same change occurs in Donna, despite only having shared one adventure with the Doctor, telling him in 'Partners in Crime' that she had to wake up to her same old life. When she met the Tenth Doctor in 'The Runaway Bride', she demonstrated a lack of will to be impressed. Like Peri, she is constantly sarcastic, responding to his question as to why she is wearing a bridal dress by saying that she is going ten-pin bowling. She slaps the Doctor when he starts theorising the science behind her appearance in the TARDIS, demanding that he stops messing about and gets her to the church. Donna does not care for the wonders of the universe, her eyes firmly on the ground, even missing the Sycorax invasion due to a hangover. She realises that the Doctor had another woman in his ship before her, whom he says he lost, and when he asks her to trust him she wonders if that is what he said to the last one before she died. She will not be sucked into the Doctor's usual routine. When he offers to show her all of creation, she opts for her bed.

Donna meets Rose in 'Turn Left', having forgotten her adventures with the Doctor. She questions why, if this hero is so special, he took her with him. Rose responds that he thought she was brilliant, which she dismisses as stupid, before saying that it was the Doctor who showed her that – 'He did the same to me. To everyone he touches.' Despite the affection which Donna has for the Doctor, it can be confusing for a neurodivergent audience. 'Why does Donna travel with the Doctor when she hates him?' Sarah Slaven recalled being told by her autistic son Eli, because she is always shouting at him and calling him names. She found this a useful opportunity to explain to him that volume does not always indicate negative emotion, and that banter can be a means of expressing friendship. The Doctor does not always understand Donna himself. In 'The Sontaran Stratagem', she says she is going home, and he launches into a dramatic speech about everywhere he wanted to take her before realising she just means she is visiting her family. She calls him 'a great big outer space dunce', wondering how someone so clever can fail to understand something so obvious. 'No common sense!' I can hear my parents exclaiming in exasperation.

MISS OSWALD

Like Barbara, Clara is a teacher at Coal Hill School – while the Twelfth Doctor thinks of himself as a professor, his companion treats him like her student. She is cross with him in 'Deep Breath', saying that he will know it is safe to smile after she has done it, because rather than asking her directly if she wanted to meet for lunch, he left a cryptic note in a newspaper. He says that is the behaviour of 'an egomaniac, needy, game-player sort of person', believing that it was Clara who had written it for him. Just as the Fourth Doctor left Sarah in Aberdeen, the Twelfth abandons Clara in Glasgow for three weeks in 'Into the Dalek' after she sent him to get coffee. When the Doctor introduces her he does not know which word to use, not wanting to call her his assistant. She offers 'carer', which he likes because 'she cares so I don't have to.' Not that it stops her from trying to teach the Doctor to be more open-minded, correcting him that discovering that the Daleks are evil is not what they had learned. He eventually realises that if one Dalek became good it means that a good Dalek is possible, asking 'Teach' if he is right. 'Top of the class!' she proclaims. He tells her she must be an amazing teacher since she is capable of changing someone as old as he is.

Not that this lesson resolves the tension between this new Doctor and Clara. In 'The Caretaker', she tells him that he is 'a very clever man making the mistake, common to very clever people, of assuming that everybody else is stupid'. He says that he had a teacher like her once, and she informs him that he still does. He is rude about her choice of a boyfriend in Danny, whom he assumes teaches P.E. rather than mathematics, a distaste which is reciprocated. To him the Doctor is like a military officer, comparable to the Brigadier, who pushes people to make them stronger until they are doing things that they never thought they could. He observes that Clara follows him blindly, and this should concern her, a prediction proved correct in 'Kill the Moon'. The Doctor shirks responsibility for deciding whether or not to destroy the egg orbiting the Earth, informing Clara that it is 'time to take the stabilisers off your bike.' He later says that he had faith in her to make the right choice. 'Honestly, do you have music playing in your head when you say rubbish like that?' she asks him, furious that he patronised her in such a cheap way.

The Doctor is convinced of his righteousness to an extent which almost pushes Clara away for good. Danny recognises in her the same look he had when he left the army, but he warns her that she has to wait until she is not angry because no one can finish with a person while their emotions are still running high. She wonders how he became so wise – 'Same way as anyone else. I had a really bad day.' We all learn from experience – sometimes even the Doctor needs a jolly good smacked bottom.

Clara decides to go on one last trip with the Doctor, to say goodbye. He takes her to a luxury space train in 'Mummy on the Orient Express', but he notices her 'sad smile'. He is confused by this mixed expression, showing two emotions at once as though she is malfunctioning. The autistic boy Eli felt similarly confused by the Tenth Doctor's facial expressions in 'The End of Time Part Two', especially his 'happy crying.' His mother explained this to him by saying that an excess of emotion and confusion can bubble up and cause tears to spill out. But when Clara tries to explain her feelings to the Doctor, that she thought she hated him, he starts talking about destroyed planets while looking out of the window. She says that 'hatred is too strong an emotion to waste on someone that you don't like.' He asks sheepishly if he can talk about the planets again, like an autistic child fixated on their special interest. She lets him distract himself from a situation he finds uncomfortable, and after they reconcile, he tries harder to show an interest in her life. In 'Under the Lake' he says that she needs a relationship, compelled to mention it out of his 'duty of care', something she knows he takes very seriously. 'So can I stop now?' he asks. 'Please. Please do.' She appreciates that he makes an effort to comfort her, but knows that he will never fully understand.

Clara hurts the Doctor in 'Dark Water'. After Danny is killed, she finds all seven TARDIS keys and threatens to destroy them if he does not bring her boyfriend back. She admits it is fair enough when he says, 'Go to Hell', before he explains that he means it literally – does she think he cares for her so little that her betrayal would change anything? Her eyes 'inflate', which the Doctor does not like, and when she tells him that she does not deserve a friend like him, he apologises and says he is exactly what she deserves. Yet after finding the ex-soldier, in 'Death in Heaven' Danny tells Clara to 'watch the blood-soaked old general in action' as he demands that he switches on his emotional inhibitor. The Doctor hands Clara the sonic screwdriver, to which Danny remarks, 'Typical officer. Got to keep those hands clean.' He finds a way for her boyfriend to return to the living, but instead Danny sends back a child he killed in action. Clara lies, saying that he made it home, just as the Doctor lies that he found Gallifrey. She asks if they can break a habit and hug to say goodbye, and he comments, 'Never trust a hug. It's just a way to hide your face.' The Doctor struggles to navigate complex emotions and changing needs, wishing to return to how things were but knowing he can never turn back the clock. Not in any way that matters.

THE DOCTOR WHO CAME FOR TEA

It is permissible for the Doctor to be rude when they are a man, but not as a woman. The Thirteenth Doctor adds a new word to her vocabulary in 'The Woman Who Fell to Earth': sorry. She is sorry to the humans she meets that bad things are happening, that they have had bombs planted inside them, and that she has not figured out what is going on yet. It is a word which I am told I overuse, like a nervous tic or vocal stim, overcompensating for the anxiety I feel in social situations. This Doctor asks the same of herself in 'Arachnids in the UK': 'Maybe I'm nervous. Or just socially awkward. I'm still figuring myself out.' She makes no assumption that she will be asked to hang out with her new friends. Yaz invites her for tea, enthusiastically responding, 'Definitely! Yes, I would. Thanks. I love tea. Tea at Yaz's? Amazing. Are you coming? Are we all going for tea at Yaz's?' One of the most significant changes in the Doctor's attitude in this scene is her excitement at the prospect of owning a flat: 'I should get one, I'd be good in a flat. I could get a sofa. Imagine me with a sofa, like my own sofa, I could get a purple one and sit on it. Am I being weird?' Of course this is not true, knowing that she could never be settled.

The Doctor needs constant stimulation and activity, moving from one focus to another in a manner consistent with ADHD. After losing the TARDIS in 'The Impossible Planet', Rose says that it would not be so bad if she settled with the Tenth Doctor on the nearest planet. 'Me, living in a house. Now that, that is terrifying.' He would rather die than take out a mortgage. Alex Hewitt told me those diagnosed ADHD tend to procrastinate and find it difficult to complete tasks ahead of deadlines. 'Far from simply being lazy, this is an actual cognitive deficiency,' he said. 'Working on a number of Big Finish projects as a writer and producer is occasionally mentally taxing, yet because it is *Doctor Who* I find it easy to motivate myself because I hyperfocus on things I am interested in.' During the slow invasion in 'The Power of Three', the Eleventh Doctor is forced to live with the Ponds – 'Every time we flew away with the Doctor, we'd just become part of his life. But he never stood still long enough to become part of ours.' He has no understanding of their everyday existence, imagining that they mostly kiss when they are at home. He lasts about an hour occupying himself by creosoting the garden fence, playing with a football, mowing the lawn, vacuuming… Everything which he later describes to Rory's father Brian as 'so fabulously human.' I have always found it difficult to engage with menial household chores, or to pay attention when someone is explaining anything related to finance. If it does not stimulate my brain, I cannot see the point, much to the frustration of my nearest and dearest.

'No, Amy, it's definitely not the Fifth Moon of Sinda Callista. I think I can see a Ryman's.' The unthinkable happens to the Doctor in 'The Lodger' – he has to pay rent. Well, he hands over a paper bag of notes to his landlord, Craig Owens, and hopes it is enough. He lacks more social awareness than usual as he attempts to appear like a normal tenant, and Craig asks if anyone has told him he is a bit weird. 'They never really stop', the Doctor replies. Jokes are made about the Doctor's sexual naïveté, describing it as 'completely normal' that Craig spends his time with a friend who is a girl, and saying that if he brings a partner back to the house he will shout, 'I was not expecting this!' Amy, as his 'neurotypical' advisor on how to 'pass as an ordinary human being', speaks to him from the TARDIS – watch telly, play football, go down the pub, and definitely lose the bow tie. Yet the Doctor is capable of seeing things which Craig is ignorant of, such as Sophie's interest in him and her desire for a life beyond the sofa, enabling him to serve as a matchmaker. When he returns in 'Closing Time', the Doctor channels his Second incarnation by telling Craig that he does not like the way he has redecorated, failing to notice that it is a different house. He describes it as a social call, something he has not tried before, and talks openly about the script of small talk: 'This is the bit where I say I'm fine too, isn't it? I'm fine, too. Good. Love to Sophie. Bye.' He demonstrates an ability to affect Craig by telling him that he loves him in order to distract his friend from the Cyberman ship behind him. The Doctor claims that people seem to be more socially amenable when they have a baby, which is why he usually takes a human with him. They will never quite manage to fit in, but during their extended domestic interludes, the Doctor makes social adjustments to their behaviour, and sometimes shows more awareness of matters of the heart than Earthbound people.

Clara tells the Twelfth Doctor in 'Mummy on the Orient Express' that she wants him to come for dinner. He asks why she thinks he would not do that, and she fears he might find it boring. Different Doctors have varying approaches to something as human as sharing dinner or staying for Christmas. The First Doctor says in 'The Daleks' Master Plan' that he rarely gets time to celebrate, but declares that he must raise a toast since it is Christmas Day. He turns to the camera and makes a direct address to the audience, saying, 'Incidentally, a Happy Christmas to all of you at home!' The Ninth Doctor informs Rose that he does not do that in 'World War Three' when she tells him that her mother is cooking, joking that she should let her simmer. She wants to get to know him, but he has better things to do, because to him it is never 'just tea.' After their adventure in 'The Next Doctor', Jackson Lake demands that the Tenth Doctor join him for dinner 'in memory of those we've lost.' The lonely Time Lord changes his mind, just this once, and goes with him. Madge Arwell similarly convinces the Eleventh Doctor to spend Christmas with those he loves in 'The Doctor, The Widow and The Wardrobe'. He knocks on the door of the Ponds and is greeted by Amy, who says it has been two years since they last saw him. Rory informs him that there is already a place set for him at the table, and as he goes inside he touches his face, feeling that it is wet with tears – human, after all.

Donna asks the Doctor why it is always a big goodbye with him in 'The Star Beast', saying that he could do such outrageous things like having tea or dinner and a laugh. He could do something completely new: have friends. The Doctor has never liked farewells, but sometimes it is for the best. Writer Juno Dawson told me that Tegan's exit from the TARDIS in 'Resurrection of the Daleks' has stayed with her: 'She tells him she can no longer witness the bodies piling up around them. "It's stopped being fun, Doctor!" she wails, and I often apply that rule to my life too – if it stops being fun, then get out.' As the Fifth Doctor reflects, 'It's strange. I left Gallifrey for similar reasons. I'd grown tired of their lifestyle. It seems I must mend my ways.' He uses the loss of his friend as an opportunity for self-reflection, on how the way he leads his life has an alienating effect. Bill asks the Twelfth Doctor if he knows what the hardest thing was about knowing him in 'Twice Upon a Time'. 'My superior intelligence. My dazzling charisma. Oh! My impeccable dress sense', he suggests. 'Letting you go', she replies. Few companions ever want to leave the Doctor for good, yet his need to keep moving forwards prevents him from going back. It makes him afraid, but as Clara says at the end of 'Listen', he is always going to be, even if he learns to hide it, because fear is like a companion. But it can also bring us together, bring us home, for, as the First Doctor himself said in 'The Daleks', 'Fear makes companions of us all.'

At the end of 'The Giggle', the Fourteenth and Fifteenth Doctors list everything that they have been through, acknowledging that they never stop to say, 'What the Hell?' The benefit of bi-generation is that the Fourteenth is able to recuperate and heal, allowing the Fifteenth to move on. Donna says that his old face came back to show him the way home. When he joins his new family for dinner in the garden, including Mel whom the Seventh Doctor told he could never live life the way she does, he expresses contentment: 'I fought all those battles for all those years, and now I know what for. This. I've never been so happy in my life.' Autistic Whovian Esme did not buy it:

> *The burden of being the Doctor is permanently being outside all of this, having glimpses of intimacy and love and relationships, but they are transitory. On an autistic level that speaks to me because I feel like that with a lot of my*

> *relationships. Friendships can feel quite transient in that way. Feeling that kind of metaphysical distance between people. You can spend lots of time with people but there's still this gap that you can't close. I do have community and more permanent relationships, but I still feel a massive sense of isolation. I like it when the Doctor embodies that because it gives them a particular depth that they don't have otherwise. If they are just a fun person who hangs out with people without consequence or meaning, it becomes a bit pointless.*

I feel conflicted. I agree that the Doctor is at a remove from these human experiences, but I also like that he is able to engage with them at times. I know what it feels like to live in a world which does not feel as though it was designed for me, but I always appreciate it when someone offers me their hand and invites me inside. It is not something neurodivergent people take for granted or expect, which makes it all the more moving when it happens. It appears that I have that confusing oxymoronic phenomenon on my cheek – a tear of joy.

CHAPTER EIGHT
LOVE & MONSTERS

Martha Jones: **Is that what happens, though, seriously? Do you just get bored of us one day and disappear?**
Jack Harkness: **Not if you're blonde.**
Martha Jones: **Oh, she was blonde? Oh, what a surprise!**

'Utopia'

Yes, he be liking de redheads!

The Toymaker in 'The Giggle'

'What do you imagine "falling in love" is like?' Oliver Sacks asks Grandin in *An Anthropologist on Mars*. 'Maybe it's like swooning – if not that, I don't know', she replies. He changes the question to 'What is "loving"?' and she describes it as caring for another person. 'I think lots of times there are things that are missing from my life,' she says. 'Is this painful?' 'Yeah … I guess.' It is easy to feel sympathy for Grandin. She does not quite grasp the concept of love, but what matters more is the sense that there is something she is missing out on which she cannot name. It is possible for neurodivergent people to fall in love and to have sexualities, but until they experience it for themselves it can be frightening and, indeed, alien.

In 'The Aztecs', a woman named Cameca says that the First Doctor brings her joy – 'A gentle companion, and most dear to me.' She prepares cocoa, informing him that sharing the drink has a special meaning, that they are engaged to be married. The Doctor chokes. He ends their engagement when he leaves, breaking her heart. 'You're a very fine woman, Cameca', he tells her, 'and you'll always be very, very dear to me.' He has the kindness to let her down gently, albeit having a devastating romantic impact on her. It is an influence which the Doctor often has, no doubt the result of their intellectual prowess, courage, and inherent goodness which attracts people across the universe regardless of their physical appearance. Yet it is not something that they find themselves able to reciprocate, their sexuality and ability to fall in love constantly a source of frustration and amusement.

Love can be an insuperable barrier between the Doctor and their friends. In 'Fury from the Deep', Victoria Waterfield decides to stay with Maggie and Frank Harris as a stable family unit away from the dangers of travelling in the TARDIS. Jamie protests, upset that she will leave in a display of romantic affection. The Second Doctor ignores him, saying that she must make up her own mind as it is her life. Jamie talks to Victoria alone, hugging and kissing her as they say goodbye. When they leave her, the Doctor says, 'I was fond of her too, you know, Jamie.' He is unaware that their feelings towards Victoria are different, incapable of empathising with his male companion. It is reminiscent of the First Doctor's reluctance to say goodbye to Susan when she decides to stay with David, and the Third Doctor shuffling away awkwardly when Jo does the same. Few things mystify the Doctor during the classic era so much as affairs of the heart.

In 'The Five Doctors', the Fifth Doctor says, 'The TARDIS is more than a machine, Tegan. It's like a person. It needs coaxing, persuading, encouraging.' Leela questions the Fourth Doctor's relationship with his ship in 'Image of the Fendahl' after he tells her not to call K9 'he', which she claims is hypocritical since he calls the TARDIS 'she'. He says it is entirely different, stating that he is 'in complete and constant control of her' right before the 'old girl' throws them sideways. The TARDIS is the Doctor's only enduring companion, justifying his personification of her during their travels. This is actualised in 'The Doctor's Wife', in which the TARDIS Matrix is placed within the body of a woman named Idris. The Eleventh Doctor reveals that the first time he touched her console he said that she was 'the most beautiful thing I had ever known.' Asking what he calls her, she informs him that her name is 'Sexy'. He questions her lack of reliability, to which she says that she always takes her Doctor to where he needs to go – she was unlocked when he stole her on Gallifrey because she chose him. When he tells Amy that the TARDIS is a woman, she jokes, 'Did you wish really hard?' Long after everyone else has gone, it's just 'a boy and his box, off to see the universe.'

Just as the Third Doctor named his motorcar Bessie, the TARDIS is more than just a vehicle to them. In 'Thin Ice' the Twelfth tells Bill to choose a dress from the wardrobe. 'So the TARDIS has dresses and likes a bit of trouble? Yeah, I think I'm low-key in love with her', she says. 'Me too', he replies. It is a machine, not a human, which gives the Doctor a sense of the concept of love. This might be satisfying, were it not so obvious that they are sad to be missing out on the one experience the universe has to offer which they have not yet had.

SONG FOR TEN

The first time the Doctor demonstrates a real desire for romantic companionship is in 'The Girl in the Fireplace'. He meets Reinette Poisson after stumbling off a spaceship into her bedroom. Moments go by for the Tenth Doctor as years pass for the French aristocrat – she tells him it is impolite for him to have not aged a day before she pushes him against a wall and kisses him passionately. Where the First Doctor rejected the advances of a human woman, this incarnation happily 'snogged Madame de Pompadour.' He enters her mind, and she finds a way into his, observing 'such a lonely little boy. Lonely then and lonelier now', asking him how he can bear it. He is thrilled at the prospect of taking her away with him to see the stars, not for a second thinking of the historical ramifications. For once 'the slow path' does not scare him, yet he returns too late. After reading Reinette's final letter, urging him to hurry back as her days grow short, Rose asks him if he is all right. 'I'm always all right', comes the blatant lie. Neurodivergent fan Ian Palmer told me that rewatching this episode with his wife brought him to tears, which he said is unusual for him:

> *One aspect of the Doctor is explicitly shown here and that is how lonely they are. How they go through life with brief moments of friendship but they always end quickly. This is like me. There are only a couple of people that I've been friends with for more than a few years, when the relationship inevitably ends with some kind of issue and falling out, normally over something I have no idea about. I have gone through my entire life feeling out of place, like some kind of alien, in literally every social situation I've been in. Even in my family, I am the odd one out and the black sheep. That sense of not belonging and loneliness is still with me.*

The Doctor always carries a fear of impermanence. They explain this by saying that they will outlive every mortal they meet, which is true, but no relationship they have comes close to lasting a human lifetime. They are afraid of endings, so they push people away, terrified of getting their hopes up for romance only to have them dashed.

Reinette's fling with the Doctor is a microcosm of his relationship with Rose. While Jackie suspects a non-platonic relationship between the Ninth Doctor and her daughter, this is largely shown to be humorous until 'The Parting of the Ways'. He coolly says, 'I think you need a Doctor' before kissing her to absorb the golden energy from the heart of the TARDIS which is destroying her. Perhaps there is an amorous dimension to their relationship after all, which becomes more explicit as Rose and Mickey drift apart during the Tenth Doctor's first series. By 'Doomsday', after Rose has been sucked into a parallel universe, she is certain of her feelings towards the Time Lord. She hears him calling her name in a dream, and they drive to Dålig Ulv Stranden – Bad Wolf Bay – in Norway. Just as the Doctor did not care for the impact taking Reinette with him might have on history, he tells Rose that he is burning up a sun to say goodbye. He describes her ability to live life day after day as 'the one adventure I can never have', and she is heartbroken at the thought of him being alone again. 'I love you', she says, and the Doctor characteristically replies, 'Quite right, too. And I suppose, if it's my last chance to say it, Rose Tyler – ' Perhaps he was going to say it before he vanished, but that seems a step too far away from type.

I relate to such bumbling circumlocution in attempting to express myself. As does author Kate Fox, who told me that this connected to her alexithymia: 'All of that unexpressed grief resonated so much and was really crucial for me in being able to access my own many years of unexpressed grief and loss.' Director Graeme Harper said that it was difficult for David Tennant to perform the scene without tears: 'I think he had a battle trying to stop them from flooding down his cheeks.' There is a tension in the performance of the Doctor between the emotional expression of the human actor portraying them and the parameters of the character. It simply would not be the Doctor were he to cry and profess his undying love to Rose. The most explicit representation of his feelings is found in the lyrics of a song called 'Love Don't Roam' which is heard playing at Donna's wedding reception in 'The Runaway Bride': 'But of all the strange, strange creatures / In the air, at sea, on land, / Oh, my girl, my girl, my precious girl, / I love you, you understand.'

In 'Journey's End', the Doctor has a half-human double – one who, like the Ninth Doctor, was born in battle, full of blood, anger, and revenge. This Doctor also needs Rose to make him better. She is reluctant to accept him at first, but realises that he shares her Doctor's soul. He will age and die just as she will, unlike the two-hearted Time Lord. For final confirmation, she asks him what he was going to say to her the last time they saw each other in Norway, and the human Doctor whispers something in her ear which causes them to kiss. Our Doctor has to leave them, knowing that he will never be able to live as this other version can. It is a projection of another existence, one uninhibited by his timeless mind.

MARTHA JONES

It took the Tenth Doctor time to realise the full extent of his feelings towards Rose, and after accepting them it left him mournful and heartbroken. He has no intention of feeling the same way about Martha, but that does not stop her from falling for him. The Doctor lacks awareness of the impact his actions have on her – when they meet in 'Smith and Jones', he tells her that it means nothing when he gives her a long, hard kiss for the purpose of a genetic transfer. 'That was nothing?' she wonders, the damage done. Despite protesting that she only goes for humans, in 'The Infinite Quest' her 'heart's desire' is revealed to be the Doctor.

He takes her on a trip to say thank you in 'The Shakespeare Code', informing her that she is not replacing Rose. Martha flirts with him when they realise they will have to share a bed, but he keeps muttering that Rose would say the right thing. He describes Martha as a novice so she cannot be expected to be good enough, informing her that he will take her home tomorrow. 'Great', she says crossly, blowing out the candle. Yet she is delighted when the Doctor praises her for recognising that the fourteen sides of the Globe correspond to the number of lines in a sonnet, and ignores Shakespeare when he advises her to entertain a man who will actually kiss her. She remains optimistic, enjoying her time with him on New Earth in 'Gridlock' until he reveals that he last went there with Rose. 'Ever heard the word "rebound"?' Martha enquires. Of course not.

Shakespeare is not the only human to observe the dissonance in feelings between the unhappy coupling. Showgirl Tallulah Francis tells Martha in 'Daleks in Manhattan' that her boyfriend Laszlo waits for her after her performances and leaves a rosebud on her dressing table, making her envious. She recognises that Martha loves the Doctor because it is obvious in the way she looks at him, but to him it is not. Tallulah takes this to mean that he is 'into musical theatre' – would that it were so simple. Even after discovering that Laszlo has been turned into a pig slave, he remains in a relationship with Tallulah. 'There's someone for everyone', Martha remarks. 'Maybe', the Doctor coldly replies. After taking her home in 'The Lazarus Experiment', she informs him that she cannot continue to be taken along for a treat and needs to be more to him than just a passenger. They hug and he reassures her that she means more to him than that, although not in the way she longs for. On their next adventure in '42', Martha tries to get over the Doctor by kissing Riley, a misguided attempt to make him jealous.

Martha's heart is further broken when she is forced to witness John Smith fall in love with Joan during 'Human Nature'. In the story's second part, 'The Family of Blood', the relationship which the school matron believed herself to be in unravels. She asks John to tell her about his childhood, to which he offers objective facts about Nottingham rather than anecdotes. John is devastated when he asks Martha why the Doctor needs a companion, and she tells him that the Time Lord is lonely, realising that this is what he too must become. He wonders what sort of a man this Doctor must be if he did not consider the possibility that his human self might fall in love. Martha confesses her feelings for the first time, saying that while the Doctor does not so much as look at her, she does not care because she loves him. John warns Joan of this, that his new self will not be capable of loving her as he did – he sees a vision of their potential future, getting married, having children, and dying in bed as an old man. The life that the Doctor can never know. After the fob watch is opened and the Doctor returns, Joan cannot look at him: 'He was braver than you in the end, that ordinary man. You chose to change. He chose to die.' He invites her to go with him, saying that he is capable of everything that John was, but she knows that to him she will always seem small. In 'The End of Time Part Two' the Doctor visits Joan's great-granddaughter Verity Newman, named after the architects of *Doctor Who* just as John Smith's human parents were. She has published Joan's diary as *A Journal of Impossible Things*, and the Doctor asks her if Joan was happy in the end. 'Yes. Yes, she was', Verity replies. 'Were you?'

At the end of 'Last of the Time Lords', Martha can no longer stand it. She spent years training to be a doctor, but instead she is chasing a man who will never reciprocate her feelings. The Doctor is confused by the very human way in which she explains her decision, comparing herself to her friend Vicky who loved a man called Sean. She told Vicky to get out, so now she has to follow her own advice, but unlike the Doctor's other companions, she gives him a mobile phone and tells him if it rings he had better come running. When they meet again in 'The Sontaran Stratagem', Martha is in a relationship with Tom Milligan, who works in paediatrics in Africa – the Doctor is baffled, with Donna explaining, 'She's engaged, you prawn.' Martha is upset by Jenny's death in 'The Doctor's Daughter' because she 'thought for a moment there you'd finally found something worth living for.' He tells her there is always something worth living for, and after they say goodbye she looks at her engagement ring, reminding herself of the happier existence she chose for herself when she left the TARDIS. The Doctor never meant to hurt her. One wonders if he ever knew her true feelings.

THE GIRLS WHO WAITED

'Oh, you are sweet. Doctor. But I really wasn't suggesting anything quite so long term.' Amy wants something rather different from Martha when she runs off with the Eleventh Doctor on the night before her wedding. When they meet in 'The Eleventh Hour' after she has grown up, Amy appears before him dressed in a police uniform as part of her work as a kissogram. She asks him why he chose her to go with him in the middle of the night. 'Fun', he says, a word with varying associations to the ancient Time Lord and the young human woman. She attempts to confide in him in 'The Beast Below' about her intentions by obliquely asking if he has ever run away from something because he was scared, or not ready, or just because he could – he refers to the time he ran away from Gallifrey, not exactly the same scenario as Amy's marriage.

She finally confesses in 'Flesh and Stone', and he asks her why she left her engagement ring behind. 'Why did I leave my engagement ring when I ran away with a strange man the night before my wedding?' 'Yes.' 'You really are an alien, aren't you?' She tries to find a word that even he can understand, which turns out to be a passionate kiss. He protests that he is 907, which she takes to mean that it has been a while since he last had sex. He says that the most important thing in the history of the universe is that 'I get you sorted out right now.' 'That's what I've been trying to tell you.' More *Carry On Time Travelling* than *Doctor Who*, methinks.

The Doctor does not know how to cope with Amy's advances, seldom having experienced someone so confident before. In 'The Vampires of Venice' he pops out of a cake intended to contain a stripper for Rory's stag party, telling him that his fiancée kissed him. He says that Rory is a lucky man because she is a great kisser – 'Funny how you can say something in your head and it sounds fine.' The unravelling situation causes him to panic, and in an attempt to make amends he takes them to Venice. He tries to explain Amy's actions as resulting from relief after their encounter with the Weeping Angels, which is not true. 'And you kissed her back', Rory says. 'No. I kissed her mouth.' By trying to make things better the Doctor makes them worse, getting lost in a scenario entirely alien to him. Amy gives up her intentions with the Time Lord, embracing a friendship which Rory is too submissive to protest. They are Amy's boys, whether he likes it or not.

The tension of this love triangle is tested further in 'Amy's Choice'. The Dream Lord preys on Amy's anxieties, telling her that the Doctor has always loved a redhead, including Elizabeth the First – 'Well, she thought she was the first.' She believes that her friend trusts her, but the Dream Lord points out he has never even told her his real name. He forces the Doctor to question his use of the word 'friends', saying that they never see him again once they have grown up, because 'the old man prefers the company of the young, does he not?' Amy decides that she would prefer to die in a reality without

Rory than live in it, confirming her loyalty to him. But the Dream Lord raises questions about the dynamic which the Doctor creates with his companions, relating to the function they serve for him and the secrets which he keeps, despite asking them to trust him. The Doctor is a fantasy for Amy, a childhood imaginary friend called 'the Raggedy Doctor'. Her obsession ostracises her, leading her to be seen as problematic by adults who send her for psychological assessments. It is not only the Doctor who fails to recognise the distinction between intention and action, choosing to escape into fantasy rather than face reality.

In 'The Angels Take Manhattan', the Doctor enjoys a picnic with Amy and Rory. He reads a book out loud to them, a mystery featuring the Private Detective Melody Malone whose physical description delights the Doctor – 'Yowzah!' Rory remarks that only he could fall in love with a character in a book, failing to recognise the similarity to his wife's adolescent affections for her Raggedy Man. The Doctor does not notice Amy's reading glasses, recognising that something has changed in her appearance but not knowing what, and when she points them out he bluntly tells her he does not like them because they make her eyes look 'all liney.' He panics, realising his error, and says she looks fine. The Doctor is disgusted when the couple kiss in front of him, before continuing to read to Amy. He tears out the last page in a finifugal act – a resistance to endings and change characteristic of neurodivergent people. I seldom read books to the end, even reading the first twelve books of *A Series of Unfortunate Events* and refusing to pick up the thirteenth novel during childhood for the same reason. It is at the end of this episode that the Doctor loses Amy and Rory, emotionally devastating him. He had found in them a friendship built on flirtation, repartee, and banter – all things which had been out of the Doctor's reach hitherto. Losing them made him lonelier than ever.

The Doctor is left alone with River, his wife and closest companion – the one with whom he shared his name. She whispers it to the Tenth Doctor in 'Forest of the Dead', their encounters taking place in reverse-parallel order in each other's timelines. River is frustrated by the emotionality of the Doctor's younger self, and has to convince a man who has never met her before to believe that she will become the person he trusts most. It breaks her heart to discover that the whole time the Doctor knew her he was aware of how she died, although he also knew that he would save her with a neural relay placed in a sonic screwdriver. Amy is more perceptive of River's relationship to the Eleventh Doctor than he is in 'The Time of Angels', witnessing the way they flirt by debating how to fly the TARDIS and describing her unique attitude to the Time Lord as 'heel, boy!' River asks Amy if she thinks that with the Doctor their relationship could be anything as simple as marriage. It impresses her when she says yes.

The Doctor hurts River in 'The Impossible Astronaut' by showing up after she witnessed his death at Lake Silencio. She informs him that it is cold, 'even by your standards', and slaps him. She enjoys the dynamic between them, secretly correcting his flying of the TARDIS as they materialise in the Oval Office, lying that she is 'just admiring your skills, sweetie.' The Doctor demonstrates a characteristic lack of awareness of River's sarcasm, informing her that she might learn something. He even admits that he kind of likes the fact that she does not mind shooting people in 'Day of the Moon', but when she kisses him he is shocked and says that 'there's a first time for everything.' 'And a last time', comes her wistful reply. The Doctor matures through their relationship, following her lead and always relying upon her to make the first move. Despite his age, he is inexperienced, but demonstrates a greater enjoyment of and capacity for intimacy than previous incarnations.

He is delighted to discover in 'A Good Man Goes to War' that River is the daughter of Amy and Rory, meaning that she has Time Lord DNA due to her parents' prolonged exposure to the Untempered Schism. Suddenly finding himself in the position of knowing River before she knows him in 'Let's Kill Hitler', the Doctor has the upper hand. He is more of a mythic figure to Melody than he was to Amelia, who only knew of the Doctor through her friend. There is a flashback to Mels at school, echoing the memories of Ian and Barbara dealing with Susan: why did the Titanic sink? 'Because the Doctor didn't save it. Except you don't know about the Doctor because you're stupid.' She has a different provenance to her classmates, trained as a weapon to kill the very man who has become the object of her fantasies. Years later, long after their wedding, the Doctor teams up with River in 'The Angels Take Manhattan'. Her arm is caught by a Weeping Angel, but she manages to get free. The Doctor asks how she achieved this without breaking her wrist since it was written in the book, meaning she must have changed the future – she says it is called marriage. But when he takes her hand she gasps in pain, realising she lied. 'When one's in love with an ageless god who insists on the face of a twelve-year-old', she says, 'one does one's best to hide the damage.' The Doctor is old but he feels young, which is why he keeps younger companions. His face is chosen to match, making himself appealing to those he wants to share his adventures with. River chooses to accept this dynamic, knowing that she can never hurt him or let him see her aging for fear that he will panic and leave. The Doctor says it must hurt. 'Yes. The wrist is pretty bad too.'

'I think I'm going to need a bigger flowchart', remarks the Twelfth Doctor upon realising that River does not recognise him in 'The Husbands of River Song'. She shows him her diary, telling him that she is sad because the book is nearly full, and the man who gave it to her would know how many pages she would need. Maître d' Flemming says to River that she should know where the Doctor is because she is the woman he loves. She responds by saying that while she loves the Doctor, he does not go around falling in love because 'if you think he's anything that small or that ordinary, then you haven't the first idea of what you're dealing with.' She describes it as being like loving the stars – 'You don't expect a sunset to admire you back.' As she continues to describe how the Doctor is not sentimental enough to be there with her, she finally recognises him.

Despite lacking the affectionate nature of the Tenth or Eleventh Doctors, this version performs the most romantic act of all – he uses the Halassi Adrovar to commission the building of a restaurant opposite the Singing Towers on Darillium where the couple spend their last night together. He tells River that she looks amazing, to which she says that he has no idea whether she looks amazing or not. He says she has moved her hair about a bit, and she replies, 'Well done. It's very sweet of you to try.' She knows that this form of interaction does not come easily to him, and is appreciative of the effort he makes. She asks if he is crying, and he blames the wind. She says nothing is ever just the wind, to which he dispels the magic of the music by saying that the wind blows through the cave system and harmonises with the crystal layer. He clings to scientific fact in an effort to mask his true feelings. When he reveals that a night on the planet lasts twenty-four years, she says that she hates him. 'No, you don't', he responds. About as close to a declaration of love as the Twelfth Doctor could ever get.

THE IMPOSSIBLE GIRL

'Is there a word for total screaming genius that sounds modest and a tiny bit sexy?' Oswin asks in 'Asylum of the

Daleks'. 'You call me the Doctor', the Eleventh confidently declares. He meets her double in 'The Snowmen', a Victorian governess called Clara, soon after losing Amy and Rory. He walks away from her, muttering to himself, 'Those were the days.' He believes that he is content to be lonely, but Vastra knows better, saying that he must have made his usual impact on a young woman, encounters which always begin with the same two words: 'Doctor who?' This version of Clara has a romantic interest in him, flirting by saying that he likes her because she does not listen when he tells her what to do. He asks who said he likes her, and she points out that he gave it away by blushing when she kissed him. 'Shut up!' he utters in an attempt to escape the situation, only encouraging her. After handing Clara an umbrella which she uses to pull down the ladder to the TARDIS, she observes that the Doctor is a foot taller than her and would not have needed it. 'I never know why. I only know who', he explains, before handing her a key. As with Oswin, the Doctor does not save her, failing to learn his lesson yet again.

When the Doctor meets the modern Clara Oswald in 'The Bells of Saint John' she is working as a nanny. He observes that she should be doing 'young things, with young people.' 'You mean like you, for instance?' she retorts. 'Down, boy!' He tells her to shut up, just as he did to her Victorian predecessor. The light-heartedness of their friendship masks the Doctor's purpose in engaging Clara – to find out who this 'Impossible Girl' really is. She is capable of holding her own, however. In 'The Rings of Akhaten' the Doctor tells her that she reminds him of someone who died, and she says that she is 'not a bargain-basement stand-in for someone else. I'm not going to compete with a ghost.' It is important for all of the Doctor's companions to assert this position to break the cycle that began all those years ago when Susan left her grandfather.

The empathic psychic Emma Grayling warns Clara about the Doctor in 'Hide'. This neurodivergent woman has the ability to sense feelings, which the Doctor observes makes them the most compassionate people but also the loneliest. Clara tells him to stop talking as he does not realise the impact such an observation is having on Emma. The women confide in each other, with Clara asking her why she cannot see how Alec Palmer feels about her: 'People like me, sometimes we get our signals mixed up. We think people are feeling the way we want them to feel, you know, when they are special to us, when really there's nothing there.' She is aware of the way in which her mind works which makes her fearful of how it might mislead her. I have felt this way in all kinds of relationships, knowing that I do not always recognise signals and therefore worry that I am misreading someone. Clara says that she does not think there is anything between her and the Doctor, which Emma says is good because she must not trust him – 'There's a sliver of ice in his heart.' Emma goes on to ask Alec to tell her what she is thinking, and he says he cannot because he does not have her gift. She says he does not need it, he just needs to look at her. She further realises that the Doctor only came there to find her, and he asks about Clara. She tells him she is perfectly ordinary, very pretty and very clever, and more scared than she lets on. He asks if that is all, shocking her – 'Is that not enough?'

In 'Journey to the Centre of the TARDIS' the Doctor confronts Clara, saying that since they are about to die she might as well tell him who she is. He holds her tightly, realising she has no idea what he is talking about. Nothing frightens the Doctor more than a lack of understanding. It transpires in 'The Name of the Doctor' that Clara was broken into a million pieces to try to save the Doctor, to guide him from the day he decided which Type 40 capsule to steal on Gallifrey. She introduces him to her family as her boyfriend at Christmas in 'The Time of the Doctor', to which he says that he might be a bit rusty in some areas and will need to glance at a manual. He lacks social awareness, asking Clara if he should project holographic clothes onto the visual cortexes of her family so they too do not see he is naked. Such frivolity disappears in 'Deep Breath' after he regenerates. Vastra is surprised that she thought he was young, informing her that one might as well flirt with a mountain range. Clara is insulted, never having been interested in pretty young men; the only pin-up she had on her wall when she was fifteen was Marcus Aurelius. She struggles more with the changed personality of the Twelfth Doctor than his visage. At the end of the episode, she receives a phone call from the Eleventh who reassures her that they are the same Doctor. It hurts him because she looks at him and cannot see him, so she hugs him. This Doctor is not sure if he is a hugging person now. Clara says that he does not get a vote.

PLANET OF INCELS

Most of the Doctor's brushes with romance are hapless, although their attempts to influence and control women point to a more sinister intent. There is a prevalence of neurodivergent men amongst involuntary celibate or 'incel' communities, referring to those who denigrate and objectify women out of a belief that they are owed something due to their biological status as men. An early example of such a figure in *Doctor Who* is the outlaw Sharaz Jek in 'The Caves of Androzani'. He calls Peri his 'exquisite child' whom he wishes to keep eternally young, possessing her for his personal satisfaction. Peri asks him why he wears a hood, causing him to unmask and reveal his disfigured face which prompts her to scream. He claims that his ugliness is the reason why he lives amongst androids, for they do not see him the way she does.

'We could think of the future', he says, to which Peri replies, 'What future?'

One in which women are fully subordinated to men, one imagines, just as is planned by incels in online communities. Howie Spragg is one such individual in 'The God Complex', theorising that the hotel is in Norway because he believes a conspiracy theory that the US government has cities hidden in the mountains. Rory tells him that it is amazing that he has come up with a theory even more insane than what is actually happening. When he enters the room containing what he is most afraid of, he finds it filled with young women laughing at him. 'What's loser in K-K-K-Klingon?' one of them says. The mocking of his appearance and stammer, and no doubt his neurodivergence stereotypically signified by the reference to *Star Trek*, is shown to have fuelled an obsessive and pathological misogyny.

Nick in 'Eve of the Daleks' is portrayed similarly. He goes to a self-storage unit every New Year's Eve with objects left at his flat by ex-girlfriends, a ruse to see Sarah, the owner of the warehouse. She tells him that she wishes she was at a party, and he says it is better where they are because he hates parties, people, and drinking. Sarah is disturbed to discover that he has catalogued the items from his exes on shelves by name, prompting Yaz to ask if the women are still alive. He reveals that he only visits when Sarah is at the desk because he has 'an embarrassing crush' on her. She tells him that this is 'so stalkery', while he prefers the term 'unrequited.' He is unaware of the creepiness of his behaviour, failing to see how what he views as romantic behaviour is actually sinister and off-putting.

At least Nick lacks the confidence to act on his impulses. Alan Budd in 'The Robot Revolution' goes further in his treatment of Belinda. He echoes Adric when he says that he knows that 'girls aren't good at maths', and tells her that she has to be known as 'Miss' because she is not married. When he proposes to her, he says that she will not be allowed to wear tight clothing or text people after 20:00. Finding herself on Missbelindachandra One, Belinda encounters the AI Generator, a nod to the obsession of certain incels with the capabilities of artificial intelligence as a means of suppressing human creativity and independent thought. Realising it is actually Al, short for Alan, she says that he has 'taken coercive control and made it complete control of the whole planet', that is, the 'planet of the incels.'

Ruby dates podcaster and conspiracy theorist Conrad Clark in 'Lucky Day'. He reveals that he is part of a group called Think Tank which aims to bring down UNIT by revealing that alien threats to Earth are not real. 'What's behind your mask, Conrad?' Kate asks him, seeing only an 'angry little man' working for personal gain on the basis of a lie. The Fifteenth Doctor is furious when he confronts him, describing him as a coward who uses people's insecurities and fears as currency. He breaks his own rules and tells him that he is going to die 'boiling in anger and poison' aged forty-nine 'alone and unloved'. He will be forgotten as the world moves on without his kind. It is a powerful warning to men who turn their belief that they are misunderstood or ignored into resentment and a superiority complex. It is men like this who attempt to keep the fandom of *Doctor Who* for themselves, excluding women and those they perceive as different. Let them be included in this book not even as 'a footnote, just ashes on the wind.'

THE SAPPHIC ERA

Many of the neurodivergent fans I interviewed identify as queer, including myself. Love and sex were abstract concepts to me until adulthood. After I transitioned I had an overwhelming sense that I had some catching up to do, to try to find out what all the fuss was about. It is essential for me to be in a relationship with someone who not only accepts my neurodivergence, but cherishes and celebrates it. The power dynamics I have criticised in this chapter are shifted in a lesbian relationship. There is something uniquely beautiful and equal to love between women which is demonstrated several times in *Doctor Who*. While it was edited to be less explicitly sapphic than Rona Munro's original script, 'Survival' portrays a tender and romantic encounter between Ace and the Cheetah Person Karra. 'Smell the blood on the wind. Hear the blood in your ears. Run, run beyond the horizon and catch your hunger!' A call to give in to desire and act on impulse. The Master stabs Karra with a sabre tooth, causing her to turn into a human again. 'I can hunt in the dark', she says as they call each other 'sister', mourning the loss of their burgeoning relationship.

No such chastity was needed for the portrayal of Vastra and Jenny's marriage in the NuWho era, although their only on-screen kiss is explained narratively as a transference of air between them rather than an act of passion. Bill, on the other hand, is never coy. In 'The Pilot' she falls for Heather after they meet in a bar, a crush which causes the young woman to remain attached to her across space and time. Her dating life is explored further in 'Extremis', with Bill appearing more confident than her date Penny. While trying to reassure her that she has no reason to feel guilty, the Pope suddenly enters her bedroom and frightens the poor girl away. Bill is cross with the Twelfth Doctor, although he later informs her that Penny is not, in fact, out of her league and she should call her that night – a savviness he no doubt learnt from Clara. When we see the women together again in 'The Pyramid at the End of the World', Bill explains to Penny that her tutor is an alien. She asks if she is completely mad, to which Bill asks if it is working. Penny admits, 'A little bit.' 'Not so mad, then.' Whoever said autism cannot be sexy.

It is an effect which the Thirteenth Doctor has on Yaz, incidentally but nonetheless powerfully. In 'Arachnids in the UK', Najia asks the Doctor how she knows her daughter, wondering if they are seeing each other. Yaz informs her that they are friends, a fact which remains consistent until she begins to discuss her true feelings in 'The Haunting of Villa Diodati'. Claire Clairmont confides in Yaz that she wishes to know if Lord Byron has feelings for her by reading his private writings. Yaz suggests she just asks him, but Claire replies, 'His answers only increase the enigma.' She tells her that she knows someone like that, and Claire asks if she would trade her 'enigmatic person' for someone 'reliable and dull.' Jack Harkness is the first to spot how Yaz truly feels for the Doctor, from the way she shoved her in 'Revolution of the Daleks'. She says that it felt cruel to be shown something which she could not have any more after the Doctor left, wondering if she would rather have never known her because being without her is worse. Jack says that the joy is worth the pain, and she has to enjoy the journey while she is on it. She stays with the Doctor when Ryan and Graham decide to leave, comforting her when she says that she could change the timeline so they can all have more time together. 'It's okay to be sad', she says, giving the Doctor permission to embrace how she feels.

Travelling without the rest of their fam allows Yaz to grow closer to the Doctor. In 'The Vanquishers' the Doctor apologises for shutting her out, and says that she wants to tell her everything about herself. I find this extremely moving, having been fearful that revealing my unmasked self to women I have dated and telling them about the traumas of my past might push them away. Still, Yaz does not confess her true feelings to the Doctor. Dan asks if she has done so in 'Eve of the Daleks', and while it is obvious to him, he admits it might not be 'to a good-hearted weirdo'. She tells him that she does not know what to do because she has never admitted it to anyone, not even herself. He says that one never knows what might happen so she should act sooner rather than later. The subject is finally broached in 'Legend of the Sea Devils'. 'Yaz, I can't fix myself to anything, anywhere, or anyone. I've never been able to. That's what my life is.' She says that it is not because she does not want to, but because she is afraid that one day it will hurt. 'My Nani says courage is knowing something will hurt and doing it anyway', Yaz replies. 'Mind you, she also said it's the definition of stupidity.' For the Doctor, this is too giant a leap into the unknown. She asks for them to live in the present, although she confesses that she wishes this could go on forever. Ella Road, who co-wrote the episode with Chibnall, told me that she received letters from fans after it aired: 'One guy said that his teenage daughter, who is queer, was over the moon to see the complexity of queer love and ambiguous female friendship explored on screen in a mainstream show.' She said that representation had great importance, to see the Doctor not only as female, but as a lesbian battling anxiety.

The Doctor and Yaz sit atop the TARDIS eating ice cream before the Doctor regenerates at the end of 'The Power of the Doctor':

> *A wise person once said to me, 'Goodbyes only hurt because what came before was so special.' Oh, and it's been so special. You, and Graham, and Ryan, and Dan. Nobody else got to be us. Nobody else got to live our days. Nobody. And my hearts are so full of love of all of you. Oh, I have loved being with you, Yaz. And I have loved being me. I think I need to do this next bit alone.*

'Let's not say goodbye', is all Yaz can manage. It is a moving speech, but one which no doubt feels unsatisfying. At the end of her life the Doctor does not recognise that Yaz wanted the Time Lord for herself. She decides to be on her own rather than let the woman who loves her share that moment. Communication is everything in a relationship, and it can be made difficult, even impossible, by anxiety and neurodivergence. But if I can offer a piece of wisdom from my own romantic adventures – just tell the girl you love her, before you run out of time.

CHAPTER NINE
THE BEAST BELOW

Peri Brown: **He's not himself.**
The Sixth Doctor: **Then who am I?**
Peri Brown: **I wish you wouldn't keep wandering off like that.**
The Sixth Doctor: **See it more as a mental stroll in a park of psychic tranquillity.**

'The Twin Dilemma'

The thing I love most is the impact this show has on the fans, the people who watch it. Their love for the show, and their gratitude for it, is quite beyond expectation. I have now, after all these decades, had so many people write to thank me for helping them to get through a truly difficult time. That Doctor Who kept them going, that Peri saved their life. And all of this sounds incredibly dramatic, but it has happened so many times that you do completely have to believe that this is the truth.

Nicola Bryant said this to me when I asked her about the impact *Doctor Who* has had on her life. She has a particular interest in 'the way the brain is wired', and cherishes the mental health benefits the show gives to its fans. I would not go so far as to say that *Doctor Who* saved my life, but it has sustained me. The show gave me something to invest in when I was being bullied at school, to escape from a reality which was too horrible to bear. Despite drifting away from it during the first two series featuring the Twelfth Doctor, the third arrived at the right time – the Doctor was starting at university concurrently with me, and I connected to Bill as a queer, wide-eyed student with a passion for the past. Then the Thirteenth Doctor came along, contending with social problems as a woman when I was navigating my own changing body. After I moved to London and faced a new start in my life, I connected to the fandom community, developing existing friendships and making new ones through the show. I started writing about *Doctor Who* and contacting people who had been involved in its production, asking them what it meant to them as a means of understanding my own connection.

Not long before I started work on this book I had an accident which left me with a physical disability. I had already been diagnosed with Complex PTSD years before, but now I needed more help, contending with an array of traumas experienced since childhood. During my time at home I started rewatching *Doctor Who* with my mother and brother as I had since 2005. It was deeply nostalgic, and I scribbled notes about the show's connection to my neurodivergence which developed into the book you are reading. I had several surgeries, and during my hospital stays it was again to the Whoniverse I turned, finding comfort in its familiarity. I have talked about my relationship with the show at length with my therapist, including the sense of purpose and drive given to me by writing this book, and the conversations it has allowed me to have.

I was grateful to Alexis Harrow for her openness in discussing the relationship between *Doctor Who* and her mental health. She is thirty-one years old and is diagnosed with autism and ADHD. 'My diagnosis has been an overall positive in my life, providing validation, explanation, and confidence', she told me. 'However, it doesn't stop it from being a disability. It impacts my everyday life, from my work, my relationships, my self-worth, and identity.' She first watched the show in 2005 with 'Father's Day', an episode which resonated with her as her own father had died the year before. After watching the Ninth Doctor regenerate, she told her mother that she felt as though she had watched her best friend die. 'With my diagnosis in adult life, I look back on these times with clarity and understanding of why I reacted the way I did. I want to hold young Alexis with understanding arms, validating her feelings.' I connect to that – I would not be writing this book if I did not feel that I owe it to my younger self, to help her to make sense of the way she connected with *Doctor Who*. And yes, how she still does, no matter how grown-up she might be.

THE DAISIEST DAISY

In 'The Time Monster', Jo and the Third Doctor are tied together with Atlantean chains. If the Master opens the floodgates of Kronos' power, he tells her, then order will be swept away. Jo says that this makes everything seem pointless, inspiring the Doctor to tell her a story about 'the blackest day' of his life. When he was a boy he lived in a house perched halfway up the top of a mountain. Behind it lived an old monk who, it was said, had learned the secret of life. One day the Doctor asked the monk for help, sitting in silence as he told him everything that was troubling his mind. The monk pointed at a daisy, and suddenly the Doctor saw it through different eyes, 'simply glowing with life, like a perfectly cut jewel' – 'That was the daisiest daisy I'd ever seen.' When the Doctor says that he is sorry for bringing Jo to Atlantis, she replies that she is not.

At university I took mindfulness classes. I sat in the lotus position and slowed down my breathing, focusing on the body and taking notice of each sensation and thought as it came. Simple acts such as washing up dishes became peaceful, enriching experiences, moments of respite from the chaos of my brain. After my accident, I found myself more appreciative of things I had previously taken for granted, and stopped worrying about what I was missing out on by focusing on what I had. Sometimes I lose that feeling, and I force myself to pause and remember the gratitude I felt. Like the Doctor, I want to see and experience everything with a voraciousness driven by fear that I shall run out of time. But when one really looks at what one has, the impact is overwhelming. It is the closest one can come to a belief in divine design, noticing even the finest details of the tiniest flower. For those of us who are neurodivergent, this can be challenging, but even more rewarding.

The Fourth Doctor's joie de vivre confuses Romana in 'The Armageddon Factor'. She checks the radiation levels outside the TARDIS and remarks that there must be a nuclear war going on, while the Doctor says it is more likely a party – 'Think positive. Why do you always assume the worst?' When she informs him that she is being realistic, he dismisses this as 'empirical poppycock. Where's your joy in life? Where's your optimism?' K9 defines this attitude as a 'belief that everything will work out well. Irrational, bordering on insane.' The Doctor needs to believe that the best is possible until he knows what is actually going on. Take the example of Schrödinger's cat, that one does not know if it is alive or dead until one opens the box. The Doctor would not give up until he had explored every way to open the box believing the cat to be alive. It is what motivates him to never give up in the face of adversity, effectively masking how he might really feel.

In 'The Girl in the Fireplace', the Tenth Doctor instigates a mind meld with Reinette. He says that if there is anything she does not want him to see she can imagine a door and close it. This makes me think of the archive inside my mind, with memories I want to suppress locked away. When I was diagnosed with CPTSD, I found it impossible to stop the chains on those files breaking free and flooding into my consciousness when triggered by certain actions, such as loud knocking. I engaged in a course of Cognitive Behavioural Therapy, which helped me to restructure my thought processes to focus on the present rather than the past, and Eye Movement Desensitisation and Reprocessing which enables the processing of traumatic memories. To strengthen the chains, and block out unwanted thoughts through the building of doors. I continue to struggle with post-traumatic stress, but these techniques have enabled me to feel more in control of my memory recall, and to calm myself quickly when flashbacks do take over. 'It's the way it's always been. The monsters and the Doctor. It seems you cannot have one without the other', Reinette observes to Rose. I carry my own monsters with me, but 'one may tolerate a world of demons for the sake of an angel' – for the daisiest daisy one might see.

A line from 'Our God, Our Help' by Isaac Watts comes to mind when I think of the burden of the lonely Time Lord: 'A thousand ages in thy sight / Are like an evening gone.' The Doctor has an omniscience, an ability to hold the history of the universe within their mind. It can cause them to fail to recognise the gravity with which their companions hold certain facts, unable to understand why to a mortal they are depressing. In 'Hide', Clara asks the Eleventh Doctor how he can be okay after watching the life cycle of the Earth from birth to death. She realises that to him she is a ghost – 'We must be nothing.' Yet the Doctor is not eternal, and he too fears the end. He cries in 'The Name of the Doctor' when Trenzalore is mentioned, the place he is buried. There he finds a tear in the fabric of reality left by his journey across the universe. The words of his predecessors are heard coming through, ending with the Third Doctor observing that 'daisiest daisy' as a reminder of everything he has been through, and to hold on to the hopefulness of life and wonder which drove him away from Gallifrey in the first place. An endless quest for beauty and the sublime.

When I am depressed, I immerse myself in culture. Nothing makes me cry like an overwhelming work of classical music, such as Mahler's 'Resurrection' symphony or Elgar's *The Dream of Gerontius*. I happily take myself to the opera or ballet and pour out my soul, feeling as though the back of my brain is being massaged which induces hot tears to pour. I can detect the slightest error in pitch from the first clarinettist and feel enraged by people rustling paper or muttering behind me due to my misophonia, a hypersensitive trait of autism. Like the visualisations created in Disney's *Fantasia* (1940), I am synaesthetic, seeing the music explode to life in colour and light before me, sometimes taking on the form of narrative which fuels my visual imagination. It is this sensibility for music and art which I love most about being neurodivergent, an experience which I would not give up even if I have to contend with the disabling aspects as well.

The Eleventh Doctor sits in front of the Time-Lord painting *Gallifrey Falls No More* in 'The Day of the Doctor', and Clara asks if he wants a moment alone with it, observing 'those big sad eyes.' Several paintings have caused me to cry during my life – from the tragic expressions of the girls in Joseph Wright of Derby's *An Experiment on a Bird in an Air Pump* to the all-consuming colour of Rothko's *Seagram Murals*. The Doctor reflects that he would be a great curator when he retires, at which point an old man bearing the face of the Fourth Doctor appears, having done just that. It is a rare moment of stillness for the Doctor, of contemplation and appreciation for something beautiful. It allows him to continue without burning out.

MOVING VINCENT

Dr Black tells a group at the Musée d'Orsay in Paris about *Wheatfield with Crows*, one of the final paintings of Vincent van Gogh. He describes the artist's last months before his death in 1890 as the most astonishing of his career, works produced without hope for praise or reward. Two children go to the *Portrait of Dr Gachet* and one informs the other that this was the doctor who cared for Van Gogh during his madness. The Eleventh Doctor approaches *The Church at Auvers* with Amy, noticing a monster in the window which compels him to pay its creator a visit. 'Vincent and the Doctor' is a remarkable study of mental health and creative genius, often cited as one of the show's finest episodes. I was taught about Van Gogh at school in Year 8, exploring his impressionistic use of colour and light. I connected to the artist's vision through my own hypersensitive perception of the world, not least the synaesthetic effect which music has on my mind's eye: 'It's colour. Colour that holds the key. I can hear the colours. Listen to them. Every time I step outside, I feel nature is shouting at me.' The episode was broadcast around the same time that I wrote a biographical essay on Van Gogh, which fleshed out his troubled life in a way which clung to my imagination and never let go.

At that age, like Vincent, I was being assessed by doctors and therapists who struggled to make sense of the way my brain worked. 'It seems to me there's so much more to the world than the average eye is allowed to see', Vincent says, which is how I felt not being understood by others. Few people around me related to my passions for classical music and art, only my grandmother. She took me to my first classical concert when I was a child, to hear a programme which included Rachmaninov's second piano concerto and Nielsen's 'Inextinguishable' symphony. The former work stirred my emotions, but it was the latter which enraptured my subconscious – the final movement features an uproarious 'battle' between two timpanists which thundered in my ears. I love dissonant, almost violent instrumental music, from Stravinsky's *The Rite of Spring* to the hard bop of Art Blakey. Such music drowns out the noise in my brain and of the world around me, focusing solely on the crashing of drums and cymbals. I recall seeing my grandmother, otherwise a stoic individual, weep at a performance of Elgar's *Cello Concerto in E minor* – seeing her tears gave me permission to openly express the emotions I felt. It was our private language, a means of communicating beyond the limitations of words. When Amy tells Vincent that she is fine, he informs her that he can 'hear the song of your sadness', causing her to cry inexplicably. Those of us who are neurodivergent can often sense things that others cannot.

Vincent shares with the Doctor and Amy his perception of nature. They lie on the ground and hold hands, as the sky transforms into the blazing swirls of yellow and orange against a sea of deep blue depicted in *The Starry Night*. 'We are so lucky we are still alive to see this beautiful world', he says in a speech reminiscent of the story told to Jo by the Third Doctor in Atlantis. Only Vincent can see the Krafayis, the monster which embodies the illness of his mind. He recognises that the creature only lashed out because it was scared, 'like humans who lash out when they're frightened.' I can see this in people who have abused me, that it was because I was different that they were motivated to violence. This allows me to forgive them, so they cannot continue to have a hold on me. It was with an optimism for the future that I am able to withstand their attacks. I cannot allow them to prevent me from achieving success, and being amongst those who understand and accept me.

The final sequence of the episode struck a deep chord with me, in which Vincent travels in the TARDIS to the Musée d'Orsay to see his works on display. Dr Black describes why Van Gogh is the finest painter of all time: 'He transformed the pain of his tormented life into ecstatic beauty.' Such words of praise cause Vincent to weep, with the Doctor suddenly panicking that he has overwhelmed him. Amy is naïve, believing that their act of kindness would change the course of history, but the Doctor would never have done it if he had believed things would alter significantly:

> *The way I see it, every life is a pile of good things and bad things. The good things don't always soften the bad things; but vice versa, the bad things don't necessarily spoil the good things or make them unimportant. And we definitely added to his pile of good things.*

He observes that they made some small changes, including a note on one of Van Gogh's still-life paintings of sunflowers dedicating it to Amy. The Doctor relates to the complexity of Vincent's depression, that even when one can see the future it does not necessarily affect how things are in the present. He offers hope and reassurance, something which no medical doctor could give to Van Gogh.

DEATH AND TRANSFIGURATION

Artificial means of 'curing' depression are critiqued in *Doctor Who*. 'The Happiness Patrol' considers Thatcherism and the idea of enforced emotions in an Orwellian dystopia called Terra Prime where sadness is punishable by death. The British Prime Minister is doubled by Helen A, a tyrannical figure who fails to see the contradiction of coerced happiness through fear. The Seventh Doctor confronts Helen A, describing her candy-coloured metropolis, with its party games and infectious muzak, as 'cosmetic', warning her that 'happiness is nothing unless it exists side-by-side with sadness.' She experiences this for herself when she discovers that her pet Fifi is dead. It is only through contrast that the concept of goodness exists, that without pain and suffering there cannot be the opposite. Helen A lacks empathy with those who do not share her approach to emotions, an exaggerated actualisation of a stereotypical neurodivergent resistance to feelings.

The Tenth Doctor is horrified to discover that in the underbelly of New New York in 'Gridlock' pharmacists are selling mood drugs. These are patches which chemically induce emotions, including 'Happy' and 'Anger'. A woman purchases 'Forget', choosing the strength she requires in order to carry on her life without knowing that her parents have gone on to the motorway, seemingly never to return. Novice Hame shows the Doctor the Senate, populated with the skeletons of people who died after taking a new mood called 'Bliss'. A virus mutated inside the compound and became airborne, wiping out the population in seven minutes – a bitter irony. The episode exposes the advantage taken by pharmaceutical companies of those who are mentally vulnerable, considering how they can be manipulated and harmed by those who seek profit rather than offering meaningful help.

For Bill's first trip onboard the TARDIS, she tells the Twelfth Doctor that she wishes to see the future because she wants to know if it is 'happy.' He takes her to one of Earth's first space colonies, which is staffed by Emojibots which serve as an interface to microbots known as Vardy. It is their job to ensure that all humans remain happy, but after a woman died and her family started grieving, they recognised this emotion as hostile and killed them. People wear emotional indicators on their backs, which the Doctor observes makes sense because if one could see it then it might affect one's mood. In their basic form, emojis are simplistic representations of human emotions. When I was a child being assessed for autism, I was shown emoticons on cards and asked to identify the emotion being expressed. But they can also be confusing, expressing nuanced ideas and associations for which one must be familiar with an entirely different language. Texting and posting on social media can be a minefield for neurodivergent people, allowing for miscommunication.

Christopher Boone, who is autistic, recalls in *The Curious Incident of the Dog in the Night-Time* by Mark Haddon that he was shown pictures of a sad face and a happy face when he was a child. He identified them easily, but struggled with more complex illustrations. He believes he would be a good astronaut, due to his intelligence and understanding of how machines work, and because he would be comfortable floating away on his own in a tiny spacecraft. The novel inspired a Big Finish story by Nev Fountain called *The Curious Incident of the Doctor in the Night-Time*, in which the Sixth Doctor encounters an autistic boy named Michael. Like Christopher, he struggles to understand the 'invisible rules' which other people are born with inside their heads. The Doctor tells him that he also hates these rules and is always breaking them. Where Michael offends Peri by telling her that she has a boy's name, because he knows two boys called Perry, the Doctor informs him that this is 'very logical.'

Their connection allows the Doctor to comfort Michael in his grief. The boy says that he knows his father is dead, but he does not understand why he must 'go away as well', to which the Doctor responds that he is now in 'a very special place'; that is, the past:

> *A lot of people think the past is a sad place, but I visit it a lot and let me tell you I find it just as exciting as the present and the future. Your father lives there now, and all the moments*

> ***where he is a living, breathing, loving father are there too. All stored safely, and they will never go away.***

Michael asks if he can visit him, and the Doctor says that anyone with his mental abilities can do so just by closing their eyes. In 2014 a video was sent by Peter Capaldi in role as the Twelfth Doctor to a nine-year-old autistic boy called Thomas Goodall whose grandmother had recently died. He told him that bad and sad things happen to the Doctor and Clara when they are travelling, and that they are on his side. The message made Thomas smile for the first time since his grandmother's death and gave him courage to attend her funeral. Grief can be very complex for neurodivergent people to navigate, and both of these examples reveal how *Doctor Who* is able to guide us through them. It can be helpful for us to make sense of what is happening in the real world through a connection to fiction, to see internal feelings externalised in a way which appears logical.

In 'The Doctor, The Widow and The Wardrobe', the Eleventh Doctor gives Madge Arwell and her children, Cyril and Lily, a tour of their renovated home. He has built a child's haven, including 'a sciency-wiency workbench', torches for secret reading, and a 'zone of tranquility'. Everything the Doctor could want. Madge confides in her caretaker, saying that she does not know why she keeps shouting at her children. He tells her it is because 'every time you see them happy, you remember how sad they're going to be, and it breaks your heart', knowing that she must tell them that their fighter-pilot father is dead. Madge believes that there is no point in her children being happy now if they will be sad later, to which the Doctor assures her that they should be allowed to be happy now precisely *because* they are going to be sad later. She embraces the children and says what she always says: 'This Christmas is going to be the best Christmas ever.'

There is no instruction manual for grief. Alexis Harrow told me that *Doctor Who* has helped her to navigate the loss of her parents, allowing for a form of emotional release. She said that the last time an episode made her cry was 'Rosa', broadcast two years after her mother died. The song 'Rise Up' by Andra Day plays over the end credits, which made her think of 'my mum and the horrendously hard times we had, and how I would do it all again in a heartbeat, to be with her.' She said that the grief carried by Graham and Ryan after the death of Grace moved her, although she was confused by the Thirteenth Doctor's insensitivity. 'The Doctor has been around for thousands of years and has experienced the full spectrum of human emotion', Alexis observed. 'The same Doctor who tried to offer comfort to Vincent van Gogh. I just felt the Doctor would be more empathetic.'

In 'Arachnids in the UK' Graham tells the Doctor that grief needs time, and he wants to travel in the TARDIS rather than remaining in a house filled with memories. Ryan says in 'The Tsuranga Conundrum' that the last time he saw his father, Aaron, was a year ago. He had found his mother dead in the kitchen when he was thirteen years old, and he felt abandoned by his father – 'I never knew life threw that sort of stuff at you. I never knew that when it does, sometimes adults don't cope either.' Aaron attempts to reconcile with Ryan in 'Resolution'. He goes to shake the Doctor's hand and she bluntly says, 'You weren't at Grace's funeral', refusing to engage with someone who had let her friend down. He talks to his son and tells him that he ran away from him out of shame, and by the end of the episode Ryan forgives his father and says that he loves him. Families can be challenging to navigate, and people struggle to cope with overwhelming emotions and responsibilities no matter how old they are.

In 'Can You Hear Me?' the god Zellin moulds his form to provoke fear from humans, extracting nightmares from the scared and vulnerable. Ryan visits his friend Tibo at his flat, which he notes is uncharacteristically dirty. Tibo says that he is having a difficult time and nightmares featuring Zellin. He is upset that his friend seemingly abandoned him, and Ryan dreams of the elderly Tibo saying that he waited for him to come back and he never did. In Graham's dream, he is back at Sheffield City Hospital, with his nurse Grace informing him that his cancer has returned and asking him why he failed to save her life. Zellin informs the Doctor that the best part of humanity is 'the cruelty of their own minds directed towards themselves.' She retorts that the greatest thing about humans is that they live with fear, doubt, and guilt but they always prevail – that out of mental struggles comes strength. The episode shows how humans have always battled the same demons, but through understanding and kinship, they can be overcome.

Yet as Alexis noted, the Doctor struggles at the end of the episode to find the right words to offer Graham when he shares his nightmare. 'I should say a reassuring thing now, shouldn't I?' she says. 'I'm still quite socially awkward, so I'm just going to subtly walk towards the console and look at something. And then, in a minute, I'll think of something that I should've said, that might've been helpful.' The Doctor is capable of grand speeches about humanity, but when it comes to being a good friend she panics and forgets her bedside manner. She blames her social awkwardness, but it betrays a deeper fear within herself of things ending and of losing people which she cannot articulate. Clearly she has lost the cue cards which Clara made for the Twelfth Doctor. The scene is surprising because this female Doctor seemed more socially capable than her male predecessor, but it is a reminder that she similarly struggles at times to find the right thing to say. I relate to this scene – I never quite know what to do when someone confides in me. I have spoken to people who have started crying with grief as they told me about a loved one they lost, and I felt a panic in my brain as I did not know what one could possibly say which would help. The Doctor suddenly starts talking about *Frankenstein*. I fear that I would attempt a similar change of subject.

I contacted Emma Sullivan, the director of 'Can You Hear Me?' and 'The Haunting of Villa Diodati', to discuss neurodivergence and *Doctor Who*. She told me that she used to work in schools where she taught neurodivergent children how to make films. 'There is a really amazing school in South London called the Michael Tippett school', she said. 'A lot of the kids there were non-verbal, but they do communicate with Makaton. It's a great place, magic.' This is a form of visual communication using gestures and images to express feelings, like a physical embodiment of emoticons. She told me about a group of neurodivergent children who love the film *Avatar* (2009) and are able to express themselves by talking about the world of Pandora. It helped them to build friendships and relate to other children who loved the film, improving their mental health and abating loneliness. Emma told me that she can see such social structures being made possible through *Doctor Who*. The show gives those who find it difficult to express themselves a language, something they can point to in order to make sense of their emotions. It might seem like a non sequitur for the Doctor to mention *Frankenstein*, but I can see her intention – she related what Graham had told her to the human fears of change and death embodied by Mary Shelley's novel. It might not make sense to her fam, but it makes sense to me.

CHAPTER TEN
NIGHT TERRORS

Bill Potts: **I thought I could hear the music, but I can't, can I? They're in another time.**
The Twelfth Doctor: **Music's funny like that.**

'The Eaters of Light'

Crimson. Eleven. Delight. The smell of dust after rain. Crimson, eleven, delight, the smell of dust after rain. Crimson, eleven, delight, the smell of dust after rain.

Amy Pond in 'The Doctor's Wife'

Sometimes I start talking and I cannot stop. I start reeling off fact after fact, moving from one subject to another as my brain kicks into overdrive. Like the Doctor waxing lyrical about edible ball bearings in 'The Idiot's Lantern' it can seem as though I am malfunctioning, causing the person I am talking at to insist I come up for air. How does it feel to be inside my head? 'Brilliant! Fantastic! Molto bene! Great big universe, packed into my brain. You know you could fix that Chameleon Circuit if you just tried hotbinding the fragment links and superseding the binary, binary, binary…' Just as Donna does in 'Journey's End' before her brain starts to hurt, I get stuck on certain words and sounds which repeat over and over until I feel like I will collapse. While Donna is able to have it taken away, there is no such solace for the Doctor and me.

In 'The Sensorites', the inhabitants of the Sense Sphere experience a neurodivergence from the humans who visit them. They bond with Susan through their shared telepathic abilities, but the First Doctor fails to empathise with their hypersensitivity. The Sensorites cringe when the Doctor shouts, with Susan explaining that they register the noise as an attack. While the Doctor describes this as 'inhuman' and 'monstrous', Susan explains to them that they 'didn't mean to use sound as a weapon.' Neurodivergent relationships to sound and music are often the result of heightened levels of sensory processing sensitivity. In the 1990s, the psychologists Elaine and Arthur Aron developed the SPS framework to explain why some people have increased reactivity, both positive and negative, to physical, social, and emotional stimuli – described as a highly sensitive person (HSP). The symptoms of being an HSP are related to our depth of processing, needing to take time to perceive and process external and internal input such as sound, light, feelings, and information. The Arons estimated that this categorisation accounts for about 15 to 20 percent of people.

Being hypersensitive led me to co-found Stims Collective with neurodivergent filmmakers Georgia Kumari Bradburn and Sam Chown Ahern which curates 'relaxed' cinema screenings for a neurodiverse audience. This involves keeping the lights on at a low level, decreasing the volume, and allowing people to move freely, including in a quiet area outside the auditorium. Many neurodivergent people adjust their personal sound levels in and out of the cinema through earplugs or headphones. Some sounds are violent, sudden, and atonal, which prompt distress and overwhelming sensory negativity, which is why 'relaxed' environment guidelines encourage venues to turn off hand dryers, for example, or request that audiences do not applaud. However, other sounds, especially music, can have a powerful positive impact on neurodivergent people. In the Arons' Highly Sensitive Person Scale questionnaire, both 'I am made uncomfortable by loud noises' and 'I am deeply moved by the arts or music' are likely to be true of an HSP.

A lot of neurodivergent people also show symptoms of misophonia, which typically displays itself as visceral irritation triggered by noises such as chewing. The distress caused can, for many, be alleviated by music, in much the same way as dissonance can be resolved. Where a scene in a restaurant or other busy environment can be too loud, the same volume of classical music might be non-distressing, even pleasant. Many neurodivergent people play loud music through headphones to drown out or 'resolve' the hubbub of life. When the Second Doctor is thinking, or angry, and trying to calm himself, he plays his recorder. This frustrates others, including the Brigadier in 'The Three Doctors', who does not understand why the Doctor is so distressed to have lost 'some damn fool flute!' The Twelfth Doctor similarly plays his electric guitar, especially when he is sad. In 'Hell Bent' he enters Eddie's Diner and starts to play a song called 'Clara', although he cannot remember the woman it is about. These means of sensory comfort have a self-contained, individual logic which others fail to understand.

TREATISE ON HARMONY

'Indifference to music's emotional power may occur in people with Asperger's syndrome', writes Sacks in *Musicophilia*, his study of psychology and music. He takes Grandin again as his subject, saying that she was fascinated by musical form especially in the compositions of J.S. Bach. 'Music, she said, did not "move" her, move her to the depths, as it apparently could (she had observed) with other people.' Yet Sacks found that Grandin's experience was contradicted by a period he spent during the 1970s working with young neurodivergent people in a hospital ward. He brought in a piano, and discovered that it was only through music that he could make contact with the non-verbal children.

In the *Torchwood* novel *Into the Silence* by Sarah Pinborough a non-verbal child called Ryan stays at the Havannah Court Autism Centre after his mother, Adrienne Scott, found his needs too complex to manage. Despite not talking, the child sings beautifully: 'As always when her boy sang, the haunting emotional quality he created with his voice made it almost impossible for anyone seeing him for the first time to really believe he could be so disconnected from people.' He imitates the emotions of the singer without seemingly being capable of articulating his own feelings. After Adrienne is killed by an alien from the Silent Planet, Ryan sings the 'Pie Jesu' from Fauré's *Requiem in D minor* and touches the creature's face. Captain Jack claims that the alien is comparable to the autistic child, seeking connection by following the music, and he allows it to take Ryan with it back through the Rift. The representation of autism is clunky, and the mother's attitude to her son is difficult to read. However there is resonance to the idea of a neurodivergent individual identifying more readily with an alien than neurotypical humans, with music as the only means of getting through.

'The drumming. Can't you hear it? I thought it would stop, but it never does. Never ever stops. Inside my head, the drumming, Doctor. The constant drumming.' The Master is plagued in 'The Sound of Drums' by a rhythm even the Tenth Doctor says he cannot hear. In 'Last of the Time Lords' he claims that it entered his mind as a child when he looked into the Time Vortex, describing it as a call to war. It is still there in 'The End of Time', in which Rassilon describes the pattern as 'a rhythm of four. The heartbeat of a Time Lord.' The Master's insanity is the result of a sensitivity to his own body and time itself. 'Music can be pleasant, but a simple repetition like that, it's merely a distraction from the inevitable. Hope is its own form of cruelty', says the Landlord in 'Knock Knock' after a record gets stuck, preventing his tenant Pavel from being absorbed into the house. He taps his tuning fork to awaken the insects he found in the garden as a boy. Maestro uses this implement in 'The Devil's Chord' to unlock the song hidden in Ruby's soul – 'Carol of the Bells', as heard on the night when her mother left her at the church on Ruby Road. The episode begins with a lesson about the sinister tritone which was banned by the Mediaeval Church, believing it to be capable of summoning the Devil. Like the Master's drumbeat, humans have an arpeggio placed inside their minds by the Toymaker in 'The Giggle'. The Seventh, and then Eighth, Doctor's record player sticks on the word 'time' in 'The Movie', breaking the peace they have created in the TARDIS. I think of the words my brain gets stuck on, spiralling earworms of musical phrases which refuse to leave. It all gets too much.

'Well this is gay. Why all the music?' the Second Doctor asks the Pilot of the colony he visits in 'The Macra Terror'. He informs him that they regulate their day with music, bringing them together in unison. Connection through music is an essential component of 'Gridlock', which sees the return of the Macra. The people of New Earth are stuck in their cars on the motorway, isolated in small groups or on their own. Yet every day they share in the daily contemplation, singing hymns such as 'The Old Rugged Cross' and 'Abide With Me' together in an act of solidarity. I find Christian music to have a reassuring effect, attending Evensong to hear the choir singing. It brings people together in harmony, a shared language which ignores difference.

Chloe and Trish Webber sing the Australian nursery rhyme 'Kookaburra' to drown out the drawing of their abusive father and husband in 'Fear Her'. The Siren in 'The Curse of the Black Spot' uses her wordless song as an anaesthetic for her patients in a sick bay, and in 'Cold War' the elderly Grisensko encourages Clara to sing 'Hungry Like the Wolf' by Duran Duran with him to give them courage.

Clara tells him that might work if this was *Pinocchio* (1940), but music is always shown to bring comfort even in the most challenging moments. Abigail performs 'Silence Is All You Know' in 'A Christmas Carol', her voice resonating in the ice crystals which causes them to align as clouds and trigger snow to fall. The Eleventh Doctor tells Clara in 'The Rings of Akhaten' that the people are singing 'The Long Song' to the Old God, a lullaby without end which feeds him while he sleeps. The ending of 'Twice Upon a Time' sees Captain Archibald Hamish Lethbridge-Stewart return to the trenches as the Christmas truce begins in 1914 when German soldiers sang 'Stille Nacht', echoed by the British as 'Silent Night'. 'For one day, one Christmas, a very long time ago, everyone just put down their weapons, and started to sing. Everybody just stopped. Everyone was just kind', the Twelfth Doctor says. In 'The Eaters of Light' he tells Missy that while she understands the universe, she has never learned to hear its music. She opens her mind and heart to the Pictish tones, causing a tear to emerge. Music holds enormous power in the Whoniverse, with compositions being capable of resting gods, opening the skies, and ending wars. It brings courage and companionship where all else fails, affecting even the most hardened Time Lord.

'Neurodivergence plus confidence plus liberalism and a splash of libertarianism. Is that the Doctor?' Murray Gold wondered when I asked him about his thoughts on the relationship between the show he has worked on as composer since 2005 and neurodiversity. He told me that he tries not to think too much about his work, with which he has 'an intensely personal relationship' filled with endless doubts and insecurity:

> *Sometimes I think my openness and curiosity are my secret weapons. People have spoken about a directness and*

> *transparency to my music. I wouldn't disagree with this. Honestly if anyone says my music is terrible, I would most likely agree with them and apologise – a lot of people did when I started working on Doctor Who. But I suspect there might be something quite sincere, honest, and critically not-phoney about it.*

This is something which came up in several conversations I had with neurodivergent fans of the show, who said that they appreciate the emotional hand-holding offered by Murray's scoring. They concur with his assessment that there is something friendly, generous, warm, and benevolent about the music of *Doctor Who*, reaching out both to the characters on screen and the audience at home. He told me that he thinks that the forcefulness of his music connects to 'the moral crusade' which is strong in children – 'They are very Manichaean and seem to really dislike moral ambiguity.' Some view the music as overly manipulative, but for others this is desirable – for those who struggle to navigate the complexities of human empathy and emotion, to have it guided through clear orchestral music is beneficial. One knows that the Doctor and their companions are joking around when the music is jaunty, and sincere when it becomes sentimental and grandiose. Many fans of the show listen to the music in isolation – I have been playing through the soundtracks on a loop as I write, motivated by the *Sturm und Drang* of 'I Am the Doctor' and 'The Shepherd's Boy'. They are made up of Wagnerian leitmotifs which perfectly capture each character, allowing them to appear in one's mind even when detached from visuals.

I was particularly devastated by 'Doomsday', which soundtracked Rose's exit, the haunting vocals keeping me awake at night and always making me cry. I equally appreciated the subtlety of Segun Akinola's music during the Thirteenth

Doctor's tenure, which luxuriated in the vast atmosphere of interstellar landscapes and changed the tone of the programme. I sit with these scores and close my eyes, transporting myself to another planet where I feel calmer and safer than I do on this Earth. It blocks out the noise which disturbs my brain, and grounds me in a familiar territory, one which is at the same time both strange and known.

WHAT DREAMS MAY COME

Neurodivergent Whovian Stuart Dodgson is a music teacher, trumpeter, and conductor. His earliest memories of *Doctor Who* are of the opening titles featuring the Fourth Doctor. 'I used to play with my toy bricks and pretend they were Daleks', he told me. 'I put two together, one on top of the other, and then, in my mind, they were Daleks. I must have seen 'Destiny of the Daleks' which was broadcast in September 1979. I had just turned three.' When I describe vivid memories from when I was two or three years old, people tell me that cannot be possible, but for many neurodivergent people it is. I suspect there is a connection between Stuart's love of music and the vibrancy of his visual imagination, just as there is in my own mind.

Sometimes the photographic quality of my memory can be beneficial, yet it can also make it more difficult to process trauma and forget the past. When I was undergoing Cognitive Behavioural Therapy I found it useful to visualise a place where I felt peace and comfort – standing in the garden of my grandparents' house during the spring as a child, my bare feet sinking into the grass and the smell of lavender filling the air. I use essential oils to take me there, to calm me when I am overwhelmed or experiencing flashbacks. On several occasions in *Doctor Who* humans are advised to focus on something homely to keep them calm during a crisis. In 'Time-Flight', Hayter tells Angela to fight the telepathic crystal by focusing her mind on something she is sure of, such as her family or fish and chips. The Ninth Doctor takes Rose back to Earth in 'The End of the World' to reassure her that everything is still as it was in her own time. She smells chips and decides she wants to eat some before going back into the TARDIS. The newly regenerated Tenth Doctor reassures her that 'fish and chips, sausage and mash, beans on toast' are all waiting for her at home if she wants to go back in 'Born Again', as he does in 'Planet of the Dead' for the people he is trying to save – 'Food and home and people. Hold on to that, because we're going to get there. I promise. I'm going to get you home.' As Dorothy says, tapping her ruby slippers together in *The Wizard of Oz* (1939), there's no place quite like it.

In *Explaining Humans*, Pang describes disturbances to her sleep. 'I can't stop feeling anxious about the colour orange and the texture of biscuits in my head, and the smell of new shampoo on my pillow', she writes, relating insomnia to ADHD and her obsessive thoughts and fears with autism. My nightmares are anxiety-fuelled hellscapes created out of endlessly frustrating dream logic, sometimes pleasant but more often bizarre contortions of projected reality. Stuart told me that he was terrified by 'Kinda' as a child: 'I remembered the black space that Tegan was trapped in for all my childhood, and the duplication of her and not knowing which one was real.' The Mara sought physical existence by taking over a host through their dreams. While Tegan believed she had rid herself of it, in 'Snakedance' the malevolent being returned. It is discovered that the Great Crystal is the source of the Mara's power, absorbing what was in their minds, the 'restlessness, the hatred, the greed' and amplifying it. Like stimming, the only way to purify it is through the Snake Dance. It is unsurprising that such a villain haunted a neurodivergent child such as Stuart, whose visual imagination and sensitivity were already heightened. Ace asks the Seventh Doctor what his pet hates are in 'Ghost Light' after he takes her to a house which frightened her when she was thirteen years old. He cites burnt toast and bus stations before mentioning unrequited love, tyranny, and cruelty. Celery might comfort the Fifth Doctor and ultimately save his life, but for me the smell, taste, and texture is intolerable, as is the sound which organza makes when rubbed together. Such intense feelings were noted in my autism assessment when I received my diagnosis.

Luke is confused when Sarah is frightened in 'The Day of the Clown', having witnessed her remain stoic throughout *The Sarah Jane Adventures*. She tells him that when she was a child her Aunt Lavinia had a room of toys including a clown marionette which appeared to watch her during a storm. It was the first time she cried for her parents, who died when she was a baby. Luke's bad dreams are the subject of 'The Nightmare Man', overhearing his mother tell K9 that she will not miss him when he leaves home because he was only good for crosswords and emptying the bins. Both Smiths demonstrate an anxiety about abandonment, of being ostracised on the basis of their backgrounds and the uniqueness of their minds.

The manipulation of fear is explored in several *Doctor Who* stories. In 'The Satan Pit', the Tenth Doctor describes the Beast as 'a good psychologist' capable of playing on the basic fears of darkness and childhood nightmares to become a manifestation of every myth of the Devil. It lists each anxiety which consumes the members of the crew, including the captain who is 'scared of command' and the scientist 'still running from Daddy.' Each room of the hotel in 'The God Complex' is reserved for the greatest fear of its guests, labelled underneath their portraits in the lobby: defeat, having their photograph taken, Daleks, other people's socks, et cetera. Clara asks the Twelfth Doctor why she is experiencing a feeling of dread in 'In the Forest of the Night', to which he says that the woods have haunted the scary stories humanity has been telling each other for centuries. The Bogeyman in 'Space Babies' is a literal embodiment of the myth used to frighten children, roaring at seventeen hertz, the exact pitch which makes one scared. It is seen to be essential, for without our fears we are not driven towards success.

There is no time for nightmares in 'Sleep No More', in which Professor Rassmussen's Morpheus cabinet enables users to concentrate their entire nocturnal experience into a single five-minute burst. The machine is designed to boost productivity, creating a generation of Wide-Awakes who are artificially well-rested. The Twelfth Doctor quotes *Macbeth*: 'Sleep, that knits up the ravelled sleeve of care. The death of each day's life, sore labour's bath. Balm of hurt minds, chief nourisher in life's great feast.' He calls the invention an abomination for removing this vital part of existence, something which even he needs. My productivity refuses to follow a regular pattern. I have intense bursts of energy in which my brain works incredibly quickly and can produce large volumes of writing, but it will always be followed by a period of burnout in which I can scarcely do anything. Sleep is essential for managing these fluctuations, despite sometimes wishing that I had a Morpheus cabinet so I could carry on working through the night.

Eight-year-old George overhears an old woman struggling with her shopping bag in the lift adjacent to his bedroom in 'Night Terrors'. The sound terrifies the boy, calling for his mother who says that he needs to lock it away in the cupboard with everything else he does not like. He insists that she must 'do the thing'; that is, switch the light on and off. She does it four times, but he informs her that it must be five. His father, Alex, tells the Eleventh Doctor that it is difficult to admit that one's child has a problem, describing him as 'a funny kid' who has never cried. The Doctor discovers that George is a Tenza, an alien which came to Earth out of a need for a nest. After something scared him, it began a cycle of fear, that his parents are rejecting him. After asking how he can keep George if he is not human, Alex embraces the boy and says, 'Whatever you are, whatever you do, you're my son, and I will never, ever send you away.' George is an excellent representation of how it can feel to be neurodivergent as a child. Without diagnosis or an ability to express oneself, it can be an isolating experience as one is made to feel different or abnormal by parents who anticipate a certain path of development. George is hypersensitive, with an overwhelming visual imagination which makes everyday objects and sounds horrifying. It takes the Doctor to communicate with him through a shared understanding of the world, and to open his parents' minds to a different way of being human.

WORLDS OF FICTION

'If you make up the right story, then you think it will keep them safe and they'll all come home. That's okay. You're not the first person to ever have done that.' The Twelfth Doctor reassures Ashildr in 'The Girl Who Died' after he finds her playing with puppets in her room. I had a collection of *Doctor Who* figures when I was younger which lined my windowsill, standing guard on the threshold of the outside world. They were players in an array of adventures, from battles to talent contests and fashion shows. My childhood games kept me safe and occupied, giving me a sense of control over a world of my own design. When I was not playing, I was reading. In 'The Mind Robber', Jamie finds a machine which visualises works of literature on a screen, including *Treasure Island* and *Little Women*. The world they have discovered, populated by fictional heroes and villains from Gulliver to Medusa, is overseen by the Master of the Land of Fiction, a writer once capable of churning out five thousand words a week whose brain is the source of creative power for the entire operation. My toys would often leave the Whoniverse and venture into Narnia or Middle Earth, melding my imaginary worlds together to create endless possibilities. It was a realm in which I could easily lose myself.

The First Doctor stumbles into a fictional place in 'The Chase'. He describes it as preconditioned, created exactly as one might expect to find in a nightmare, a world of dreams. He tells Ian that he is convinced they are in an area of human thought, while the camera reveals to the audience that they were actually at 'Frankenstein's House of Horrors' at the Festival of Ghana in 1996. It is strange that the Doctor jumps to such a fantastical conclusion, perhaps the result of wishful thinking. They encounter the Monster created by Victor Frankenstein, a character who recurs in *Doctor Who*. The Seventh Doctor's regeneration into the Eighth is intercut with a morgue worker watching the 1931 film adaptation of *Frankenstein* on a television. It is the animation scene, in which the scientist proclaims, 'It's alive!' Luke is described by Sam Lloyd in 'The Mad Woman in the Attic' as having been made 'like Frankenstein', to which Luke of course informs him that he is like the creature, not the scientist.

While the comparison in these scenes is intended to refer to the bringing to life of a corpse in the former and the fusion of human elements by which Luke was created in the latter, Frankenstein's Monster is a useful analogy to neurodivergent experience. After escaping from their creator, they must learn about the world in a way which is constantly complicated. They attempt to learn language and how to interact with human beings – in the 1931 film, the Monster meets a little girl by a lake. They throw flowers on to the water together, observing that the pretty objects float. The Monster in turn throws the girl, but is horrified when she sinks and drowns, committing a deadly faux pas. A neurodivergent person might believe that they have understood a social convention, yet make a mistake which to them appeared logical.

The Cyberium enters Percy Bysshe Shelley's mind in 'The Haunting of Villa Diodati', causing him to have a vision of a death god rising from Hades – the Lone Cyberman. When Mary Shelley asks the Thirteenth Doctor what a Cyberman is, she describes, 'Someone altered. Organs, flesh surgically replaced with mechanical parts without consent. It drives them insane, so they alter the brain too, switch off all emotion.' Yet Ashad is unfinished, his flesh elements visible – he tells the Doctor that she irritates him, which she describes as too human for a Cyberman. The encounter inspires Mary to write her novel, a reflection on that which defines a soul: 'You didn't want to be this way. They hurt you, this modern Prometheus. You loved once. And were loved in return. You do not wish to kill.' He informs her that she is wrong to see the best in him, just as the girl by the lake should not have trusted the Monster. She attempts to get close to the lonely creature, but in so doing puts herself in danger.

Fear of being alone is what keeps the Doctor moving, although they too put all who travel with them in peril. A glimpse of their nightmares is seen through a telepathy device used by the Master in 'The Mind of Evil', revealing a Dalek. Yet this is less nuanced than later explorations of the Doctor's anxieties. In 'It Takes You Away', the Thirteenth Doctor tells Yaz that as a child her fifth grandmother told her a bedtime story about the Solitract, an exiled conscious universe: 'Think of it like a kid with chickenpox – nuclear chickenpox – who wants to join in but always ends up infecting everyone else.' This seems a more accurate description of what the Doctor fears about themself, that they can never truly be trusted. The Dream Lord in 'Amy's Choice' is a manifestation of this anxiety created by a speck of psychic pollen from the Candle

Meadows of Karass Don Slava which fell into the time rotor of the TARDIS. He tries to destroy the faith which Amy has in him, knowing that she should know better than to trust her Raggedy Man.

The Twelfth Doctor ruminates on his nightmares on two occasions. In 'Listen' he theorises that everyone experiences the same dream in which one wakes up to believe there is someone hiding in the dark. After sitting up, a hand grabs their ankle from underneath the bed. Clara finds herself in the barn on Gallifrey where the Doctor slept as a child because he did not want others to hear him crying at night, terrified of being forced to join the army rather than going to the Academy. When the boy sits up she instinctively grabs his ankle, and tells him that it was just a dream. She says that fear is a superpower, knowing that he will return to that barn in 'The Day of the Doctor' when he will be very afraid – 'But that's okay. Because if you're very wise and very strong, fear doesn't have to make you cruel or cowardly. Fear can make you kind.'

There is a portrait of Clara, cracking and peeling, on the wall of the castle inside the Doctor's Confession Dial in 'Heaven Sent'. A fly lands on it, which prompts the Doctor to recall another childhood memory, of a veiled corpse covered in flies on a hot day. 'So, who's been stealing my nightmares?' he asks. He is pursued by the Veil slowly to force him to make his confession, realising that he is in a 'fully automated haunted house' like the one he mistook for a mental reality in 'The Chase'. He admits that he has been lying by telling people that he left Gallifrey out of boredom, rather than because he was scared. He recites a story by the Brothers Grimm, 'The Shepherd Boy'. The emperor asks the boy how many seconds there are in eternity. He replies that there is a mountain of pure diamond, on which every hundred years a little bird sharpens its beak. When the entire mountain is chiselled away, the first second of eternity will have passed. 'You must think that's a Hell of a long time', the Doctor says. 'Personally, I think that's a Hell of a bird.' What frightens and overwhelms us can make us stronger, more resilient to a world which neurodivergent people have to carve their own way through. There is no manual for us, so we need to figure out the rules for ourselves, but ultimately many of us are able to push forwards. Sometimes it just takes a few adjustments to get things right.

CHAPTER ELEVEN

THE GOD COMPLEX

The Twelfth Doctor: **I'm terrified.**
Clara Oswald: **Of what?**
The Twelfth Doctor: **The answer to my next question, which must be honest and cold and considered, without kindness or restraint. Clara, be my pal and tell me, am I a good man?**
Clara Oswald: **I don't know.**
The Twelfth Doctor: **Neither do I.**

'Into the Dalek'

The Doctor is far from perfect. They differ from the traditional hero in that they do not have an infallible moral compass. They are not an absolutist, capable of bending the rules of good and evil in order to make sense of an array of ethical problems. If the Doctor has powers, they are of intelligence, experience, and kindness above physical strength. 'The Doctor is someone flawed and hurt and lonely striving constantly to be better than they know they might be, to be on everyone's side, to find the beauty and value in everything in and of itself', Rob Burton observed to me. Yet Alexis Harrow noted something more sinister in our conversation:

> *The Doctor is very happy to let atrocious things happen to keep the status quo. The Doctor is a hypocrite. This is one of the*

> *biggest things that I think conflicts with my neurodivergence and my want for there to be a black-and-white good and bad.*

It can be challenging for neurodivergent people to accept a flawed hero, and to move on when they do something bad. I was reluctant to accept the Twelfth Doctor – he was arrogant and rude, and when he asked Clara if he was a good man I no longer felt certain of the answer myself.

One area of the Doctor's morality which is contradictory is their approach to violence. The Thirteenth is their most vocally pacifist incarnation, chastising Ryan and Graham in 'The Ghost Monument' for wanting to use guns. 'You can't out-think bullets', says Graham, to which she responds, 'Been doing it all my life.' Yet the Doctor has not always condemned violence. The First seems to contemplate smashing the skull of a wounded man with a rock in 'An Unearthly Child', and although he reassures Ian in 'The Daleks' that, despite the Thals not being armed, 'the mind will always triumph', he forces them to fight their enemies. 'You know, I am so constantly outwitting the opposition, I tend to forget the delights and satisfaction of the arts, the gentle art of fisticuffs', he says to Vicki after duelling an assassin in 'The Romans'. The Third Doctor employs his skills in Venusian karate, capable of permanently paralysing someone by jabbing his thumb next to their collarbone.

These moments of aggression can be justified as self-defence, such as the Fifth Doctor's parrying and dodging of Sir Gilles Estram in 'The King's Demons'; the same incarnation who protested the possibility of him attacking Ann in 'Black Orchid' by saying that 'it wouldn't be cricket.' But his successor is actively hostile, believing himself to be superior to others. In 'The Twin Dilemma' the Sixth Doctor says that one should not 'finish up face down in a pool of one's own blood. Especially blood as noble as mine.' He wields a sonic lance in 'Attack of the Cybermen', in which he tells Peri to shoot a police officer. He even murders Shockeye by smothering him with cyanide-soaked cotton wool in 'The Two Doctors', and after causing two attendants to fall into an acid bath in 'Vengeance on Varos', he delivers a Bond-like quip: 'You'll forgive me if I don't join you.' This extraordinary change of character causes Valeyard to accuse the Doctor of having 'a well-known predilection for violence' in 'The Mysterious Planet' during 'The Trial of a Time Lord', with him admitting that he occasionally resorts to a modicum of force.

His successors lack such an explicit will to violence, although there are exceptions. The Seventh Doctor gleefully presents Ace with an electrified baseball bat for 'Dalek hunting' in 'Remembrance of the Daleks', and uses his umbrella to disarm the Cyberleader in 'Silver Nemesis'. The lack of humanoid features of the Doctor's robotic enemies seems to justify these actions, repeated again when the Ninth Doctor happily locks and loads a gun in 'Dalek'. 'What're you going to do, throw your A-Levels at 'em?' he mocks Adam, the opposite mantra to his later female self. He contradicts this approach in 'The Doctor Dances', revealing that he destroyed the weapon factories of Villengard to make way for a banana grove – 'I like bananas. Bananas are good.' The Tenth Doctor wields a sword after his regeneration in 'The Christmas Invasion', challenging the Sycorax leader to a duel. After extending mercy to him, the leader attempts to fight again, with the Doctor casually throwing a satsuma at a button which causes him to fall to his death. 'No second chances. I'm that sort of a man', he coolly says without looking back. The violence of the Doctor is one of the most noticeable areas in which their personality shifts, contradicting the most essential elements of their character.

TO BE A GOD

The neurodivergent inclination to view morality in binary terms can lead to the belief that they must be right to follow strict rules. When I was growing up, I had an almost evangelical approach to faith – I hung on every word of church sermons and readings from the Bible, struggling to grasp the nuances of metaphor and allegory. I was determined to lead a life free from sin, and I viewed those who did not as inferior. It made for a very lonely existence, which coupled with burgeoning dysphoria and sexuality led to deeply unhealthy self-hatred. I was terrified of God, who was very real to me, as was the threat of hellfire and brimstone. Through conversation with priests and the adoption of a more agnostic, relativist approach to faith, I managed to move away from this adolescent conservatism to a morality which was kinder to myself and others. Such a blind and immature approach to Christianity is understandable to me now as the result of an autistic desire for clear, inviolable laws – something which getting older taught me was not possible, or, indeed, right.

Barbara is certain of her beliefs in 'The Aztecs', in which she is mistaken to be the reincarnation of a priest as a god called Yetaxa. The First Doctor warns her that she must not interfere in a human sacrifice, but she defies him by forbidding it from taking place. She does not consider the value which the man felt in being offered to the gods, causing more harm than she intended. Yet the Doctor leans into the divine power granted to him when he is mistaken by Achilles for Zeus in 'The Myth Makers'. He tells the hero to not hinder him or he will strike him with a thunderbolt, and informs Agamemnon that he has supernatural knowledge by saying that he knows his wife to be unfaithful.

The Doctor has fought many false gods, those who are convinced of their righteousness to a megalomaniacal degree. The Fourth Doctor encounters Sutekh in 'Pyramids of Mars' who destroyed his own planet, Phaester Osiris, and belittles the Time Lord as a 'grovelling insect.' He describes Sutekh's bringing of death as stemming from a fear of being rivalled in power by other intelligent lifeforms. Monarch similarly expresses a belief in his superiority in 'Four to Doomsday', claiming to have transcended 'flesh time' and desiring to travel beyond the Big Bang in the belief that he will meet himself there as creator of the universe. The Seventh Doctor faces the Gods of Ragnarok in 'The Greatest Show in the Galaxy', who order him to entertain them in a bid to stay alive. The Emperor of the Daleks in 'The Parting of the Ways' calls the Ninth Doctor 'the Heathen' for refusing to supplicate himself to his divinity, and Tzim-Sha argues that the Thirteenth Doctor herself made him a god in 'The Battle of Ranskoor Av Kolos'. Like Sutekh and Monarch, it is supernatural knowledge which the villain believes to have granted him such powers, just as the First Doctor cited himself when attempting to pass for Zeus.

Omega is a similar figure in the mythos of Gallifrey, claiming to be the creator of the Time Lords. In 'The Three Doctors', he demands for his mask to be removed, yet this is not possible because he lacks corporeal existence. Omega seeks to retrieve this in 'Arc of Infinity', meeting the Fifth Doctor in the Matrix which stores all of Time Lord knowledge. It is faith in Omega which justifies the god complex of the Time Lords themselves, that they are omniscient and have a duty to maintain the universe without direct interference. It is this central tenet of Gallifreyan law which the Doctor repeatedly breaks. At the end of 'The War Games', the Time Lords hold a trial for the War Lord, a rare event. The Second Doctor is brought forward as a witness, and is glad to see that justice still prevails on his home planet, although he remarks under his breath that 'they've lost their sense of humour.' The Doctor sees himself as more human than the rest of his people and capable of a less rigid approach to the rules – something which I also learned to embrace as I matured. The Time Lords exile the Doctor to Earth, for he cannot sit back and observe evil as they do.

The Doctor is more compliant with the orders of the Time Lords during his time at UNIT. The Fourth is employed on several missions, including averting the creation of his greatest enemy in 'Genesis of the Daleks' and finding the Key to Time. Yet the Sixth is tried again for his transgression of the First Law of Gallifrey. In 'The Mysterious Planet' he objects to the idea that the Matrix contains all knowledge, but rather all Time Lord knowledge, protesting that this is insular complacency – 'A micro-organism in a drop of water might think it knows the universe. All it knows is that drop of water.' He is more accepting of the limits of his mind than his brethren, and in 'The Ultimate Foe' he condemns them explicitly. He says that he should never have left Gallifrey because his own civilisation has been corrupted by ten million years of absolute power. Yet the Master reveals to him that Valeyard is actually an amalgamation of the darker sides of his own nature, placed on trial by himself. The evil he seeks to condemn is shown to also exist within the Doctor. No matter how far they run from Gallifrey, they can never shirk their heritage.

The Doctor attempts to assert his authority during his trial by citing his position as Lord President of Gallifrey, although he is informed that in his absence he was deposed. In 'The Deadly Assassin', this position is described as being passed down from Rassilon, the founder of their modern civilisation. He found the Eye of Harmony, which balances all things, sealed with the Great Key, an ebonite rod carried by the President on ceremonial occasions. The Fourth Doctor claims his right to the inheritance of Rassilon in 'The Invasion of Time', although he promptly decides to leave Gallifrey again – when Andred reminds him that he has access to the Matrix, the greatest source of knowledge in the universe, he replies, 'Well, I do talk to myself sometimes, yes.' Despite his arrogance, the Doctor has no desire to be a god. Borusa manipulates the Game of Rassilon in 'The Five Doctors' so that he can become President Eternal. Yet when he puts the Ring of Rassilon on his finger, granting immortality, he becomes a stone figure on the side of the Tomb of Rassilon. The First Doctor encourages him to do so, realising that it is a trap designed to do away with those who seek to live forever. Chancellor Flavia arrives to inform the Fifth that he has been appointed President, but he decides to give her full deputy powers until he returns. 'You mean you're deliberately choosing to go on the run from your own people in a rackety old TARDIS?' Tegan asks. 'Why not?' the Doctor replies. 'After all, that's how it all started.'

THE MASTER

'I am usually referred to as the Master', says the Doctor's intellectual equal when he arrives on Earth in 'Terror of the Autons'. He attacks the showman Luigi Rossini, whom he calls an 'insolent primitive.' A Time Lord appears before the Third Doctor to inform him that his enemy is near – 'You are incorrigibly meddlesome, Doctor, but we've always felt that your hearts are in the right places.' The Master's, by contrast, are not. In 'Colony in Space', he admires a civilisation which used genetic engineering to develop a super race. He wants the Doctor to join him in his pursuit to control the universe, to which he replies that he wishes to see it, not rule it. The Master's eugenicist beliefs are reminiscent of Francis Galton, who inspired the founding of the Eugenic Education Society in 1906. This institute endorsed involuntary euthanasia of the 'feeble-minded' alongside funds for the wealthy to reproduce. The British government voted in the Mental Deficiency Act in 1913 to begin segregation based on proximity to cognitive normality, a precursor to the 'Law for the Prevention of Hereditarily Diseased Offspring' instituted by the Nazis in Germany in 1935. Compulsory sterilisation was prescribed for neurodivergent people, followed by Aktion T4 in which the disabled were systematically exterminated. There is no room for neurodiversity in the Master Race.

'The Master is definitely an outsider, and there is that tension where the Doctor hates to admit that they relate to the Master more than they do to human beings', Esme Hayes remarked to me. 'The Doctor does hate the Master and thinks he's a dickhead but he has this kind of intuitive understanding.' She is correct to observe a unique affinity which exists between them. 'Well, he used to be a friend of mine once. A very good friend. In fact, you might almost say we were at school together', the Third Doctor admits to Jo in 'The Sea Devils'. I reflect on the 'friendships' I had when I was at school, often with other children who were obsessed with *Doctor Who*. I know some of them to have been diagnosed with autism, and the rivalry which came from trying to outsmart each other always caused any friendliness to break down. It is a complex form of interpersonal relationship which I see reflected in the dynamic between the Doctor and the Master.

After Professor Yana remembers his true identity and regenerates at the end of 'Utopia', he summons the Tenth Doctor to face him in 'The Sound of Drums'. The Master admits that he likes it when he uses the name he chose, which the Doctor describes as a 'psychiatrist's field day.' He reminds him that he also chose his: 'The man who makes people better. How sanctimonious is that?' He envies the Doctor for witnessing the Time War, saying that he must have felt like a god. Instead he says that he is lonely, and points out that all they have now is each other, to which the Master mockingly wonders if he is asking him out on a date. His response to the Doctor's sentimentality is to laugh at him for sounding gay, deflecting the truth of his own feelings of isolation. As the Toclafane descend, he says to his old friend in mock biblical speech, 'And so it came to pass that the human race fell, and the Earth was no more. And I looked down upon my new dominion as Master of all, and I thought it good.' I can hear my childhood self decrying his blasphemy. The Master believes he has a biological right to build a new empire lasting one hundred trillion years in 'Last of the Time Lords', a promise reminiscent of Adolf Hitler's declaration of a thousand-year Reich. He is defeated by the power of prayer, of the people of Earth thinking of the Doctor's name in unison to impact the Archangel Network. The Master curls into a ball like a child going into meltdown, and the Doctor embraces him. He utters the unthinkable: 'I forgive you.'

After the Master becomes Missy, her friendship with the Doctor becomes more explicit. When the Twelfth Doctor asks for her motivation in 'Death in Heaven', she says that she needs to make him see that they are not so different so that she can have her friend back. She gives him the power to decide the outcome of every war through the control of her Cybermen, asking if he trusts himself to act for good. It is Missy who makes him understand his moral position, that he is an idiot with a box and a screwdriver just passing through, helping out and learning all the time. She says that Gallifrey has returned to its original coordinates, and asks him to go with her, 'just like the old days'. In 'The Magician's Apprentice', Missy reveals to Clara that the Doctor gave his Confession Dial to her as his closest friend. She describes their attempts to destroy each other as 'sort of our texting', but when Clara mockingly replies, 'Must be love', Missy explodes: 'Oh, don't be disgusting. We're Time Lords, not animals. Try, nano-brain, to rise above the reproductive frenzy of your noisy little food chain, and contemplate friendship. A friendship older than your civilisation, and infinitely more complex.' She asserts the bond between her and the Doctor, of their divergent experience of life and the universe, something which a human can never understand.

'Come on, Lady Version. I honestly don't know what you see in him', the Master says to Missy upon his return in 'The Doctor Falls'. 'Likewise', comes her snide response. The Doctor makes a speech begging them to be kind. The Master says he did not listen, but Missy has changed. All he has ever wanted is for her to stand with him, to which she says, 'Me too. But no. Sorry. Just, no. But thanks for trying.' Yet when she finds herself alone with her male predecessor, she stabs him in the back. She says that the Doctor is right that it is time to stand with him, claiming it to be where they have always been going. He responds by shooting her with his laser screwdriver – 'Our perfect ending.' The Master never makes up their mind, desiring competition with the Doctor since they compared grades at the Academy on Gallifrey. Intellectual rivals, sparring across the universe.

THE RIGHT TO KILL

In 'Genesis of the Daleks', the Fourth Doctor is informed that the Time Lords allow him to enjoy his freedom if occasionally he does something for them in return. They foresee a time when the Daleks have destroyed all other lifeforms, causing them to instruct the Doctor to return to Skaro at the point of their creation and destroy them. He discovers that they are not machines but genetically mutated beings engineered by Davros from the humanoid Kaleds. He is left only with the option to wipe out the race altogether. He holds two wires in his hands which will detonate the explosives in the incubation room containing the Daleks. 'Have I that right?' he asks, and Sarah says he cannot doubt it. He wonders what the universe without them would be like, for good has come from fear of the enemy:

> *Listen, if someone who knew the future pointed out a child to you and told you that that child would grow up totally evil, to be a ruthless dictator who would destroy millions of lives, could you then kill that child?*

'Do I have the right?' The Doctor asks a second time. In 'The Magician's Apprentice', the Twelfth Doctor wonders how scared an individual must be to seal each of their own kind inside a tank, as Davros had done. He seems to believe that his younger self was wrong to decide that out of evil there must come something good, and that he should have destroyed the Daleks when he had the chance. Davros gives him that opportunity again in 'The Witch's Familiar', asking the Doctor if he is ready to be a god. He says that he came to see Davros out of compassion as he believed him to be dying, and when he informs the scientist that Gallifrey has returned, he is shocked when he congratulates him. Davros switches off his blue eye to use his own sight to look at the Doctor and ask him if he did right by protecting his own kind. He shares the Doctor's own inner quandary: 'Was I right? I need to know before the end. Am I a good man?' Out of trust, he gives Davros enough regeneration energy to allow him to open his eyes, but it is a trap. The episode ends with the Doctor using the TARDIS not to kill the child Davros, but to save him. 'I'm not sure that any of that matters, friends, enemies. So long as there's mercy. Always mercy.' This is the Doctor's guiding moral principle, something the Daleks never give.

It is difficult, then, to witness our hero break it. In 'Remembrance of the Daleks', the Seventh Doctor uses the Hand of Omega, which the Time Lord creator used to manipulate the stars, to turn Skaro's sun supernova and wipe out the Dalek homeworld. 'We wanted to live forever, so the Doctor made sure that we did', narrates Son of Mine at the end of 'The Family of Blood', telling of how the Tenth Doctor never raised his voice as he carried out their punishments – wrapping the Father in unbreakable chains forged in the heart of a dwarf star, tricking the Mother into the event horizon of a collapsing galaxy, trapping the Daughter inside every mirror, and suspending the Son in time as a scarecrow keeping watch over the fields of England. 'The fury of the Time Lord, being kind.' The scientist Kahler-Jex is being hunted by the Gunslinger as a war criminal in 'A Town Called Mercy', having experimented on humanoid subjects and fused their bodies with weaponry. Pointing a gun at Jex, the Doctor says he genuinely does not know if he would not kill him. Amy stops him, asking when murder became an option:

> *But they keep coming back, don't you see? Every time I negotiate, I try to understand. Well, not today. No. Today, I honour the victims first. His, the Master's, the Daleks', all the people who died because of my mercy!*

Jex informs him that in his culture they believe that in the afterlife one's spirit carries the souls of everyone they have wronged up a mountain, which is why he fears death. 'We all carry our prisons with us', he says. 'Mine is my past. Yours is your morality.' The Doctor's anger gets the better of him at times, frustrated by the lack of a clear answer of what is right.

'Waste no more time arguing about what a good man should be. Be one.' This line from *Meditations* by Marcus Aurelius is recited by Clara at the beginning of 'The Day of the Doctor', a mantra to exist for good rather than overthink it. The greatest moral question of the Doctor's life lies before him in the Moment which will end the Time War by wiping out the Time Lords and the Daleks alike. The interface tells him that he will always carry the trauma of his decision with him, one day counting all the children who died on Gallifrey because of him. While the War Doctor accepts their decision, the

Eleventh refuses, bringing together all of their predecessors to alter their personal history, simultaneously ending the War and saving their home planet.

It terrifies the Empress of the Racnoss in 'The Runaway Bride' when the Tenth Doctor reveals that he is from Gallifrey, for the Time Lords destroyed her kind. He allows her children to burn and drown, watching over the carnage with rage. Donna tells him that he can stop, and later says that she was scared because he was able to watch those creatures die as though he was 'a stranger.' She makes him promise her that he will find someone to travel with 'because sometimes, I think you need someone to stop you.' The Doctor appears frighteningly dispassionate, a clinical detachment which his companions cannot bear. Donna refuses to go with him, but comes to regret it, finding normal life to no longer cut the mustard. They reunite in 'Partners in Crime' during their concurrent investigations into Adipose Industries. She asks if they are going to blow up the blobs of fat, to which the Doctor says that they are just children and cannot help where they come from – a revelation to Donna after he was happy to watch the children of the Racnoss suffer.

THE RIGHT TO SAVE

More complex for Donna is the Doctor's morality when it comes to changing history. In 'The Fires of Pompeii' she wants to save everyone, knowing that Vesuvius will soon erupt, but he tells her that they must not. After developing a friendship with Caecilius and his family she begs him to save someone, 'not the whole town. Just save someone.' The TARDIS appears like a *deus ex machina* as the Doctor is cast in blinding light, reaching out a hand to Caecilius as ash from the volcano falls on him like snow. It is a step too far, however, an act which would surely have seen him put on trial if the High Council still existed. He and Donna are honoured by the Caecilius family as their household gods, having bestowed himself with a divine right.

This complex worsens in 'The Waters of Mars' when the Doctor visits Bowie Base One in 2059, another fixed point in which all of the crew were killed. He tells Adelaide Brooke that she begins a journey which takes the human race to the stars as her work inspires her granddaughter to become the pilot of the first lightspeed ship to Proxima Centauri – information he describes as 'consolation.' She asks the Doctor to help her, and after he decides to do so, she questions it. He says that she can inspire her granddaughter face-to-face now. 'You can't know that. And if my family changes, the whole of history could change. The future of the human race. No one should have that much power', she says. 'Tough', proclaims the Time Lord Victorious. He says that he has often saved 'little people' but never anyone as important as Adelaide, which horrifies her. She takes matters into her own hands, shooting herself upon entering her house, forcing the Doctor to realise he has gone too far.

Adelaide is far from the first person to have died as a direct result of the Doctor's actions. Davros deems it his final victory in 'Journey's End' to show the Doctor himself – that he takes ordinary people and fashions them into weapons, his 'Children of Time', not dissimilar to the creation of the Daleks. Harriet Jones dies in his name, and Davros asks how many more have done so. The Toymaker stages the deaths of his companions in the form of a puppet show in 'The Giggle' to show Donna the damage her friend has done since he left her. The Doctor tries to justify each in turn, to which the Toymaker cries, 'Well, that's all right then!' As far back as 'The Daleks' Master Plan' companions were shown to be expendable – Bret, Katarina, and Sara are all killed during the course of the serial, which the First Doctor deems 'a terrible waste.' They are not aware of the impact they have, and the fear their power inspires. When the Eleventh appears in 'A Good Man Goes to War' he tells the army to point a gun at him if it helps them to relax – 'You're only human.' He meets a soldier called Lorna Bucket, who as she lies dying tells him that they met in the Gamma Forests. He lies and says he remembers her, turning to Vastra to ask who she was. She was brave, she says, and the Doctor observes that they always are. It falls upon River to force him to understand the consequences of his actions:

> *When you began, all those years ago, sailing off to see the universe, did you ever think you'd become this? The man who can turn an army around at the mention of his name. Doctor. The word for healer and wise man throughout the universe. We get that word from you, you know. But if you carry on the way you are, what might that word come to mean?*

River says that she was a babe in arms, the child of the Doctor's closest friends, when she was stolen to be turned into a weapon out of fear of him. It can be challenging for neurodivergent people to understand the relationship between cause and effect, narrowly focused on their own actions and intentions without appreciating the impact they have on those around them. I have had this explained to me throughout my life, just as River does with the Doctor. It can be difficult to hear, but always vital.

'So is this how it works, Doctor? You never interfere in the affairs of other peoples or planets, unless there's children crying?' Amy figures him out in 'The Beast Below'. She chooses to forget that she knows Starship UK is built on the back of the last Star Whale because she knows that if they stay the Doctor will have to choose between humans and the creature. He is furious that she took it upon herself to save him from that decision. He decides to euthanise the whale by passing an electrical charge through its brain, knowing that he must then find a new name because he will no longer be the Doctor. Amy realises that if they release the whale it will voluntarily continue to carry the ship, recognising a similarity to the last of the Time Lords – all the pain, misery, and loneliness has made it kind. She has a deep faith in the Doctor akin to religion, ever since she waited for him as a child. This faith is tested in 'The God Complex', just as the Seventh Doctor broke Ace's trust in him in 'The Curse of Fenric'. 'I took you with me because I was vain. Because I wanted to be adored', he admits, telling Amy Williams to stop waiting for him.

A child cries again in 'The Girl Who Died'. Clara observes that they stop when the Doctor decides to stay and help the village against the Mire. He tells her that he is sick of losing people after Ashildr dies, saying that he can do anything but is not supposed to. He notices his reflection and realises that he chose the face of Caecilius as a reminder of his power to save anyone he wants. To Hell with the Time Lords – yet as Rassilon discovered, immortality is a curse and not a blessing which Ashildr comes to resent the Doctor for granting her. In 'Face the Raven' he encounters her again, as Me. Clara takes Rigsy's chronolock which means that her soul must be given to the Quantum Shade, a fact which the Doctor refuses to accept. He rages at Me, telling her that he will rain Hell on her for all time, to which Clara points out that his 'reign of terror will end with the sight of the first crying child and you know it.' She tells the Doctor to listen to her, and his eyes move about frantically, refusing to make eye contact. He appears to be going into meltdown. 'You're going to be alone now, and you're very bad at that', she says, repeating that he needs to listen to her and do what she says. 'You don't be a warrior. Promise me. Be a Doctor.'

LAWS REWRITTEN

Clara knows that she has to enforce eye contact with the Doctor to ensure he is paying attention. She demands it of him again in 'Hell Bent' when she needs to know how long the Doctor spent trapped in the Confession Dial. Ohila says that it was four-and-a-half billion years, which the Doctor explains by repeating that he had a duty of care. He returned to Gallifrey, lying on his childhood bed in the barn, and brought down Rassilon to rule his home once more just to bring Clara back. They steal a Type 40 capsule, and he panics as he realises his plan to start her heart again has not worked. Before he loses his memory of her, he offers some advice – never be cruel or cowardly, laugh at everything, and never eat pears because they are too squishy and make your chin wet. Clara flies off with Me back to Gallifrey, albeit 'the long way round', their capsule's Chameleon Circuit stuck in the guise of an American diner. The rules are kept, but they can be bent.

The lore of Gallifrey was altered for the Thirteenth Doctor, causing her to have an existential crisis. The Master tells her in 'Spyfall Part Two' that he destroyed their home after discovering the lies they had been told about the founding fathers. She learns this for herself in 'The Timeless Children' after entering the Chamber of the Matrix. Before the Time Lords existed there was a Shobogan explorer called Tecteun who discovered a boundary into another unknown dimension or universe. There lay an abandoned child which she adopted, an infant capable of regeneration. Tecteun studied them and spliced into herself this genetic ability which began the Time Lord race. This child was, of course, the Doctor. Memories of her incarnations before the First Doctor are revealed to have been wiped from her memory owing to her work with the Division. She meets Tecteun in 'Survivors of the Flux', 'the woman you used to call Mother', telling her that she should have left her because she might have been retrieved by her own people. 'You judge me for giving you the journey of your lifetime', Tecteun replies. 'What do you do, Doctor? Pick people up, take them with you? You adopt them, use them, for reassurance, for company. They're your experiments, just as you were mine.' The Doctor could retrieve her memories from a fob watch in which Tecteun stored them, just as the Tenth Doctor's identity was once hidden by the Chameleon Arch. She wonders if she really wants to know.

'Why do you want this diagnosis?' the doctor asked me. Many have questioned the value of diagnosis, but for me it was an affirmation. I know that my mind works in a different way to others, which allows me to articulate and understand myself. It means that when I find something challenging or overwhelming I can get the help and adjustments I need without always needing to explain or justify myself. I can identify the strengths of my brain and hone them, allowing myself to flourish in ways I struggled to navigate prior to knowing more about autism. I think of my relationship with my grandmother and recognise that our affinity was created by a shared neurodivergence. It makes me interested in my heritage, in where I have come from, and the influence I might have on my own children. By talking about autism and neurodiversity I inspire questioning in others about the typicality of their own minds, sometimes leading them to seek diagnosis. I cannot open the fob watch of my past and change things, but I can accept my present and who I am today.

CHAPTER TWELVE

ROGUE

The Fifteenth Doctor: **It doesn't matter where I come from, because I am absolutely lovely, aren't I? That wasn't rhetorical, Pops.**
Poppy: **Yes, you are.**
The Fifteenth Doctor: **And do you want to know my secret? There's no one like me in the whole wide universe. No one like me exists, and that's true of everyone. It's not a problem, Captain Pops. It's a superpower. High five!**

'Space Babies'

In the 1999 Channel Four drama *Queer as Folk*, Vince asks his boyfriend how many actors he can name who have played the Doctor. He manages Jon Pertwee and Tom Baker before demanding to know why it matters. Vince uses this question to determine whether or not to break up with him, which he does. A neurodivergent fan asked the same of David Tennant in a 2025 episode of ITV's *The Assembly*, taking it in turns to name them all. It is the most basic question a Whovian can ask, appealing to a neurodivergent love of listmaking and trivia – many of us, of course, have every episode or even every cast list memorised. To use it as a determining factor in a relationship is striking, yet for Vince it is something to be taken very seriously.

The 2001 play *Regenerations*, written by Daragh Carville and broadcast on BBC Radio Three, follows the relationship between two gay male fans at a *Doctor Who* convention in Belfast. One is frustrated that the other clings to his obsession with what he deems a children's programme, paralleled by his own Catholic guilt around his sexuality. Less sympathetic is the sketch 'The Kidnappers' starring Mark Gatiss and David Walliams, broadcast during 'Doctor Who Night' on BBC Two in 1999, in which two Whovians capture Peter Davison. Mark asks David if it would be all right to kiss Peter, before switching the light off. Homosexuality and *Doctor Who* had become synonymous, be that as the subject of mockery or celebration. Queer groups include the Sisterhood of Karn which has met regularly in Soho since 1994, and the Gallifrey Cabaret which tours across the United Kingdom. Russell T Davies, who wrote *Queer as Folk*, was the lead writer for the revival of *Doctor Who* in 2005, and returned to the role in 2023. He regularly works with queer writers and directors, and with the casting of Ncuti Gatwa as the Fifteenth Doctor, depicted the Time Lord as queer themself.

'The Doctor doesn't have love for a gender, in my mind', Bella Madge said to me. 'It was always for the people he brings along. It always felt non-sexual.' This was true of the Doctor in the classic era, although it is easy to see why the character held a gay appeal prior to NuWho. They were always an outsider who never settles down, who wears camp clothing and enjoys the platonic company of women. These attributes are taken further in the characterisation of the Fifteenth Doctor. However his confident sexuality is a contradiction to many of the elements discussed in this book in relation to neurodivergence. Ian Palmer expressed this to me:

> *I'm unsure about this Doctor as he lacks the quirkiness and eccentricities. He's too normal and socially well-adapted compared to other incarnations. I feel like we are lacking their alien side. It's also the first time I am not seeing myself in them. It's sad that they have been changed so much, it's like a deliberate choice to remove the neurodivergence from the character and that feels alienating to me as a fan.*

This is a view which most of the neurodivergent Whovians I spoke to expressed. None of them said that they disliked the Fifteenth Doctor and Gatwa's performance, but there was consensus that he is not the Doctor in the same way as previous incarnations. It is never about their gender, their sexuality, or the colour of their skin – it is about how their mind works.

LET'S DANCE

The closest precedent to the flirty Fifteenth Doctor was Captain Jack, a Time Agent first seen in 'The Empty Child' spying on Rose and remarking, 'Excellent bottom.' He promptly turns to his companion Algy and says that he has an excellent bottom too. Rose is swept off her feet by Jack – he takes her onto the roof of his invisible spaceship, tethered to the Elizabeth Tower, where they drink champagne as London burns. The Tenth Doctor is petty when Jack returns in 'Utopia', describing his vortex manipulator as a space hopper compared to his TARDIS sports car. He informs the Captain that he left him behind after Rose brought him back to life in 'The Parting of the Ways' because he was 'wrong', meaning that his existence violates the laws of the Time Lords. It seems he reserves the rules for the man he can never be – suave, charming, and never without company. There is a flirtation between them, at least from Jack's perspective. When he says he could go and meet himself, the Doctor replies that he is the only man he will ever be happy with, prompting Jack to describe his new regeneration as 'kind of cheeky.' There is more than a glint of jealousy in the Doctor's eye.

Jack's difference to the Time Lord is asserted in *Torchwood* through his blasé approach to violence. In 'Cyberwoman' he points a gun at Ianto and says that if he does not kill Lisa he will kill them both. 'You act like a hero but you're the biggest monster of all', his sometime lover replies. His romantic attachment to Ianto is unusual, as Jack frequently neglects his companions by disappearing and reappearing in the nick of time. His immortality distinguishes him from humans just as it does for the Doctor, giving him a different sense of consequence. The coldness of his behaviour is contrasted by the mortal Gwen Cooper, who is down-to-earth and caring. She has a typical, heterosexual domestic life which informs her approach to saving the world in a way which Jack cannot understand.

The Ninth Doctor asks Rose why she trusts Jack in 'The Doctor Dances', and she tells him that he is like him 'except with dating and dancing.' He informs her that he has indeed danced in his nine hundred years of life, a word which becomes a euphemism for sex. Rose is taken aback when Jack flirts with Algy, with the Doctor informing her that he is a fifty-first-century man so he is more flexible with his dancing. He fumbles 'Moonlight Serenade' but finds 'In the Mood' more his tempo, remembering his moves and they dance together. When Rose says that she thinks Jack would like to take this one, the Doctor says he is sure that he would, but with whom? The Doctor's envy for the ease with which Jack interacts with his companion and other people frustrates him, something which he finds himself to lack a capacity for.

Such a change to the Doctor's character was introduced in 'The Movie' in which the Eighth incarnation takes on the role of a Hollywood leading man. He kisses Dr Grace Holloway, an action justified by the assertion by both the Master and the Doctor that he is half-human, on his mother's side. The Ninth flirts with Jabe from the Forest of Cheem in 'The End of World', gifting her air from his lungs and saying there is more where that came from. The Tenth kisses Astrid Peth twice in 'Voyage of the Damned', first after she grabs him by the lapels, and second initiated by him after she is rendered as stardust. He is attracted to Lady Christina de

Souza in 'Planet of the Dead', who responds in French when he says, 'Allons-y!' prompting him to remark that they were made for each other. After informing the Doctor that she was lying when she said she hated him, Christina pulls him in for a kiss, to the applause of their fellow passengers. The Eleventh advises the young Kazran Sardick in 'A Christmas Carol' to be awkward and rubbish at kissing Abigail because he is going to be anyway and might as well do it on purpose. He is perplexed by the two of them kissing at a Hollywood party, asking if they breathe out of their ears, yet he has lipstick on his face from Marilyn Monroe whom he dashes off to marry. After the Tenth marries Elizabeth I in 'The Day of the Doctor' and they kiss, the War Doctor asks, 'Is there a lot of this in the future?' The Eleventh has to admit, 'It does start to happen, yeah.'

GAY ALL OF A SUDDEN

When the Tenth Doctor's face returns as the Fourteenth in 'The Star Beast', he takes note that his approach to intimacy and relationships has changed. He tells Shirley Bingham that Donna is his best friend and he loves her. 'Oh. Mmm. Do I say things like that now?' Shirley remarks that it sounds like a good thing for him to say. His queerness is stated explicitly in 'Wild Blue Yonder', with the Doctor agreeing with Donna that Isaac Newton was 'so hot.' He asks her if that is who he is now, to which she jokes, 'Well, it was never that far from the surface, mate.' After his bi-generation, the Fifteenth Doctor wears his newfound sexuality with pride. The same Time Lord who struggled to dance with Rose is seen tearing up the dancefloor of a nightclub in 'The Church on Ruby Road'. He uses terms of endearment such as 'babes', and tells Ruby that he learnt escapology by spending 'a long, hot summer with Harry Houdini.'

Edward Smyth said that he does not see this as inconsistent with neurodivergence, knowing lots of neurodivergent people who love loud music and going clubbing. 'He feels like a very modern ND person, he has this real charm and beauty. But he is also very sensitive and cries a lot. He feels like he has got this real eccentricity, almost ADHD qualities.' He compared this to the Eleventh Doctor and the constant whirring of his brain and frantic movements. There have always been variations in the Doctor's taste. The Third enjoys drinking wine and eating cheese in 'Day of the Daleks', as does the Fourth in 'City of Death' when he takes Romana to a place he knows which does a wonderful bouillabaisse in Paris. Yet the Fifth refuses the invitation of a cocktail in 'Black Orchid', preferring to take a cold drink with him to his bath, and when the Eleventh drinks wine in 'The Impossible Astronaut' he spits it out like a child, claiming he thought it would taste more like the gums. His dancing skills have always been haphazard, as demonstrated by John Smith bumping into another couple while waltzing with Joan in 'Human Nature', and the Eleventh's performance of the 'drunk giraffe' at Amy's wedding in 'The Big Bang' and with the children of Christmas in 'The Time of the Doctor'.

The Fifteenth Doctor bears no such lack of finesse in his movements or hesitance in joining a party. He is thrilled upon arriving at a dance in 'Rogue', telling Ruby that he has given her psychic earrings which beam the choreography into her motor system: 'It's like instant *Strictly*.' He has popular culture knowledge which would have eluded his predecessors, accepting Ruby's Gen-Z reference to *Bridgerton* rather than Austen. Rogue behaves more like the Doctor we know – when the Time Lord says, 'Honey, I'm here for fun', the bounty hunter retorts, 'Then go and pursue your facile pleasures and leave me alone.' When Rogue tells him that he lives in solitude, the Doctor observes, 'Baby, I can see', adopting the role typically assumed by the companion. He lip syncs to Kylie Minogue before brandishing his psychic paper which, as it did for Jack and Rose, functions as a dating profile. The Doctor is flustered, which Rogue likes, allowing him to let his guard down and be more flirtatious. When the Doctor decides to create a scene in the ballroom by dancing with his fancyman, Rogue does not understand. The Doctor knows that they are scandalous and is proud of it, kissing Rogue before he loses him. Suddenly the Doctor is back to his usual self, this new incarnation experiencing his first trauma and heartbreak – 'It is what it is, so onwards.'

THE DOCTOR RETURNS

There are other times when the Fifteenth Doctor behaves in a fashion which can be identified with the neurodivergent traits of his predecessors. In 'Boom' he goes on a tangent about Villengard, saying that he once had to deactivate a mine at a lesbian gymkhana, underwater, for a bet – 'Sorry, wrong moment for this story.' The faith of the Anglicans infuriates him, observing there are no Kastorians but an algorithm programming hardware to kill the marines so that they need to keep buying more. He describes faith as a 'magic word that keeps you never having to think for yourself', but later tells Splice that he is sorry her father is dead to which she replies that he is not gone. He says that just because he does not like faith does not mean that he does not need it, a balanced approach between his reliance upon empiricism and his experience of the universe. He has a meaningful quote to hand, 'What survives of us is love', the final line of 'An Arundel Tomb' by Philip Larkin. Certainly a more Doctor-like reference than a Netflix Original.

At the end of 'Empire of Death', Ruby discovers that her birth mother is a nurse called Louise Alison Miller. The Doctor repeats one of his favourite tenets, that the most ordinary person is the most important person in the universe, yet when they find Louise, he is reluctant to allow Ruby to approach her. He claims to know better, saying that she is happy with a man called Mike – 'The point is is that she has had over seven thousand days to come and find you, and she never has.' He believes that Louise made her choice and they should respect that, although it is out of a selfish fear of losing his friend if she decides to remain with her mother on Earth. Ruby defies the Doctor and is proved correct, embracing her mother and rekindling her family. He admits that her life is out there now and her own adventure is just beginning, although he says he will see her again. She points out that he never went back to find his own granddaughter, which this older and wiser Doctor admits was a mistake. He says that Ruby changed him by encouraging him to discuss his family in ways that he never did before. They were both foundlings, a heritage shared and yet altogether different. The Doctor may look human, but he finally remembers that he is not.

When the Doctor must spend a year at the Sandringham Hotel with Anita in 'Joy to the World' to break a bootstrap paradox, he tells her that he has never lived life one day after the other in the right order. A situation which would have driven his predecessors to madness is something he claims to love, enjoying the Christmas he spends with his human companion. He reminds us of his true nature when he makes Joy Almondo angry to break her link to the briefcase. In Holmesian fashion, he says that one can tell everything about a person from their choice of hotel room, and Joy's was the loneliest and saddest he had ever seen. He pushes further, asking if her mother chose her name as an ironic joke. She says that her mother died alone in hospital during the COVID-19 pandemic, which the Doctor mocks. He uses her rage to his advantage, saving her in the process, but more importantly in pursuit of his mission. It is calculating and cruel, pushing all the right buttons without a care for the impact it will have on Joy.

Belinda does not stand for the Doctor's usual way with humans. He wins her over as a friend in 'The Robot Revolution' after she asks if having a second diaphragm is better or worse to which he replies, 'If you start deciding which body is best, you're going down a very dangerous path.' As a nurse she is more interested in the Doctor's binary vascular system than anything else. When he points out the TARDIS is bigger on the inside, disappointed that this does not impress her, she says that she is aware of that and now she needs to get home before her shift starts. After he says that he thinks they are connected somehow, she asks, 'Is that what you say to all the girls?' She realises that he is dangerous, that a woman who trusted him died and he tested her DNA without permission. The Doctor is not sure how to handle such self-assurance. He cannot relate to her preference for domestic life and struggles to navigate his ship more than usual with the help of a Vortex Indicator or Vindicator, perhaps as an excuse to keep Belinda onboard for longer.

At their final stop before Earth, 'The Interstellar Song Contest', Belinda tells the Doctor that they are going to stay. She excitedly recalls that she used to watch Eurovision when she was little with her parents, an anecdote the Doctor cannot help but one-up by saying that he was there in 1974 when ABBA won. He later describes himself as Belinda's 'protector', a position she would surely dispute. Yet she is delighted, and a bit scared, to see the Doctor get angry after learning about what had happened to the Hellions. They are an ostracised race whose planet was bought by the Corporation so they could harvest the Hell Poppy to flavour PoppyHoney, which sponsors the Contest. The Hellion performer Cora shows Belinda the stubs of her horns which were cut off by force, attempting to pass as a different species to avoid being banned from singing. Her plight resonates with minorities who need to disguise their true identity to be accepted in society, establishing a perpetual state of anxiety for fear of being unmasked. The Doctor tells Belinda that hearing of the deaths of three trillion people 'triggered' him, bringing back the trauma of Gallifrey through a vision of Susan. The Doctor connects to this fear, of being discriminated against on the basis of his biology or his mind, and it compels him to act with anger and, controversially, violence.

When they return to Earth in 'Wish World', the Doctor and Belinda have been brainwashed by the Rani. The reality created by Conrad is this Doctor's ultimate nightmare – he lives in a house with his wife and child, wearing a bowler hat and pinstriped suit for work, under the name of John Smith. He is stifled beyond recognition. The only people who escape from Conrad's vision are those he ignores as a result of his perception bias, disabled people like Shirley who live in an underground community, and Donna's transgender daughter Rose who vanishes altogether. It is a vision of Rogue which snaps the Doctor out of his hypnosis, saying that he misses and loves him, one of few characters with whom the Doctor has shared such a powerful connection.

INTO THE FUTURE

When the Doctor is brought before the Rani, it is clear that they lack the bond between Time Lords evident in his relationship with the Master. In 'The Mark of the Rani' she had been exiled from Gallifrey for her experiments, which the Sixth Doctor admired, wondering what relationship they might have if he was 'particularly nice to her.' She expresses concern that the Seventh Doctor might injure himself in 'Time and the Rani', surprising him as she has expressed nothing but contempt for other Time Lords. She is experimenting on the planet Lakertya, saying that she does not see why she should abandon her research because of the side effects on an inferior species. In 'The Reality War' her latest experiment is on the Earth, using the power of doubt to crack open the Underverse and free Omega. She wants to use him as a gene bank to resurrect the Time Lords and construct a new Gallifrey, revealing that their species is infertile. When it is suggested that Poppy, the impossible daughter of the Doctor and Belinda, represents the future, the Rani says that she is contaminated with human DNA. 'He walks around like he's one of you, but you're like insects to him. Playthings. A fetish', the Rani says of the Doctor. She reminds his human friends of the difference between them which is masked by his appearance and ability to pass.

The Rani's hubris in resurrecting Omega proves to be her downfall, yet the Doctor realises he must sacrifice his current incarnation if he is to retrieve his daughter by punching regeneration energy into the Vortex. The Thirteenth Doctor appears, once again echoing the Second Doctor in their characteristic honesty by saying, 'You've redecorated. I don't like it. Does it really need to be bigger in a room defined by its bigness?' She is more scientific than this newer Doctor, advising him to 'try shifting the third strand of phenotype markers one micro-spasm to the left.' He observes that it is strange he did not know to do that, given that he is older than she is, which they both dismiss as 'timey-wimey.' 'We never change. All these faces, and we never really change', the Thirteenth says, although it does not quite feel true anymore. She is shocked when he tells her that he loves her, a word she does not recognise within her personal lexicon. 'That's why you got me', the Fifteenth explains, prompting her to say that she should tell Yaz. 'You never do. But she knows.' After she disappears, he gazes out of the TARDIS doors as he regenerates yet again.

The Fifteenth Doctor's tenure was a significant change which frustrated many of the neurodivergent Whovians I interviewed. I felt similarly for the most part, not least in the ease with which he shed tears and expressed his emotions. This might be due to him seeming less alien or more neurotypical, but crucially it is because his behaviour did not always feel consistent with the character of the Doctor. Yet I think of 'The Story & The Engine', in which stories told in a barbershop are used to fuel a vehicle. The Doctor says he once challenged Ernest Hemingway to write the shortest story he could. His own effort was 'I'm born. I die. I'm born.' The machine connects to him and episodes from his past are heard. 'My body is like a barbershop. All of them inside, telling their stories, bickering! I will not fail them!' *Doctor Who* has never been consistent, and while there are elements of each of the Doctor's incarnations which might confuse or frustrate its fans, it is the acceptance of change which remains essential to the nature of the programme we love. Difficult to accept at first, perhaps, but just like the Doctor, we always get there in the end.

EPILOGUE

THE GREASTEST SHOW IN THE GALAXY

Whizz Kid: **Hello. This is the Psychic Circus, isn't it?**
Morgana: **Yes, that's right.**
Whizz Kid: **Oh great! I've come halfway across the southern nebula to be here. I want to enter the talent contest. I know all about the Psychic Circus, you see. In fact, I'm your greatest fan.**

'The Greatest Show in the Galaxy'

Whizz Kid looks like an amalgamation of several Doctors in his bow tie, sleeveless jumper, and blue spectacles. He is a figure any Whovian can recognise, possibly even in ourselves. He was played in 'The Greatest Show in the Galaxy' by Gian Sammarco before he retired from acting to become a psychiatric nurse – the actor who brought Sue Townsend's Adrian Mole to life on television in 1985. His collection of Psychic Circus ephemera is extensive, and he sent letters to one of its founding members. Despite never actually having seen the show, he says, 'I know it's not as good as it used to be but I'm still terribly interested.' A knowing wink to the audience as ratings for *Doctor Who* hit an all-time low with the programme being cancelled soon after. It is also a rather cruel mockery of the show's own fandom, with

Captain Cook knowingly sending the boy to his death by giving him the opportunity to perform in the ring. He tells him that danger only exists for those 'without resource or imagination or panache', which of course Whizz Kid lacks. He is incinerated, leaving only the cracked remains of his glasses on the floor to the sound of wild applause.

There is a pettiness to the portrayal of Whizz Kid – he serves no real function to the narrative, only to demonstrate the stakes at play. He exists for the writers and producers of *Doctor Who* to point at its vocal, passionate fans and question if they really believe that they could do a better job. It is also an expression of pessimism, of the futility of trying to please the fans because they will never be satisfied. It is something that I have often been baffled by about the show's fandom, that so many people keep watching despite professing to no longer enjoy it. It comes from a lack of will to accept change, but more so out of an attachment to the era of the show when it first made an impression on them as an individual.

There is a charming interview from 2016 by an autistic fan called Gerard Groves with Christopher Eccleston after the actor starred in the drama series *The A Word* as the grandfather to a boy diagnosed with ASC. Gerard tells Eccleston that he was inspired by him when he was seven years old in 2005. 'So you were one of mine?' the actor asks, visibly moved by the impact his Doctor, the Ninth, had on him. They reunited in 2018 and Eccleston revealed that their meeting stayed with him, saying that autism is a 'profoundly human condition' and that we can all locate ourselves 'on the spectrum.' He admits that diagnosis and recognition was less prevalent when he was growing up. At the end of the discussion he says that loving someone who is autistic means changing for them, not the other way round.

The Ninth Doctor is also my Doctor. To me that first

series from 2005 is flawless, as I know it is to many others who were introduced to the show that year. Of course if I meet up with a group of Whovian friends of similar age to myself, we all agree on this at first. Then someone says, 'Oh, but what about "Boom Town"?', to which I say that it is a beautiful character study of Blon and the Doctor's approach to the possibility of redemption after the Time War. Then someone else will start criticising 'The Unquiet Dead', at which point a full-blown argument has broken out. 'What do you get if you put four *Doctor Who* fans in the same room?' 'Five opinions', as the joke goes. Whovians are like the varying incarnations of the Doctor, each defined by unique sartorial preferences and personality traits, yet united by our core beliefs and knowledge. 'We've got a very important inscription to translate and I think they'll get it all wrong without me', says the Third Doctor in 'The Five Doctors'. The Second points out that it is written in Old High Gallifreyan which few understand these days, to which all of the Doctors chime, 'Fortunately, I do.' I'm certain that this exchange occurs every time I join my team at the Quiz of Rassilon.

My generation of fans are the core part of the audience which Davies appealed to as showrunner, those of us who as children destroyed our copies of *Doctor Who Adventures* by tearing off the free gift and plastering our bedroom walls with the posters contained within its glossy pages. It was organised fandom which he took issue with, those who harangue writers and actors with questions and criticisms. Unlike the 1980s, regular cast and senior crew avoided conventions, preferring to be visible to fans through media outlets and BBC events while directing ire towards those who blasted the show online. In a 2008 interview with *The Guardian* Davies called these people 'mosquitoes', arguing that, 'They are not real fandom, though, they are a core of mostly men who like to complain. Fandom is bigger and richer than that, and they are only about 1,000 people who give everyone else a bad name.' Such people have also been derided by Davies as 'ming-mongs', referring to a 1987 Victoria Wood sketch lampooning the nonsensical, childish language of *Doctor Who*. The term draws problematically from the racist, patronising term 'mongoloid', which in turn has been shortened as 'mong' to mock those who have intellectual disabilities or neurodivergence. It is an offensive derision which other writers for the show have distanced themselves from, not least Davies's successor Moffat. In a 2008 interview he said, 'I am a fan myself. A proper list-making-borderline-autistic fan. I am head mingmong [sic]. I'm King Ming.' He reclaims Davies's pejorative term as an identity to be proud of, even citing neurodivergence in his relationship to the show.

Davies put a 'mosquito' in 'Rose', asserting his position on this kind of fan from the beginning of his tenure. Rose's research into the Ninth Doctor leads her to Clive Finch, a man who runs the conspiracy website 'Who is Doctor Who?' from his 'mancave' shed. His son opens the door and calls out, 'Dad! It's one of your nutters!' His wife cannot believe that a woman has taken an interest in the website, referencing the overwhelmingly male nature of obsessive fandom. When Clive is killed by an Auton, it is an attempt to put an end to the association of *Doctor Who* fans with stereotypical anoraks, replacing him with Rose who represents a fandom open to change, inclusive, and not elitist. She is the wider audience, working-class and in touch with ordinary British life, the anti-Whizz Kid.

Meet a fan of *Doctor Who* and they will ask you two questions: who is your favourite Doctor, and what is your favourite story? My answer to the latter is twofold and suitably contrarian – 'Black Orchid' is my favourite classic serial, because the Doctor plays cricket in it, and 'Love &

Monsters' is my favourite of NuWho. I remember watching *Blue Peter* when they hosted a competition to design the alien for the episode, for which I submitted an illustration of a race which disguised themselves as curtains to strangle their victims. I wonder why I did not win. The prize went to nine-year-old William Grantham and his Abzorbaloff, portrayed in the episode by Peter Kay. He is from the planet Clom, sister planet of Raxacoricofallapatorius, and like that planet's inhabitants he masks his repulsive green self under the skinsuit of a human called Victor Kennedy. The monster is an even more exaggerated caricature of Davies's 'mosquitoes', a man who literally sucks the joy out of other fans in his pursuit of knowledge about the Doctor.

The heroes of the episode, the London Investigation 'n' Detective agency – LINDA, for short – represent acceptable, endearing fandom. Ursula is the bespectacled nerdy girl with all the facts, Bliss the aspiring fan artist, Mr Skinner the writer who creates his own stories, and Bridget the shy woman who just wants to be part of a club after losing her daughter. They are joined by Elton Pope, whose chief obsession is the Electric Light Orchestra, the one who has a personal connection to the Doctor. LINDA soon socialises beyond the remit of the Doctor, including cooking and making music together. Kennedy arrives during a jam session, a man who recoils at the touch of others on account of his 'exeema.' 'You've forgotten your purpose in life', he chastises them. 'You, with your band and your cakes and your blubbing and all the while he still exists. The Doctor.' He gives them homework, to use the Torchwood files to create new databases, and forces Elton to take advantage of Jackie to learn more. She discovers that he was only getting close to her for information, which breaks her heart. He thinks of everything he lost, the importance of human life and connection which was obscured by his obsession, too late to declare his love to Ursula for she has been absorbed. 'It's not his fault, but maybe that's what happens if you touch the Doctor.'

There are times when my hyperfixations cause me to neglect important aspects of my life, be that forgetting to eat or isolating myself from others. It was part of the reason why I rejected *Doctor Who* for a while during my late teens, feeling that by clinging to the show I had stunted my development into adulthood. When I came home from school I hid in my room with my notebooks and spreadsheets, cataloguing my books or keeping records of every film I had seen. 'You've only got seventeen DVDs?' is Larry Nightingale's question to Sally Sparrow in 'Blink' when she realises that the connection between the films on his list is that she owns all of them. Larry has been obsessively watching Easter eggs which he found on the discs, and discussing them in online fora. When Sally watches the complete video of the Doctor, Larry writes down a transcript which will create the illusion that the Doctor is having a live conversation with her. He does not realise this, and his ignorance of the obvious creates humorous dramatic irony – '"The angels have the phone box." That's my favourite, I've got it on a t-shirt.' It is an affectionate portrayal of twin interests, with Larry and Sally forming a relationship and together running a shop selling antiquarian books and rare DVDs.

The episode was written by Moffat, who knows that there is something amusing about obsessive fandom and collecting, but who also has great affection for it. Metatextual representations of Whovians during his era are far less critical than those penned by Davies. UNIT scientific advisor Dr Malcolm Taylor, a creation of Davies, cannot believe he is speaking to the Tenth Doctor in 'Planet of the Dead', having read all of his files, and gets excited when his hero calls him a genius. When they meet in person he hugs him and cannot stop saying, 'I love you.' Davies believed the character worthy of his own spin-off series, yet Malcolm was seen to be a stereotyped geek rather than someone relatable to fans. The character is mentioned briefly in 'The Day of the Doctor', written by Moffat, in which Kate says that the ravens at the Tower of London 'are looking a bit sluggish. Tell Malcolm they need new batteries.'

He is replaced by Osgood, a woman who wears nods to various incarnations of the Doctor like a grown-up female version of Whizz Kid. She is overexcited by the prospect of meeting the Eleventh Doctor, with Kate prompting her to use her asthma inhaler, yet she quickly pulls herself together and becomes a vital part of events. When Missy kills her in 'Death in Heaven', she steps on Osgood's glasses in a parallel to the death of Whizz Kid. Her return in 'The Zygon Invasion' renders her a more heroic figure, still wearing the cosplay of the Doctor but no longer defined by her fandom. Ingrid Oliver told me that she adores the impact her character had on fans, especially Whovian women who had not felt represented in this way before. 'To see people dressed up as my character, men and women, old and young, from all walks of life, is such an extraordinary thing', she said. 'Aside from the conventions, I've had NASA scientists, politicians, journalists, judges, all come up to me over the years professing their love for the Doctor.' I like to wear something related to *Doctor Who*, a scarf or a badge, whenever I can to keep it close to my heart, although I will never again allow my fandom to define me.

Whovians Lizzie, Robyn, and Hassan are the embodiment of love for the show in 'Lux'. They were created as a trap for the Fifteenth Doctor and Belinda, but the strength of their obsession caused them to attain independence, even hinting at spoilers for the end of the episode. Everything in Lizzie's flat is related to *Doctor Who* – from the fez on her head to the 'Don't Blink' and K9 mugs. The Doctor and Belinda cannot believe that they are on television, with him asking the fans for their favourite adventure. They are unanimous in their choice of 'Blink', although I suspect 'Heaven Sent' would be more accurate.

James Goss fleshes out these characters in the Target novelisation. The book describes the 'ritual' of them gathering at Lizzie's place on Saturdays like a 'secret society' who take *Doctor Who* seriously – Hassan claims that the only reason his friends had not 'got' 'Legend of the Sea Devils' is because motion smoothing was on. Lizzie is able to recognise that the Doctor is forcing politeness when looking at her DVD collection because she had sat next to her father at her mother's second wedding and had seen him smile despite it killing him inside. She is heartbroken when Belinda says she is annoying, hurting all the more because she had invested in her character. The Doctor is described as empathetic, he 'sensed her tears', and leans over to hold Lizzie. He looks into her eyes: 'She'd never felt so seen in her life [...] That look of infinite understanding and sadness.' My favourite line from *The History Boys* by Alan Bennett comes to mind:

> *The best moments in reading are when you come across something – a thought, a feeling, a way of looking at things – which you had thought special and particular to you. Now here it is, set down by someone else, a person you have never met, someone even who is long dead. And it is as if a hand has come out and taken yours.*

For Whizz Kid or LINDA or any other fans to be treated so harshly by the thing they love can be hurtful. It is far more meaningful, as in 'Lux', when the show extends warmth to the people who connect with it beyond casual viewership. At the end of the episode, the trio realise that they still exist, fuelled by the strength of this love. 'They all screamed with joy because they were alive. And wasn't that the magic of *Doctor Who?*' ends the novel.

For a while I avoided revealing my obsession with *Doctor Who* to others because it baffled those who knew me. It is childish compared to many of my other interests, which I do not deny to be true. 'Black Orchid' is my favourite story. Nothing supernatural occurs – the Doctor plays a cricket match before attending a costume party at a country house. It plays out like an Agatha Christie mystery, with the culprit who attacked Ann revealed to be George Cranleigh, a botanist who after being kidnapped and tortured in the Amazon was left disfigured and mentally disabled. He is hidden away by his family, causing him to become violent and ultimately to fall to his death. It is a deeply human tragedy which occurs at the end of a serial which solely exists for the purpose of being fun. The depiction of neurodivergence is problematic and clumsy, yet it portrays the masks and surfaces which neurotypical society projects in order to be accepted.

'Black Orchid' is a microcosm of *Doctor Who* as a whole – it is silly and trivial, yet it also deals with the most essential philosophical questions of morality, relationships, and identity. It is at once both my escape from a world I have never felt entirely comfortable or safe in, and the mirrored lens through which I try to make sense of it. This book is about the show I have loved since I was six years old and why I and other neurodivergent people have connected with it so deeply for over six decades, yet it is more broadly a guidebook to approaching life from another perspective. I am grateful to those who have kept the show going for so long, but more so I am thankful for everyone who has been connected to me through it. For my parents and my brother who watched it with me at the beginning; for those who quizzed me and debated its contents at school and university; for the friends with whom I have shared my new adventures as an adult;

and for the neurodivergent Whovians who opened up to me about their experiences with powerful honesty. It is dedicated to all of you, and to my childhood self, who ended up on a planet filled with strange, strange creatures called Human Beings, and needed a Doctor to show her the mysteries of this neurodiverse universe. Over to you, dear reader – tag, you're it.

SELECTED BIBLIOGRAPHY

Abnett, Dan, *The Last Voyage* (London: BBC Audio, 2010).

Albrecht, Karl, 'Did Sherlock Holmes Have Asperger Syndrome?', *Psychology Today*, 13 October 2011.

Aldred, Sophie, ed. *Ace's Jacket: The Inside Story* (Gloucester: Chinbeard Books, 2025).

Aron, Elaine N. and Arthur Aron, 'Sensory-Processing Sensitivity and Its Relation to Introversion and Emotionality', *Journal of Personality and Social Psychology* 73.2 (1997), pp. 345-368.

Bennett, Alan, *The History Boys* (London: Faber & Faber, 2004).

Booth, Paul, Matt Hills, Tansy Rayner Roberts, and Joy Piedmont, eds., *Adventures Across Space and Time: A Doctor Who Reader* (London: Bloomsbury, 2023).

Booth, Paul, and Craig Owen Jones, *Watching Doctor Who: Fan Reception and Evaluation* (London: Bloomsbury, 2021).

Booy, Miles, *Love and Monsters: The Doctor Who Experience, 1979 to Present* (London: I.B. Tauris, 2012).

Braithwaite, Philip, *Time Lords and Star Cops: British Science Fiction Television in the 1970s-80s* (Manchester: Manchester University Press, 2023).

Britton, Piers D., *TARDISBound: Navigating the Universes of Doctor Who* (London: I.B. Tauris, 2011).

—, *Design for Doctor Who: Vision and Revision in Science Fiction Television* (London: Bloomsbury, 2021).

Čapek, Karel, *R.U.R. (Rossum's Universal Robots)* (London: Penguin, 2004 [orig. 1921]).

Chapman, Robert, *Empire of Normality: Neurodiversity and Capitalism* (London: Pluto Press, 2023).

Cherry, Brigid, Matt Hills, and Andrew O'Day, eds. *New Dawn: Essays on the Jodie Whittaker Era* (Manchester: Manchester University Press, 2021).

Cook, Benjamin, 'Everything Everywhere All At Once [Jodie Whittaker Interview]', *Doctor Who Magazine*, 621 (2025), pp. 16-41.

Cook O'Toole, Jennifer, *Autism in Heels: The Untold Story of a Female Life on the Spectrum* (New York: Skyhorse Publishing, 2018).

Crawford, Lillian, '"I got to have an affair with Kylie!" Stars share their best Doctor Who moments – part one', *The Guardian*, 20 November 2023.

—, '"Matt Smith and I twiddle knobs. I am 12 again!" Stars share their best Doctor Who moments – part two', *The Guardian*, 21 November 2023.

—, '"John Hurt and I swapped wine tips": Stars share their best Doctor Who moments – part three', *The Guardian*, 22 November 2023.

—, '"My favourite moment is me … not in a big-headed way", Stars share their best Doctor Who memories – part four', *The Guardian*, 23 November 2023.

—, '"I made the Daily Mail incredibly angry": Stars share their Doctor Who moments – part five', *The Guardian*, 24 November 2023.

—, 'The Power of the Doctor', *Doctor Who Magazine*, 611 (2024), pp. 34-36.

Decker, Kevin S., *Who is Who? The Philosophy of Doctor Who* (London: I.B. Tauris, 2013).

Dixit, Priya, 'Relating to Difference: Aliens and Alienness in Doctor Who and International Relations', *International Studies Perspectives*, 13.3 (2012), pp. 289–306.

Down, John Langdon, *On Some of the Mental Affections of Childhood and Youth: Being the Lettsomian Lectures Delivered Before the Medical Society of London in 1887, Together With Other Papers* (London: J. & A. Churchill, 1887).

Doyle, Arthur Conan, *A Study in Scarlet* (London: Penguin, 2001 [orig. 1887]).

—, *The Sign of Four* (London: Penguin, 2001 [orig. 1890]).

Félix, Paulo Victor Sousa, *Percepções Atípicas: Uma Análise de Fóruns do Site Reddit em Relação a Características Autísticas do Personagem Doctor (Doctor Who)* (Uberlândia: MG, 2025).

Fountain, Nev, *The Curious Incident of the Doctor in the Night-Time* (London: Big Finish, 2014).

Freeman Loftis, Sonia, *Imagining Autism: Fiction and Stereotypes on the Spectrum* (Bloomington: Indiana University Press, 2015).

Gibbs, Alan, "Maybe that's what happens if you touch the Doctor, even for a second': Trauma in Doctor Who', *Journal of Popular Culture*, 46.5 (2013), pp. 950-972.

Gillat, Gary, 'The Fan Gene Part One: Defining the Indefinable', *Doctor Who Magazine*, 326 (2003), pp. 12-17.

—, 'The Fan Gene Part Two: Born to Love You', *Doctor Who Magazine*, 328 (2003), pp. 12-17.

—, 'The Fan Gene Part Three: All You Need Is Love', *Doctor Who Magazine*, 331 (2003), pp. 12-17.

Goss, James, *Doctor Who: Lux* (London: BBC Books, 2025).

Haddon, Mark, *The Curious Incident of the Dog in the Night-Time* (London: Vintage, 2004).

Haraway, Donna, 'A Manifesto for Cyborgs: Science, Technology, and Socialist-Feminism in the 1980s', *Socialist Review*, 80 (1985), pp. 65-107.

Hardt, Maria-Xenia, *Heroism in Doctor Who* (Baden-Baden: Nomos Verlagsgesellschaft, 2022).

Hills, Matt, *Triumph of a Time Lord: Regenerating Doctor Who in the Twenty-First Century* (London: I.B. Tauris, 2010).

—, ed., *New Dimensions of Doctor Who: Adventures in Space, Time and Television* (London: I.B. Tauris, 2013).

Horne, Marc, 'Doctor Who in war with Planet Maggie', *The Sunday Times*, 14 February 2010.

Hunter, Sazz, 'Doctor Who as a Metaphor for Autistic Masking', *Medium*, 12 February 2023.

—, 'Why Do Autistic People Love Doctor Who?', *Medium*, 21 June 2024.

Jowett, Lorna, *Dancing with the Doctor: Dimensions of Gender in the Doctor Who Universe* (London: I.B. Tauris, 2017).

Kanner, Leo, 'Autistic disturbances of affective contact', *Nervous Child*, 2.3 (1943), pp. 217-250.

Keyes, Daniel, *Flowers for Algernon* (London: Orion Publishing, 2022 [orig. 1959]).

MacRury, Iain, and Michael Rustin, *The Inner World of Doctor Who: Psychoanalytic Reflections in Time and Space* (London: Routledge, 2013).

Manning, Leslie, 'Negotiating Doctor Who: Neurodiversity and Fandom', in Einar Thorsen, Heather Savigny, Jenny Alexander, and Daniel Jackson, eds, *Media, Margins and Popular Culture* (London: Palgrave Macmillan, 2015), pp. 153-165.

Marshall, Jackie, 'Lily', in *Doctor Who Short Trips: A Christmas Treasury*, ed. Paul Cornell (London: Big Finish, 2004).

Nelson, Jackie, 'The Remarkable Day Daphne Met the "Doctor"', *Autism Parenting Magazine*, 26 January 2024.

Nerenberg, Jenara, *Divergent Mind: Thriving in a World That Wasn't Designed for You* (New York: Harper Collins, 2021).

Newson, Elizabeth and John Newson, *Four Years Old in an Urban Community* (London: Routledge, 2013 [orig. 1968]).

O'Day, Andrew, ed., *Twelfth Night: Adventures in Time and Space with Peter Capaldi* (London: I.B. Tauris, 2018).

Pang, Camilla, *Explaining Humans: What Science Can Teach Us about Life, Love and Relationships* (London: Penguin, 2021).

Phillips, Ivan, *Once Upon a Time Lord: The Myths and Stories of Doctor Who* (London: Bloomsbury, 2020).

Pinborough, Sarah, *Torchwood: Into the Silence* (London: Random House, 2009).

Russell, Willy, *Educating Rita* (London: Methuen Drama, 2009 [orig. 1980]).

Sacks, Oliver, *The Man Who Mistook His Wife for a Hat* (London: Picador, 2011 [orig. 1985]).

—, *An Anthropologist on Mars: Seven Paradoxical Tales* (London: Picador, 2012 [orig. 1995]).

—, *Musicophilia: Tales of Music and the Brain* (London: Picador, 2012 [orig. 2008]).

Shaw, George Bernard, *The Doctor's Dilemma* (London: Penguin, 1987 [orig. 1906]).

—, *Pygmalion: A Romance in Five Acts* (London: Penguin, 2003 [orig, 1912]).

Silberman, Steve, *NeuroTribes: The Legacy of Autism and How to Think Smarter about People who Think Differently* (London: Allen & Unwin, 2015).

Slaven, Sarah, 'The Lessons Doctor Who is Teaching My ASD Kid', *PeaBillyBean*, 26 July 2012.

Stack, Mike, *Doctor Who and Gay Male Fandom: A Queer(ed) Transmedia Franchise* (London: Routledge, 2024).

Suskind, Ron, *Life, Animated: A Story of Sidekicks, Heroes, and Autism* (New York: Kingswell, 2014).

Turner, Alwyn W., *The Man Who Invented the Daleks: The Strange Worlds of Terry Nation* (London: Aurum Press, 2011).

Wells, H.G., *The Time Machine* (London: Penguin, 2012 [orig. 1895]).

Yost, Kimberly, *Courageous Companions: Followership in Doctor Who* (Leeds: Emerald Publishing, 2024).

ACKNOWLEDGEMENTS

This book came about thanks to my editor David Moloney, who read a piece I wrote in *Doctor Who Magazine* and saw potential to expand it across the Whoniverse. I am incredibly grateful for his encouragement and patience in making this project a reality. Many thanks also to Will Parkes, Helen Porter, and all at Herne Books.

I would like to thank those who helped to hone my writing over the years and supported me in my academic and freelance careers, from my sixth-form teachers to my supervisors at Cambridge, especially James Raven and Kasia Boddy. I am forever grateful for the mentorship offered to me by the team at Little White Lies and beyond, not least David Jenkins, Hannah Strong, Adam Woodward, and Leila Latif, as well as Matthew Sweet, Samira Ahmed, Queenie Qureshi-Wales, and Jane Long, all of whom introduced me to the world of broadcasting and have endured my ramblings about *Who*, culture, and autism.

In childhood I may not have understood the value of friendship, but it has sustained me in adulthood. I could not be more appreciative of the love and support I have shared with James Samuel, Linfa Kear, and Erin Baker since our school days, and those I was exceptionally fortunate to meet at university, not least Adam Reeves, Eli Hong, Ian Wang, Chlo Spinks, Hugh Oxlade, Madeleine Wulfahrt, Nadia Hourihan, Anna Cardoso, Stephanie Childress, Elizabeth Huang, Martha O'Neil, my beloved quizzers, and many others. My life has been enriched by the experiences and conversations I have had with hundreds of people I have been privileged to call friends, with particular thanks to Laura Venning, Scarlett Wingate, Jamie Mehta, Jessica Thomas, Dean Evans, Anna Churchill, Issy Macleod, Clémence Rebourg, Alice Dodds, George Attwood, Manuela Lazić, Elena Lazic, Charlie Shackleton, Guy Lodge (the man and the cat), and the rest of the 'Regression Sessions' lads. I would not have been able to overcome the many struggles of the past few years without you.

For this project I am grateful to my co-hosts and friends from *Autism Through Cinema*, including Alex Widdowson, David Hartley, Sophie Broadgate, Janet Harbord, Steven Eastwood, et alia, with special love and thanks to Georgia Kumari Bradburn and Sam Chown Ahern, my partners in Stims. I would like to thank the programmers who have supported my curation and the development of relaxed screenings in London and Edinburgh, namely Maggi Hurt, Paul Ridd, Emma Boa, Abla Khan, Alex Davidson, Jonathan Gleneadie, Harriet Waller, and Ruby McGuigan. I have been so very grateful to expand my knowledge of disability theory and experience through the reading group I run with Milo Pissarro, Colm Gallagher, and Joseph Rizzo-Naudi which has informed the writing of this book.

There is a frankly ridiculous list of people I want to thank for talking to me about *Doctor Who* over the years, many of whom are quoted in this book. They include Simon Callow, Dan Starkey, Euros Lyn, Sophie Aldred, Anneke Wills, John Leeson, Nikki Wilson, Simon Nye, Ruth Madeley, Kai Owen, Tom Kingsley, Paul McGann, James Strong, Tom Baker, Chris Chibnall, Daniel Nettheim, Catrin Stewart, Graeme Harper, Nick Hurran, Michael E. Briant, Louise Jameson, Nicola Bryant, Chris Roebuck, Ardal O'Hanlon, Terry Molloy, Simon Fisher-Becker, Jane Tranter, Steven Moffat, Sylvester McCoy, Annette Badland, Sacha Dhawan, Katy Manning, Jacqueline

King, Ingrid Oliver, Michael Troughton, Phil Collinson, Ben Aaronovitch, Greg Austin, Jimmy Vee, Julie Gardner, Neil Cross, Dylan Holmes Williams, Rona Munro, Segun Akinola, Neve McIntosh, Ella Road, Jessica Carney, Beth Willis, David Bradley, Elizabeth Parker, Martin Jarvis, Jamie Donoughue, Lalla Ward, Sheila Hancock, Sophie Hopkins, Juno Dawson, Rachel Talalay, Azhur Saleem, Vinay Patel, and Alice Troughton. I am particularly grateful for the time and thoughtfulness with which the following people spoke to me about *Doctor Who* in relation to neurodiversity: Cath Tregenna, Emma Sullivan, Stephen Gallagher, Charlie Craggs, Susie Liggat, Murray Gold, Ella Watts, Barnaby Edwards, James Strong, and Waris Hussein.

The Whoniverse, as this book has shown, would not exist without its fans. Some of the finest conversations of my life have been shared with these Whovians, and I wish I could have quoted them in full: Harry Draper, Alexis Harrow, Stuart Dodgson, Maria Assima Santos, Dominic Walsh, Rob Burton, Ian Palmer, Rob Freeman, Carolyn Arnold, Hannah Burrows, and Kate Fox, with special thanks to Esme Hayes and Bella Madge, whose feedback has been invaluable and profoundly moving.

As I hope has been made obvious, I owe so much to my closest family and friends, both in relation to *Doctor Who* and neurodivergence. This book has been discussed and debated with three in particular, and my gratitude goes far beyond the realms of the Whoniverse: Alex Hewitt, Edward Smyth, and Molly O'Gorman.

Finally, I would like to take this space to thank Nick Clanchy, for having been and continuing to be there for me; Beth Ahsunollah, for your care and kindness; James, Thomas, Ralph, and Kim Sanders, for our convention adventures and shared celebration of nerdery; my grandparents, who introduced me to so much of the culture which has defined my life, and have always loved and supported me in everything I do. And most of all, to my brother, Adam, and my parents, Helen and Matt – this book is a testament to the three of you, my TARDIS co-pilots, who have fought with me a universe of monsters. Hope makes companions of us all.

'Love, in all its forms, is the most powerful weapon we have. Because love is a form of hope. And like hope, love abides. In the face of everything.'

STORY INDEX

THE FOURTEENTH DOCTOR

Specials (2023)

THE FIFTEENTH DOCTOR

Specials (2023) continued

Series 14 (2024)

Special (2024)

Series 15 (2025)

OTHER SERIES IN THE BBC 'WHONIVERSE'

Torchwood

The Sarah Jane Adventures

Class

BBC shorts

Other spin-offs and media